TRAGEDY

BY

ASHLEY H. THORNDIKE

TRAGEDY

BY

ASHLEY H. THORNDIKE

A MARANDELL BOOK

COOPER SQUARE PUBLISHERS, INC.

NEW YORK

1965

PREFACE

THIS book attempts to trace the course of English tragedy from its beginnings to the middle of the nineteenth century, and to indicate the part which it has played in the history both of the theatre and of literature. All tragedies of the sixteenth century are noticed, because of their historical interest and their close relationship to Shakespeare, but after 1600 only representative plays have been considered. The aim of this series has been kept in view, and the discussion, whether of individual plays or of dramatic conditions, has been determined by their importance in the study of a literary type. Tragedy in the eighteenth and nineteenth centuries has attracted very little critical attention, and in those fields the book is something of a pioneer. The Elizabethan drama, on the contrary, has been the subject of a vast amount of antiquarian, biographical, and literary research, without which such a treatment as I have attempted would be almost impossible. In order, however, to keep the main purpose in view, it has been necessary to omit nearly all notice of the processes of research or the debates of criticism, and to give only what seem to me the results. To indicate at every point my reliance on my own investigations or my indebtedness to the researches of others would, indeed, necessitate doubling the size of the book. Its readers will not require an apology for its brevity, but I regret that I can offer only this inadequate acknowledgment of the great assistance I have received not merely from the studies mentioned in the Bibliographical Notes, but also from many others that have directly or indirectly contributed to my discussion.

I am indebted to Dr. Ernest Bernbaum, who very kindly read chapters viii and ix, and made a number of suggestions. I have also the pleasure of expressing my great obligations to Professors Brander Matthews, Jefferson B. Fletcher, and William A. Neilson, who have read both the manuscript and the proof-sheets and given me the generous benefit of their most helpful criticism.

A. H. T.

New York, March, 1908.

CONTENTS

TRAGEDY

CHAPTER I

DEFINITIONS

THERE is little difficulty in selecting the plays that should be included in a history of English tragedy. Since the middle of the sixteenth century there have always been plays commonly received as tragedies, and others so closely resembling these that they require consideration in any comprehensive study. How far these plays present the common characteristics of a type, how far they constitute a clearly defined form of the drama, and how far they may be connected from one period to another in a continuous development — are questions better answered at the book's end than at its beginning. Some questions of the definition of tragedy, however, may well be preliminary to a study of its history. The very term " English tragedy" involves two precarious abstractions. It separates tragedy from the drama of which it is a part, and it separates English tragedies from those of other languages to which they are related in character and origin. In attempting a definition, we may question the reality of these abstract separations by which our later discussions are to be conveniently limited; for a definition can be attained only through the distinction of tragedy from other forms of the drama, and through a consideration of the varying conceptions of tragedy in different periods and nations.

We may begin very empirically with an element common to all tragedies and roughly distinguishing them from other forms of drama; noticed, indeed, in all theoretical definitions, though its importance is often blurred and it receives only scant attention from Aristotle. He refers to the third part of the plot as " the tragic incident, a destructive or painful action, such as death on the stage, bodily agony, wounds, and the like." If his meaning of "a destructive or painful action" is extended to include mental as well as physical suffering, we have a definition of an indispensable element in tragedy and a conspicuous distinction from comedy.

This definition has had ample recognition in practice and in popular opinion, as in the sixteenth-century idea of a tragedy as a play involving deaths, and in the present common conception of tragedy as requiring an unhappy ending. These uncritical opinions, however, introduce amendments that are not quite corollaries. The happy ending has never been completely excluded. Aristotle, while pronouncing in favor of the unhappy ending as best suited to producing tragic effect, recognized the possibility and popularity of a conclusion that limited punishment to the vicious. In modern times the salvation of the virtuous in tragedy has had warm defenders, including Racine and Dr. Johnson; and the essentiality of either an unhappy ending or of deaths has been generally denied. Evidently either is a natural but not inevitable accompaniment of suffering and disaster. A tragedy may permit of relief or even recovery for the good, or it may minimize the external and physical elements of suffering; but its action must be largely unhappy though its end is not, and destructive even if it does not lead to deaths.

Our working definition, however, does not attempt to indicate the qualities necessary to excellence in tragedy or to particularize in respect to the treatment of the action. It offers no distinction, where recent critics have been careful to make one, between tragedy and what we to-day call melodrama.[1] The relation between the two is similar to that between comedy and farce. Melodrama is more sensational, less serious; it attains its effects by spectacles, machines, externals, while tragedy deals with character and motive; it reaches its conclusions through accidents and surprises, while tragedy seeks to show the cause of every effect. But the distinction is general and relative rather than specific and absolute. The use of witches to foretell actions and characters would of itself be a melodramatic device, and so it is in Middleton's "Witch," but not in "Macbeth." Congreve's "Mourning Bride" is a melodrama, judged by our standards at present, but for many years it was considered one of the great tragedies in the language. A stage presentation, in fact, almost presupposes external, spectacular, and sen-

---

[1] For a discussion of an earlier meaning of the term "melodrama" and the origin of its present use, see chap. x.

sational effects, which must vary according to the theatrical conditions and the taste of the day, as well as in response to the artistic purpose and treatment. The distinction between melodrama and tragedy, in short, is hardly more than between bad tragedy and good, or between a lower and a higher type. So far as a separation of the two has been made, it has been the result of centuries of experience. It cannot readily be fixed by rule or definition; it requires historical treatment.

Our definition, again, affords a rough rather than an exact separation from comedy. The two species cannot, indeed, be absolutely distinguished. In the theatre to-day there are many plays which one hesitates to classify as either tragedy or comedy. And there have always been, even in the Greek theatre, classes of plays recognized as neither the one nor the other. Again, a play presenting various persons and incidents is necessarily complex in material and emotional effect, and may mingle suffering and ruin with happiness and success, so that whether its main effect is tragic or comic may depend on its point of view or its general tone. The divisions of tragedy and comedy are neither mutually exclusive, nor are they together inclusive of all drama. Theoretically, there is perhaps ground for doubting whether other divisions might not be established more essential and more comprehensive. Comedy in particular comprises plays differing so widely in every respect that almost no common characteristics can be found. Yet tragedy and comedy have long been, and still are, accepted as the main divisions of the drama. The very names of the other forms, "tragicomedy," "*Schauspiel*," "emotional drama," "social drama," "*drame*," or merely "play," by their lack of distinctiveness, testify to the significance of the division of dramatic action and effects into the two classes, tragic and comic. From merely a theoretical point of view, indeed, we may recognize that a dramatic action, through its brevity and its stage presentation, if for no other reasons, has a suitability for these effects not possessed by other forms of literature. But the importance and definition of the two forms, and especially that of tragedy, depend less on theory than on historical origins and development.

If we attempt to fortify our working definition so that it may more effectively separate tragedy on the one hand from melodrama and on the other from comedy and the more or less neutral species, we are driven to consider the numerous and shifting conceptions that have marked the progress of the classical tradition in modern Europe. Although some approach to the tragic may have been manifest from the beginnings of the drama in the mimetic ceremonies of primitive culture, our present distinction between tragedy and comedy traces back to Athens, where tragedy as a form of literature had its first great development and where it received its first critical definition. Nothing closely corresponding to the two forms, as there developed and defined, is to be found in the dramas of China, India, or medieval Europe. Tragedy is an inheritance from Greece and Rome, not received by Western Europe until the Renaissance. There was, to be sure, much that was tragical in the widespread religious drama of the Middle Ages; and there were a number of plays that in content and effect might claim a place with later tragedies; but it was not until the revival of the classics that the revelation of a highly developed form of drama led to the creation of a distinct species called tragedy, in the vernacular literatures of Spain, Italy, France, and England.

The classical tradition in the beginning was affected by the mistaken theories of medieval encyclopedists and by humanistic misinterpretations of the classics. In every nation it came into conflict with the traditions of the medieval drama, and underwent great modifications; in England an amalgamation of the two traditions resulting in a tragedy widely different from either. During four centuries the changing theatrical conditions, the changing social conditions, the diversity of national peculiarities, have resulted in ideas of tragedy at variance with one another and with the classics. Shakespeare's conception of tragedy was very different from Aristotle's, and very different from Brunetière's or Ibsen's. Indeed, the conceptions formed by various of Shakespeare's contemporaries, Sidney, Marlowe, Jonson, Chapman, and Fletcher, so far as we can determine, have pronounced differences though they have common resemblances. It would require a larger book than the present one to consider adequately the differences and agreements merely of critical theory and dogma in modern Europe. Yet the

literary tradition, in spite of all these changes and variations, has remained continuous. Whether fixed in the
form of rules, or discernible only in the general resemblances of current practices, or represented by the great
models of Sophocles, Shakespeare, or Racine, it has influenced every playwright. He has striven to write more or
less in accord with some critical theory, in imitation of
some author, or in conformity to some fashion; or he
has written in opposition to theory, example, or fashion.

It is the purpose of this book to trace the course of this
tradition in the English drama, to appraise the inheritance
of each age from the preceding ages, its borrowings from
other national inheritances, and the profit and loss due
to its own invention or industry. All that may be attempted here by way of preliminary definition is a glance
at the main European course of the classical tradition
to see what have been from time to time considered the
essentials of tragedy and to ask how far there has been
any agreement in regard to these essentials.

The basis for much of modern theorizing has been
Aristotle's tentative yet searching analysis of Athenian
tragedy. Many of the peculiarities of Athenian tragedy
— its structure without acts but with a chorus, its limitation of three actors on the stage at once, its narrow
range of mythological subjects — are evidently not essential to securing tragic effect. Even the unities, whether
as observed in the Greek theatre or as defined by French
and Italian critics, may, after generations of debate, be
safely relegated as nonessential. Omitting, then, what

no one would now insist upon as requisite, we may derive from the "Poetics" something like the following: —

Tragedy is a form of drama exciting the emotions of pity and fear. Its action should be single and complete, presenting a reversal of fortune, involving persons renowned and of superior attainments, and it should be written in poetry embellished with every kind of artistic expression.

Much more than this has been derived from Aristotle by modern theorists, but this much of the classical conception has generally survived in modern tragedy. If the meaning of "a single and complete action" be stretched a little, this definition includes the plays of Shakespeare as well as those of Racine, and nearly all tragedies from the Renaissance to the present.

In one important respect, however, this definition falls short of describing Greek tragedy, and is still more inadequate for modern. Aristotle emphasized the action above the characterization, and devoted much attention to the requirements of the plot. He did not, moreover, recognize the importance of the element of conflict, whether between man and circumstance, or between men, or within the mind of man. The Greek tragedies themselves had not failed to exhibit such conflicts; the medieval drama, notably in the moralities, emphasized moral conflict; and Renaissance tragedy, wherever it showed any independence, particularly in England and Shakespeare, took for its theme the conflict of human will with other forces. The importance of this modification of the

Aristotelian view received only slow critical recognition. But it was everywhere exemplified in practice, in French classical drama as well as in Shakespeare, in plays imitating the Greeks as well as in plays revolting from their models. After a time this modification of the classical tradition came to have a distinct place in literary theory. Hegel gave it philosophical elaboration, and, in the romantic movement, when dramatists in different languages turned to Shakespeare for a model, they naturally assumed what may be called the Shakespearean definition. This important amendment to the tragic tradition may be briefly stated: —

The action of a tragedy should represent a conflict of wills, or of will with circumstance, or will with itself, and should therefore be based on the characters of the persons involved. A typical tragedy is concerned with a great personality engaged in a struggle that ends disastrously.

In the Aristotelian tradition thus amended by the Shakespearean or modern conception we have a definition of tragedy that, in spite of differences of theorists and variations in practice, is extraordinarily comprehensive. This will appear if we consider briefly the separate elements of the definition. First: Though the range of emotions has been greatly widened in modern tragedy in comparison with classical, and though the importance given to love and the admission of comedy and even farce have complicated emotional effect in a way that Sophocles could hardly have conceived, yet "pity and fear"

still serve as well as any other terms to describe the
emotional appeal peculiar to tragedy. The word φόβος,
however, hardly indicates the emotions of admiration,
awe, hate, horror, terror, despair, and dismay, which
belong to tragedy, and modern tragedy has appealed
more largely than classical to pity and sympathy. Second: The reversal of fortune has been usually found in
tragedy, though in the sense of a fall of the mighty, long
the favorite theme, it cannot be regarded as the essential kernel of a tragic action. Third: Though the action
of modern tragedies has usually been less simple than
that of the Greeks, and though double plots and many
complications have been common, yet, after the Elizabethans and the Romanticists, the tendency to-day
seems to be toward a return to the simplicity that
Aristotle had in mind. Only in rare instances, as in
"The Doll's House," has a dramatist ventured to leave
the action in a state that might be called incomplete.
Fourth: Though themes have changed and widened in
range, still the great majority have been confined to
extraordinary events and illustrious persons. Renaissance and pseudo-classical theorists interpreted Aristotle
to limit the persons of tragedy to princes or men of the
highest rank; and tragedy, even in England, long adhered to this superficial restriction. But already in the
sixteenth century there were authors who wrote tragedies
of ordinary men and contemporary events; and realism
has broken away from the literary tradition in every
generation since. Fifth: Tragedy has generally been

reserved for poetry, and often for poetry of the most embellished kind; but here again realism has resorted to a
bare style, and, particularly in the last century, to prose.

On examination, then, the particulars of the classical
tradition have shown extraordinary powers of survival,
but not one of them has gone without protest and violation. The thousands of tragedies written during four
centuries have all had marked resemblances, and all
important developments have preserved relationships to
the classical species; yet it is impossible to insist on any
one quality of that species as essential, without encountering examples of great tragedies that lack it. The close
relationships among these many plays forbid the separation of a few, distinguished by certain qualities, to be
named as tragedies, and the rest as something else; and
the great variations forbid the confident selection of any
qualities as essential in the future development of tragedy.
The modern amendments, though represented by nearly
universal practice, have not saved the classical tradition,
and are themselves coming under question. The plays
of Ibsen, which seem to have instituted the most important
development in tragedy for two centuries, return to something of the simplicity of action required by Aristotle,
and present the struggle of individual wills as did Shakespeare, but are in prose and deal with contemporary
bourgeois life, — a combination of relationships to the
tradition wholly new. While idealization in some degree
must be exercised in tragedy as in all forms of literature,
it is impossible, in the light of realistic plays, to maintain

that tragic effects can be secured only through the stories of exceptional persons. Tragic greatness, in the sense demanded by the theorists, is, indeed, scarcely more manifest in the persons of "Romeo and Juliet" than in those of "Hedda Gabler." While conflict of some kind is essential to a dramatic action, yet it may evidently be minimized without destroying the artistic impressiveness of suffering and disaster. Even the requirement that tragedy deal with the characters of individual men is being questioned. It is conceivable that plays in the future may, like Hauptmann's "The Weavers," turn from the emotions of the individual to those of a class, or may find their destructive and painful actions in the oppression, disaster, or mere unrest of the mass.

Any precise and compact definition is sure to lack in comprehensiveness and veracity. It cannot sum up the facts of the past and present, much less set rules for the future. We seem forced to reject the possibility of any exact limitations for the dramatic species, to include as tragedies all plays presenting painful or destructive actions, to accept the leading elements of a literary tradition derived from the Greeks as indicating the common bonds between such plays in the past, but to admit that this tradition, while still powerful, is variable, uncertain, and unauthoritative.

But besides this literary tradition there has been a hardly less powerful theatrical tradition. Tragedy has always owed a double allegiance, to literature and to the theatre. A tragedy is a play, not merely a dialogue in poetry or prose, but a play to be interpreted by actors before an audience in a theatre. To these three factors it has had first of all to suit itself. And these factors have constituted conditions and standards, different and not less variable and transient than those of the literary tradition. The plays of Æschylus, of Shakespeare, of Calderon, and of Racine, for example, were planned for widely different conditions, and for conditions also widely different from those now present in the theatres. Excepting Shakespeare's, no English tragedies of the sixteenth, seventeenth, eighteenth, or, one might almost say, nineteenth century, are acted in our theatres to-day. The effect of the acted drama is consequently not only different from that of the drama when read, it is also subject to other and variable artistic standards. It aims at some effects not at all literary and at some likely to be limited by its own day and theatre. A history of tragedy must take into account the differences of the theatre of one nation from that of another, and of one period from another period. It must remember that to those temporary conditions each dramatist necessarily conformed and that by them his achievement was directed. It may find some hostile to the best dramatic art, tending to promote melodramatic rather than tragic effects. It may find others that are divorced from any permanent meaning for the drama or literature. But the fact that such conditions are temporary should not breed contempt, for much great literature has been aimed not at the world or posterity but at the audience of the day. Out of temporary and varying theatrical conditions have arisen the permanent criteria for dramatic excellence.

In fact, the theatre has been a conservative influence, tending to oppose innovation and to maintain the integrity of the form of tragedy. The essentials of its literary form, its length conditioned by the time of the performance, the division into acts, scenes, or parts, and the growing importance of dialogue, have all been dependent on theatrical conditions. The characteristic qualities of national dramas have been in some measure the products of the national theatres, and only through the growing similarity of stage conditions are we likely to attain agreement in regard to the forms of drama. While there have been a multitude of tragedies that have never been acted, and some that have never been intended for acting, the attempt to write tragedy for the closet rather than for the stage has resulted either in adopting the supposed conditions of the Greek or some other foreign theatre, or in breaking away from the strict limits defined by the stage and writing lyrical medleys or dramatic monologues or imaginary conversations. As soon as tragedy has left the theatre, it has reverted to old forms or developed new and strange hybrids. Milton's "Samson Agonistes" and Swinburne's "Bothwell" are tragedies, if you will, but they have no place in the development of a national drama. Shelley's "Prometheus Unbound," Browning's "The Ring and the Book," and Landor's "Marcellus and Hannibal" are all dramatic, but they cannot be included in any definition of the species of tragedy. Object as tragedy rightly may at times to the limitations and trivialities of the theatre, it cannot safely leave its precincts without losing its own identity.

In the past nearly all tragedies of any effect on the drama's development have not only been planned for the stage but have succeeded when acted. This seems likely to be the case in the future. For the reader of a play is confronted by difficulties not found in other fiction; and, in general, only a play suited to presentation on the stage is likely to secure for a reader the visualization, the impersonations, the illusion of actuality, similar to those experienced in the theatre. The fact that the drama requires the services of theatre and actors as well as author need not lessen our recognition of the responsibility and opportunities of the one or the other. The stage affords the first test of a play's emotional appeal, and perhaps the best test of its dramatic power. The consummation of tragedy has been attained only when the dramatist has availed himself of all the aids that the theatre has offered.

Thus far our attempt at definition has had to do with what tragedy is or has been or is likely to be, rather than with what it ought to be. The more difficult question has not been shunned by criticism, and perhaps even our brief discussion ought not to omit a consideration of tragedy's function and opportunities. These certainly extend beyond the theatre and include whatever is possible for literature. As a form of literature, tragedy fulfills in general the same functions as other forms, especially as fiction, of which it is one division. It has similar opportunities and its effects are similar in kind. It must be judged by the same standards, by the nature and power of its emotional effect, and by the lasting meaning of its portrayal of life; and the census of the centuries will be necessary to establish its greatness.

Special qualities have, however, been assumed for the emotional effect of tragedy altogether apart from its peculiarities as drama or fiction. A peculiar function, a special effect, differing from other forms of literature, have been ascribed to it. Aristotle declared its effect to be the purging of the emotions, a somewhat obscure expression, surely incorrect if taken in the literal sense that Aristotle seems to have intended, but variously interpreted as referring to moral or æsthetic reactions. Modern theories have too often regarded tragedy as a sort of exposition of the moral law, illustrating the ways of providence. To-day we require of tragedy a probing into human motive, an especial devotion to the study of character under great emotional stress. But has it a special function? Tragedy deals with pain, yet seeks to give us pleasure: — this crux has been greatly emphasized by the false antithesis between pain and pleasure. As a matter of fact, though our knowledge of the æsthetic emotions is scanty, a description of the effect of tragedy is hardly more obscure than that of any other form of literature or of any other of the fine arts. In life we are enormously interested in grief and suffering and disaster, as we are also in joy, pleasure, and success. Our newspapers abound in narratives of both sorts, and so do our novels. We are stirred by the painful emotions of our fellows as readily as by their pleasurable ones. The tragic plays a large part in many forms of literature and in sculpture, music, and painting. And tragedy, dedicated to painful actions, also interests, fascinates, absorbs us. It is not diverting, amusing; it is not for daily food or recreation, but no less it ministers to an active normal human interest.

Does it carry an antidote to offset its demand upon our sympathies? Is there a katharsis that somehow transforms our pity and fear into relief and pleasure? There is something of the sort in the mere exercise of violent emotion, which in a measure carries its own relief and cure. There is something also of egotistical satisfaction, of self-congratulation that comes with the exercise of sympathy, a certain exaltation that virtue has gone out of us. There is something again of æsthetic delight in the artistic mastery which we feel in any great work of art. The harmony of the argument, the splendor of the verse, the grandeur of conception and expression may counterbalance the painfulness of the story. Yet more, tragedy may bring the inspiration of greatness and endurance, of purity and unselfishness of spirit. Its idealization of character, its revelation of beauty and power even in distress and downfall, may bring a reassurance that turns pity to exhilaration. In drama as in life there may come in moments of trial and ruin the visions of the eternities to console and exalt us.

But is it true that these elements of relief are always felt, or are always triumphant over our depression and dismay? May not the impressions of pain and destruction be unrelieved and overwhelming? What relief or exaltation is there in the first impression from "Œdipus," "Lear," or "Ghosts"? We are filled with confusion, dismay, and pity. We cannot separate ourselves from the misery. We feel the intolerable burden of the world's woe. Our sympathies struggle beneath it, vainly, despairingly. How far such emotions have any potency for actual accomplishment in deed may be doubtful to the psychologists; but surely our recognition of tragedy as one of the greatest imaginative achievements needs no other warrant than our faith that virtue lies in human sympathy, in the only atonement that we can offer, the vicarious response of our emotions to share in suffering and defeat.

From the nature of its subjects, tragedy may claim a certain preëminence in literature. If it be not truer, as is sometimes asserted, than comedy or other fiction, it has the opportunity to be more intense, more profound, more permeating in its emotional effect. As of all forms of literature, we ask for truth to life in incident, character, and word; of tragedy we ask for truth in regard to those things that affect us most deeply, — pain, disaster, failure, death. Like other forms, it may stimulate and excite, give pleasure and profit, convey new ideas and recall old, arouse questions of life and philosophy, excite multitudinous emotions; more exclusively than any other, it brings home to us the images of our own sorrows, and chastens the spirit through the outpouring of our sympathies, even our horror and despair, for the misfortunes of our fellows.

NOTE ON BIBLIOGRAPHY

The student of the theory of tragedy may extend his reading through most books dealing at all with the theatre or drama, works of literary history and criticism, treatments of æsthetics in psychology and philosophy, as well as the tragedies themselves. Only the briefest direction for such reading can be given here. Among recent works closely connected with the matter of the chapter, are: W. L. Courtney, *The Idea of Tragedy in Ancient and Modern Drama* (1900); Lewis Campbell, *Tragic Drama in Æschylus, Sophocles, and Shakespeare* (1904); Ferdinand Brunetière, *L'évolution littéraire de la tragédie* (1903) (in vol. 7 of *Etudes critiques*); and *Melodrame ou Tragédie* (*Variétés Littéraires* 1904); Elizabeth Woodbridge, *The Drama, its Law and its Technique* (1898), with bibliography. Several recent books on Shakespeare are concerned with dramatic theory: A. C. Bradley, *Shakespearean Tragedy* (1905); T. R. Lounsbury, *Shakespeare as a Dramatic Artist* (1901); G. P. Baker, *The Development of Shakespeare as a Dramatist* (1907). A book now out of date and never sound, but of wide influence still, is Freytag's *Technik des Dramas* (1881), translated as *The Technique of the Drama*, Chicago (3d ed. 1900). For a study of literary criticism in reference to dramatic theory, Saintsbury's *History of Criticism*, 3 vols. (1900–04), furnishes a compendious directory and discussion. *An Introduction to the Methods and Materials of Literary Criticism*, by C. M. Gayley and F. N. Scott (1899), furnishes full bibliographical references with comment and direction. Of great value in their special fields are Butcher's edition of Aristotle's *Poetics* (3d ed. 1902); W. Cloetta's *Beiträge zur Litteraturgeschichte des Mittelalters und der Renaissance*, Halle (1890), vol i; and J. E. Spingarn's *Literary Criticism in the Renaissance* (1899). English critical discussions of tragedy will be noted in the chapters on the various historical periods. For tragedy in relation to æsthetic theory, full references are given in Gayley and Scott; and Volkelt's *Æsthetik des Tragischen*, Munich (2d ed. 1906), supplies a valuable and comprehensive discussion and a directory and criticism of nearly all æsthetic theories since Kant. Especial mention should be made of A. W. Schlegel's *Vorlesungen über dramatische Kunst und Litteratur* (1817), translated into English in the Bohn edition; and to Hegel's *Vorlesungen über die Æsthetik*, which closes with a discussion of dramatic poetry that has been suggestive of much later theorizing.

CHAPTER II

THE MEDIEVAL AND THE CLASSICAL INFLUENCES

NGLISH tragedy makes its appearance at the very beginning of Elizabeth's reign. In the Middle Ages nearly all knowledge of the drama of the Greeks and Romans was lost, and the medieval drama developed without aid from classical precedents or models. It resulted in various forms, of which the miracles and the moralities were the most important, but it produced nothing either in form or matter closely resembling classical tragedy or comedy, and manifested no evolution toward corresponding divisions of the drama. The Renaissance gave to the world the plays of Seneca, Plautus, and the Athenian dramatists, and, after a time, some knowledge of the classical theatre and dramatic art; then, through the imitation of these models and also through the innovations and experiments which they suggested, the influence of humanism came in conflict with that of medievalism throughout Europe, in the drama as in other fields of literature. In England this conflict was still active at the middle of the sixteenth century. Miracle plays were still performed after long established fashion, and moralities continued the most important and numerous species of drama; but in

Latin imitations of the classical drama, in the theatrical activity of the schools and universities, and in the various developments of moralities, interludes, school-plays, and pageants, there were signs of a breaking away from old courses and of the adoption of new models, of the emergence of English comedy and tragedy as definite dramatic forms. Tragedy in England as elsewhere developed later and more slowly than comedy, but two years after Elizabeth's accession the first English tragedy that has been preserved was performed, and "Gorboduc" thus becomes the starting-point for a history of English tragedy.

Modern tragedy, born in the Renaissance, the product of the germinating conflict of medieval and humanistic ideas and models, has never altogether lost the marks of its heritage from both lines of ancestry. Elizabethan tragedy, in particular, reveals in every lineament, in its scenic presentation, its methods of acting, its themes, structure, characters, style, theory, and artistic impulses, the influences both of the long centuries of medieval drama and also of the inspiration of the classics and the freer opportunity for individual effort which resulted from humanism. At the beginning we must attempt to separate and define these dominant influences.

The contribution from the Middle Ages came largely from the religious drama. The folk games and plays and the performances of entertainers of various sorts contributed to the development of the drama principally on the side of comedy, and only incidentally to tragedy. Nor need the early centuries of the religious drama detain us.

Its origin in the church service, its early liturgical forms, its growth and service in the hands of the church, and its gradual secularization are of importance for us only as leading to its culmination in the fifteenth and sixteenth centuries; in England notably in the great cycles of vernacular plays performed by the guilds. It should be remembered, however, that the miracle plays never felt the least influence from the drama of the Greeks and Romans. Knowledge of the classic drama was long confined mainly to the plays of Terence, and suggested even to the most learned no idea of relationship to the familiar miracle plays; and, on the other hand, the medieval stage gave no clue to a conception of the classical theatre. As late as Erasmus the curious notion survived that the classic plays were read by the author or a "recitator" from a pulpit above, while below the actors illustrated his lines by pantomime. Almost to the middle of the fifteenth century the miracle plays comprised all that was known of stage presentation in connection with serious drama. They were still performed through the sixteenth century; the boy Shakespeare may have been a spectator at a performance by the guilds; his father and grandfather and remoter forebears had seen them or perchance taken part in them. It was this abundant dramatic practice and ancient dramatic tradition that gave to Elizabethan England its fondness for play-acting, its recourse to the theatre for both amusement and edification, and the acceptance of the drama as an important factor in its daily life.

A glance at some of the most notable differences of the miracles from classical plays reveals traits that remained potent in later drama. The miracles took their material from the Bible or from some saint's life, and their purpose was to make this material significant and impressive. They were, in fact, essentially translations of prose narratives into dramatic dialogue. Renaissance drama sought different material, but it found classical authority for basing tragedies on history, and so gave support to the medieval method of translation. In the Elizabethan period, dramatists rarely attempted the invention of their plots, but adopted and adhered to narrative sources. While they never suffered from the narrow conventionality imposed upon the authors of the miracles by the authority of the holy writ, yet something of the medieval subjection to sources was long manifest both in form and content. It is necessary to view the dramas of Shakespeare and all his predecessors as translations into dramatic form of stories already told in verse or prose.

Because of their close adherence to sources and their distinctly expository purpose, the medieval dramatists made little or no distinction between what was suited for the stage and what was not. Their duty was primarily to present the narrative; and, though individual initiative might add something interesting or amusing, nothing in the Bible seemed unsuitable to presentation on the stage, and nothing that would aid its meaning seemed unsuitable for a drama. There was no thought of restricting a play to the presentation of one crisis or a single action, and there was consequently no possibility of an approach to anything like the structure of classical tragedy. The dramatist might take advantage of the dramatic value of a given situation like the sacrifice of Isaac, or he might make a series of plays lead up to the great events of the redemption, but he was blind to any opportunity to abstract from the narrative the events that dealt with an emotional crisis and to focus them upon that as the centre of a dramatic structure. There was no notion whatever of the difference between a narrative fable and a dramatic fable. Dramatic unity and values in a miracle play, on the tragic side at least, were usually the direct results of the narrative; unity on a larger scale in the cycle was the unity of history or of exposition, not of the drama. Such was the form which the Elizabethan drama inherited, and to the end the form of Elizabethan tragedy continued a development from medieval tradition and practice, not only in its failure to adopt the unities, the chorus, and other peculiarities of classical structure, but, more essentially, in its continued inability to restrict the story provided by a narrative source to the limits of a dramatic fable. Its final attainment of an organic structure, though promoted in part by the regularizing influence of classical theory and example, was in the main conditioned by the absence of dramaturgical restrictions, permitting an epic variety of events, the lack of which Aristotle had lamented in Greek tragedy, and by the consequent opportunity for a free and characteristic development.

From the medieval drama the Elizabethans inherited not only dramatic form, but an entire method of stage presentation different from the classical. The typical medieval stage, whether in the form of the procession of pageants or the inclosed place with the stations for the various actors, had, indeed, given way to something much more like the modern platform, even before the production of "Gorboduc"; but in most particulars, in the importance placed upon costume, the historical anachronisms, the crudity but frequency of spectacle, and especially in the entire liberty as to what should be presented, medieval ideas still prevailed. In the miracle plays, heaven, hell, God, the devil, Noah's flood, the fall of Lucifer, and the Maries at the cross were all acted. The Elizabethan theatre showed scarcely less temerity.

Another far-reaching inheritance from the miracle plays was derived from their treatment of tragic themes and situations and from their pervading seriousness of purpose. Their purpose was ethical and religious edification; their theme the tragedy of sin; their situations were derived from the stories of Cain, Lucifer, Judas, John the Baptist, the Slaughter of the Innocents, and the Crucifixion. If no formal tragedy resulted, and if in inculcating the triumph of righteousness the stories of the worthies and the martyrdoms of the saints took rather the cast of tragicomedy, it was nevertheless of great significance for later tragedy that, generations before Seneca became known with his bloody stories and sententious philosophy, the drama had been the vehicle for ethical instruction and for the presentation of the most terrible and pitiful events. The miracle plays had long familiarized men with tragic action, tragic conceptions in the drama, and tragic power in the treatment of situation.

The tragic was often mingled with the comic. The dramatists mixed edification with amusement. The restraints of the sacred narrative were thrown aside for a moment, and in Herod, or Noah's wife, or the shepherds awaiting the announcement of the birth of the Messiah, opportunities were taken for the introduction of realistic portraiture of contemporary life. Horse-play and buffoonery or racy comedy often contrasted incongruously with events of momentous importance. This mixture of the comic and tragic survived in the popular drama despite the opposition of the humanists. It was indeed characteristic of medieval and Elizabethan manners and taste, and marks another important departure from classical precedent. We to-day are perhaps as near to the Athenians as to the Elizabethans in this respect. At all events, for the appreciation of Elizabethan tragedy, we sometimes need to reassert a childish and uncultivated disregard for the rapid changes of emotional tone, a liking for tears and laughter close together; or, perhaps there is ground for saying, we need to recognize the validity of the medieval taste for a comic contrast and relief in tragedy, and to accept in art the incongruities and grotesqueness of actual life.

To the moralities, the second important species of

drama in the later Middle Ages, the debt of English
tragedy is more explicit than to the miracles, but not
more essential. It is not more essential, because the
moralities were in a way the successors and the substitutes for the miracles and contributed largely to the same
effects. They were devoted to a serious purpose and presented tragic situations with a free admixture of comedy,
and they continued many of the older traditions of stage
performance and undramatic form. They differed from
the miracles chiefly in that, like so much of medieval
literature, they offered not a direct but a symbolic presentation of life. Instead of the Bible narrative, they
presented the strife of vices and virtues; instead of real
persons, personified abstractions. This change from
individual characters to abstract qualities has usually
been regarded as a retrogression by modern students,
who deem the study of the motives of individual men and
women as essential to the drama. But we have lately
been reminded that on the stage it makes little difference
whether an actor is called William or Everyman; and the
attempt at the symbolization of life offered an opportunity for freedom of invention and freshness of emotional
effect that in the miracles had been smothered by the
stereotyped repetition of the Bible narrative. The temptation and suffering of the good, the temporary triumph
of the evil, and the punishment that overtakes even the
mighty were themes which the miracle had confused with
many others. The morality gave them dramatic isolation
and emphasis.

Moreover, in substituting for a translation of the Bible narrative the symbolization of life as a conflict between folly and wisdom, or the vices and virtues, or the body and the soul, the moralities gave importance to one of the most essential elements in tragedy, that of moral strife. The world is a battlefield, the soul is beleaguered, the play is a conflict; and with this element of conflict there arises the opportunity for dramatic structure. If the story is of strife, there is likely to be a moment when the victory hangs in the balance; a reversal of fortune is implied; there is a chance for a rise and fall, a definite beginning, middle, and end. The moral conflict, moreover, encourages a study of human motive, of cause and effect in human action. In some of these plays, as "The Pride of Life," "Everyman," "The Nice Wanton," the consequences of evil are clearly traced, and the action is representative not only of the conflict of good and evil in the universe, but of the battle of will in the individual. Evidently such plays are near relations of tragedy. They at least made plain to their successors the importance of the conflict of good and evil as a dramatic theme. Their text, the wages of sin are death, has continued to be an essential part of the conception of tragedy.

The moralities, however, on the whole, made little advance, either in escape from conventionality, or in creation of structure, or in dramatic expression of the conflicts of will. They clung in the main to the dominant and already conventionalized allegory of the Middle Ages, the presentation of life as a conflict of body and

soul, although they made interesting excursions into the
fields of pedagogy and religious controversy. This allegory they treated with intense didacticism, sacrificing
all dramatic interest to enforce the lesson, though in
their later days the sermons were very generously mixed
with farce. Their importance and explicit contribution
to English tragedy arose from their historical position
just at the close of the fifteenth and the beginning of the
sixteenth century. They then served as a transition
species, conforming, by a reduction in length and in the
number of actors, to the conditions of performance
which marked the change from the medieval stage to the
Elizabethan theatre; amalgamating under humanistic
influence now with this type of play, now with that; and
imposing for a time their distinctive form and methods
on the emerging types of comedy and tragedy. Some of
the earliest tragedies, as we shall see, were direct developments from the moralities, and the influence of the
peculiarities of the morality was for a while definite and
considerable. But it soon disappeared under the demands of a new theatre and the innovations of a new art.

The inheritance of tragedy from the Middle Ages
includes an important legacy from literature entirely
apart from the drama. In the separation of the medieval
world from the classic, the terms tragedy and comedy
ceased to be connected with scenic presentation, and
were extended to cover all forms of narrative, whether
in dialogue or not. The distinction between the two,
though varying somewhat in the different lexicographers

and encyclopedists, gradually arrived at an agreement which continued to affect ideas throughout the Renaissance. There was some insistence on the restrictions that tragedy dealt with history, and comedy with fiction; tragedy with exiles, murders, important and horrible deeds, and comedy with more domestic themes or with love and seduction. There was more general agreement that tragedy dealt with persons of rank and importance, kings or great leaders, and comedy with persons of low or middle rank, and that tragedy required a more elevated and ornamented style than comedy. The most important difference, however, was held to lie in the distinction that comedy begins unhappily and proceeds to a happy conclusion, while tragedy begins prosperously and ends miserably and terribly. Thus Dante's poem was a Divine Comedy, and Chaucer in the Monk's Prologue summed up the accepted opinion of the scholarship of his day.

> "Tragedie is to seyn a certeyn storie,
> As olde bokes maken us memorie,
> Of him that stood in greet prosperitee
> And is y-fallen out of heigh degree
> Into miserie, and endeth wrecchedly."

These criteria for tragedy were fixed in the consciousness of the sixteenth century; and, though gradually correlated and amalgamated with criticism based on the newly found "Poetics," they continued to influence the theory and practice of the drama. Fitting these definitions and greatly increasing their importance and vogue, collections of tragedies attained wide popularity during the fourteenth fifteenth, and sixteenth centuries. Boccaccio's "De Casibus Illustrium Virorum et Feminarum," Chaucer's "Monk's Tale," and Lydgate's "Falls of Princes" are examples, and, far the most influential on English tragedy, "The Mirror for Magistrates." This collection, first printed in 1559 and later frequently re-edited and enlarged, suggested many themes for the historical drama. Elizabethan playwrights seeking for tragic stories turned naturally to this most famous collection of "tragedies" in the medieval sense. Consequently, the very idea of tragedy continued to carry the connotation of a sudden reversal of fortune, the fall of princes. Tragedy, indeed, has always remained very largely devoted to themes "de casibus illustrium virorum et feminarum."

Turning now from the influence of medievalism to that of humanism, we may remember that in the drama even more than elsewhere humanism denotes a revolution in the spirit of the age, an emancipation of the individual mind from the fetters that had bound intellect and imagination through the Middle Ages But we must deal first with one of the factors in accomplishing this emancipation, the reawakened knowledge of classical literature. There was some slight acquaintance with the Attic drama from the time that Greek was first taught at Oxford; the doughty Roger Ascham learned from his master Sir John Cheke to prefer Euripides to Seneca; and at the time when the study of Sophocles and Euripides was occupying the Italian dramatists, there must have been some similar response in England. Specific instances of this, however, are few and uncertain. The Greek dramatists seem to have exercised no appreciable direct influence on English tragedy of the sixteenth century; nor can their influence at any time during the seventeenth be said to have been considerable. For England, even more exclusively than for the Continent, the classical influence on the origin and early development of tragedy was confined to the ten plays which Renaissance scholarship attributed to the philosopher Seneca.

Seneca's plays, probably not intended for stage presentation, were literary exercises following the models of Greek tragedy and more especially of Euripides. By the humanist, after he had acquired some slight knowledge of the classical theatre, they were naturally accepted as plays actually performed, and their artificial and elaborate diction, which is their most conscious departure from Attic standards, was eagerly appraised as a merit. Their themes, with the exception of that of the pseudo-Senecan "Octavia," are borrowed from Greek mythology, with a strong preference for the most sensational and bloody stories of adultery, incest, the murder of parents by their children or of children by their parents. Whatever the revolting and bloody details, crime and its retribution make up the burden of each story. The plays present only the last phase of an action, and consequently open with lengthy exposition of preceding events. Much happens behind the scenes, little on the stage; there are many narrative and lyrical scenes, comparatively few dramatic. In comparison with the Athenian tragedies, they seem like prolonged rhetorical discussions of the familiar legends. Their structure involves a division into five acts, which had probably been earlier adopted in Latin tragedy and is noted in the "Ars Poetica," and the exclusion of the chorus from any participation in the action. It appears usually after each of the first four acts and indulges in philosophical reflections, hymns in praise of some deity, or lamentations. In each play a chief person or hero can be distinguished in conflict with one or more chief opponents; and each of the leading persons is accompanied by an adviser or confidant, usually a faithful friend for a hero and a nurse for the heroine. In addition to mortals, supernatural visitants, furies, gods, and especially ghosts, have a prominence that stirred Elizabethans to imitation. Though the presentation of character is not humanly vital, the long speeches and soliloquies display an elaborate analysis of moods of passion, with an absence of Athenian religion, a pagan cosmopolitanism, and an almost modern introspection. The style and philosophy were the chief recommendation of the plays to the Renaissance taste. Artificial, with constant use of antithesis, stichomythia, and hyperbole, oratorical, sonorous, bombastic, and thickly sprinkled with aphorisms and sentiments, the style seemed to the humanists to reach the height of tragic elevation and philosophic sententiousness.

The reasons for the almost exclusive adoption of

Seneca as a model seem to have been not only the comparative ignorance of Greek, but also the preference of Renaissance taste for the qualities just enumerated. Moreover, these lifeless and undramatic mixtures of rhetorical verbiage, melodramatic situations, and endless declamations had the advantage of being easy to imitate. In their encouragement to imitation and their absorption of interest away from the models of Greek tragedy, there was a danger of humanistic endeavor resulting in mere copying, a danger not altogether escaped in Italy and France, but happily averted in England.

When, on the other hand, the characteristics of these unpromising models are considered in comparison with the conventionality of the miracles and moralities, they clearly offered much provocative of literary endeavor and the development of the *genre* of tragedy. Through them secular stories, real persons, and dramatic plots took the place of the allegories and the abstractions. While they encouraged the selection of such stories as resembled the sensational myths favored by Seneca, they opened the door to history, romance, and the whole world of classical fable. Though their particular structure proved in the end impossible on the English stage, they enforced the division into acts already familiarized in comedy, and suggested the possibility of a dramatic fable in distinction from the miracles' adherence to a narrative one. Again, their presentation of character brought new persons, new motives, and new methods, calling attention to drama not as an exposition of events or as an allegory

of life, but as a field for the study of human emotion.
Their brilliant if bombastic rhetoric aroused enthusiasm
for the drama as literature and poetry; and their reflective and aphoristic style encouraged an effort to elevate
tragedy above its too familiar converse with comedy into
the realm of austere philosophy. These influences, however, were general. Every particular of Seneca's plays
had its sixteenth century imitators.

The first signs of an intelligent interest in these plays
appeared almost simultaneously at the very beginning
of the fourteenth century in the commentary of the English Dominican, Nicholas Treveth, and in the study of
the circle gathered about Lovato di Lovati at Padua.
One of this school, Albertino Mussato, about 1314, wrote
his "Eccerinis" on the fate of the Paduan tyrant, Ezze-
lino, of the preceding century. This first of the Latin
tragedies of modern times aroused the admiration of
scholars, and was followed by many other neo-Latin
imitations of Seneca. These, while keeping to the Senecan
form, often went beyond the stories of classical mythology
and chose their subjects from the Bible or from ancient
or modern history. Meanwhile neo-Latin comedy had
had a beginning and was largely stimulated by the discovery, in 1427, of twelve hitherto unknown comedies of
Plautus. All these neo-Latin plays were read and not
acted; and the actual acting, either of the classical plays
or their humanistic imitations, was not established until
the close of the fifteenth century.

The knowledge of the classical drama spread after a

time across the Alps, and Terentian comedy in particular exercised a wide influence upon the drama. Of especial interest in relation to tragedy is the new school of neo-Latin comedy which arose about 1530 in Holland and spread over Germany and into France. It applied Terentian style and structure to many of the stories in the Old Testament and to the parable of the prodigal son. To its original purpose of substituting for Terentian immorality themes edifying for youth, it soon added a Protestant tone, and in Kirchmayer's "Pammachius" (1538) entered the field of violent religious controversy. As the number of these plays rapidly increased, there resulted a secularization of treatment and the admission of Senecan as well as Terentian influence. The stories of Judith, Susannah, Goliath, and others gave opportunities for recourse to Senecan imitation; and in the "Jephthes" and "Baptistes," which about 1540 George Buchanan wrote at Bordeaux for his students to act, we have the first tragedies north of the Alps written in distinctly classical form, — a form, it should be said, derived from his study and translation of Euripides as well as from Seneca.

Seneca's preëminence as a model for tragedy, however, was in general not contested, but rather increased by the growing knowledge of Euripides and Sophocles. By the end of the fifteenth century there had been many translations of his plays in Italy; they were studied in the schools, and some had been given stage presentation. But the idea of a vernacular tragedy on the Senecan model was

not put into effect until Trissino's "Sophonisba," written in 1515. This was followed by others, until by the
time of "Gorboduc" Senecan tragedy in Italian was an
established form, and Jodelle's "Cléopatre Captive"
(1552) had marked the beginning of the Senecan *genre*
in France. The Italian tragedy had also introduced some
departures, in the choice of romantic material and in the
innovation of "tragicomedy," which supplied the Senecan model with a happy ending. But all these writers of
tragedy worked with a common purpose, to revive Senecan drama in their own day, and their plays adapted
their themes and methods to the Senecan model with the
faithfulness of disciples. These Senecan imitations, it
should be noted, were designed for special performances
under academic or courtly auspices, and not for the
popular theatre.

In England during the first half of the sixteenth century
there was a repetition of the inter-influence between the
still flourishing forms of medieval drama and the new
classical models which we have noted on the Continent.
The early Renaissance in the reign of Henry VIII awakened an interest in Seneca; and the fragment of an English play introducing Lucrece has suggested to Mr.
Chambers the possibility of an essay at Senecan tragedy
thirty years before "Gorboduc." The main force of the
humanistic influence seems, however, to have been in the
direction of comedy. The drama was no longer confined
to popular open-air presentations, but found a place at
court, in the halls of noblemen, and especially at the

schools and universities, where the comedies of Plautus and Terence and imitations both in Latin and English were frequently acted. The influence of the classical plays themselves and of the neo-Latin school and the controversial dramas of the Continent upon English moralities and interludes was extensive and distinct. This led to a multiplication and confusion of dramatic types out of which comedy emerged in such plays as "Gammer Gurton's Needle" and "Ralph Roister Doister." In Latin, but not in English, we can trace a similar movement toward tragedy. We hear of a "Dido" written by Ritwyse, master of St. Paul's, and performed by his pupils some time in the decade preceding 1532. "Absalon," written by Thomas Watson probably in the following decade, was highly praised by Roger Ascham, and, if it be identical with the play now in manuscript in the British Museum, is an example of biblical drama along Senecan lines. A non-extant "Jephthes" by Christopherson (1546), the "Archipropheta," with a romantic love episode and a clown, written by Grimald and acted at Oxford in 1547, and his "Christus Redivivus" published in 1543 as a "comœdia tragica," all belong to the same mixed species. A representative of the controversial drama appears in John Foxe's "Christus Triumphans" about 1550, which drew much from the famous "Pammachius," already translated by Bale and acted at Oxford to the great scandal of Gardiner. Of plays in the vernacular we hear of a few called tragedies, but the term was used without any exactness, and no extant play

has any just claim to the title. Ten tragedies and comedies are attributed by Bale to Ralph Radcliffe, a peda-
gogue, who in 1538 opened a theatre in his schoolhouse
and gave plays before the 'plebs.' Some of these were
certainly in Latin, but some may have been in English,
and the titles are interesting as emphasizing again the
prevailing humanistic influences. Of the tragedies, two,
"The Burning of Sodom" and "The Delivery of Susannah," are on biblical themes evidently chosen for the purpose of edification; the third, "The Condemnation of
John Huss," suggests the controversial type. Of the
comedies, four have biblical themes, while three, "Patient
Griselda," "Melibœus," and "Titus and Gisippus,"
indicate the growing search for secular and even romantic
themes. In this confusion of many species of drama,
created by a mixture of medieval and humanistic influences, there is at least no clear evidence of any English
tragedy on Senecan lines before "Gorboduc." Of the
development of the moralities toward tragedy, of which
signs are not lacking, we get the clearest examples in
plays a little later, which will be treated in the next
chapter.

Special notice, however, must here be paid to one
morality and the dramatic activity of its author. John
Bale, born 1495, a converted Carmelite who became
bishop under Edward VI and an exile during the reign
of Mary, and who died not long after the accession of
Elizabeth, was one of the most vigorous of Protestant controversialists and apparently the leader of what

may be called the Protestant drama. His forty-six plays "in idiomate materno" seem to have been intended for presentation, and, while exhibiting classical influence, doubtless in the main followed medieval models. Of the five extant, written presumably about 1538, three, "God's Promises," "John the Baptist," and "The Temptation of our Lord," are miracle plays; one, "The Three Laws," is a morality. The fifth, "King John," inspired in its satirical and Protestant elements by "Pammachius" and perhaps also by Lindsay's "Three Estates," is the first example of a morality showing an approach to the later historical drama. It is in form a controversial morality, divided into two long parts or acts, but it follows roughly a chronological outline, and among its abstractions presents the king himself as the champion of Protestantism against the pope and Pandulph. Although the direct influence of the play on later drama cannot be traced, it is a notable advance, of which there were perhaps other examples, toward the treatment of English history and of individual persons rather than abstractions in the popular drama.

The humanistic activities of the sixty years before "Gorboduc" thus resulted in a breaking away of allegiance to medieval models and the introduction of new types, rather than in any direct contribution to the form or matter of tragedy. The vernacular play approaching nearest to the field of tragedy is still a controversial morality exhibiting all the traits of medieval drama, and in its innovations pointing not toward classical models, but rather to a new extension of the morality toward the presentation of national history and real persons. During this time, however, the influence of Seneca's plays had been constantly extending and had been augmented by that of the imitations in Latin, French, and Italian. The interest of Seneca in the universities seems to have increased during the reigns of Edward and Mary and to have supplanted in a measure that in Latin comedy. In 1559 the appearance of the first English translation, that of the "Troades" by Jasper Heywood, opened the way to a wider interest and to the possibility of domiciling the Senecan drama on the English stage. By 1561 translations of four other plays had been published; and, before the collected edition of 1581, all of the ten had appeared and attained a greater popularity with the reading public than they have ever since experienced.

The first English tragedy was not a modification of current forms, but a direct imitation of Seneca. The production of "Gorboduc," however, only marked another stage in that conflict between medievalism and humanism which we have been tracing. In the next chapter we shall consider the conflict between Senecan imitations and popular tragedies that still kept to the morality form, a conflict that resulted in the discarding of both Senecan and morality incumbrances and the attainment in Marlowe and his followers of a form of tragedy very different from either, though inheriting bountifully from both.

One source of classical influence other than Seneca's

plays and their imitations was of enough importance to require special mention, that of Aristotle's "Poetics." First printed in 1508, it reinforced the dogmas derived from the "Ars Poetica," and became the basis of a rapidly increasing amount of dramatic criticism. This criticism, mostly Italian, interpreted Aristotle by means of the Senecan tragedies and so reinforced their influence; but it was also greatly modified by the medieval ideas of tragedy which we have already noticed. The resultant theory of tragedy, with special regard to its misinterpretations of Aristotle, may be briefly summarized. His dictum that tragedy is the imitation of a serious action was interpreted to mean an action illustrious because the actors are persons of the highest rank, thus adopting the medieval restriction of tragedy to princes. There was less agreement in the restriction of tragedy to history rather than fiction; and over the question of the propriety of a happy ending there was considerable debate. Tragicomedies were written and defended, but critics in general recognized tragedy as restricted to an unhappy ending, which was universally interpreted to mean deaths. In regard to the function of tragedy there was great difference of opinion over the meaning of κάθαρσις, the weight of opinion inclining to emphasize the ethical aim of tragedy, that is, the reward of virtue and punishment of vice and the inculcation of morality by means of frequent precepts. From Aristotle's discussion of character there was derived the curious idea of "decorum," so important in later theories of the drama, that every character should represent a class and should always have the same characteristics, — the kings all acting after one prescribed fashion, the soldiers after another, the old men after another, and so on. From Aristotle's mention of the restriction of time to one revolution of the sun came the unities of time and place, confining the action to one city and twenty-four hours, which were soon made predominant over the third unity of action. These distinctions became fixed in Italian criticism and were given their first full expression in English in Sidney's "Apology for Poetry," written about 1580; but before that they were more or less comprehended by most English students of Seneca. Although even a scholar in 1561 would have been unable to define the unities or decorum, he would have had some confused notion of them. The scope and function of tragedy were by that time assuming in the general literary consciousness a definition approved by both medieval and classical theory and later formulated by Puttenham: "Tragedy deals with doleful falls of unfortunate and afflicted princes, for the purpose of reminding men of the mutability of fortune and of God's just punishment of a vicious life."

Such definition of medieval and classical influences as we have been attempting necessitates a somewhat unreal separation of the two forces. Evidently, in the mind of any playwright, the two combined in a confusion of impulses, of the sources of many of which he must have been unaware. Absolute restriction to the old tradition or to the new inspiration is hardly to be expected in any Eng-

lish dramatist attempting tragedy in the neighborhood
of 1562. Such an author would have open for his choice
a wealth of stories, classical, medieval, or Italian, as yet
untouched by drama; and, though he might choose a
story whose events paralleled some Senecan plot, he
would be likely to adhere closely to his narrative source
after the medieval fashion. Even if he strove loyally after
the Senecan form, his knowledge would be hardly sufficient to prevent departures from strict classical standards.
Seneca does not always clearly observe the unities or
remove violent action from the stage, and his Elizabethan
follower would naturally err on the side in accord with
popular dramatic tradition. Of the chorus, reduced in
importance by Seneca, he would find it difficult to make
much use. On the other hand, the adapter of the morality
structure to tragic purpose would perhaps fail to derive
anything from Seneca except his bombast and sensationalism. For whatever audience the dramatist was writing,
he would have many spectators demanding the fun,
horse-play, and crude horror of medieval tradition, while
his own literary aspirations might lead him to prefer
lofty declamation and aphoristic phrasing. But, whether
his knowledge was large or small, he was likely to combine in his conception of tragedy, as did Puttenham, both
the Christian idea of evil, thwarting good and meeting
punishment, and the Senecan idea of a crime followed by
retribution or revenge. And, whether he catered to popular taste or to literary ambition, he must have contem-
plated the presentation of a reversal of fortune, persons

of royal or distinguished rank, and a catastrophe involving deaths.

It is, after all, the main contribution of humanism that through the study of the classics there had come new impetus and authority for individual effort. Art was to be based on classic precedents, but it was forbidden by the spirit of the new age to remain after medieval fashion satisfied with repetitions and translations. For the dramatist there were not only new models, but a circulation of ideas, free opportunity, and the incentive of fame. For him, too, there was a public long habituated to the drama and now well tutored in novelties and variations of the old forms, a public that no longer expected a conventionalized stage, but was possessed of what the apostle Paul deemed the chief characteristic of the classical spirit, the desire to hear some new thing.

NOTE ON BIBLIOGRAPHY

The authorities on their respective subjects are: W. Creizenach, *Geschichte des neuren Dramas*, Halle, 1893–1903 (3 vols. and index, extending to 1570, have appeared); A. W. Ward, *A History of English Dramatic Literature to the Death of Queen Anne*, 1899, new and revised edition, 3 vols.; E. K. Chambers, *The Mediæval Stage*, Oxford, 1903. These all cover the matter of the present chapter and contain bibliographies. Ward gives full bibliographical notes to editions and monographs; Creizenach's index is substantially complete for all European plays; Chambers's Appendix X contains references to editions and descriptions of all English plays up to Elizabeth's accession. Klein, *Geschichte des Dramas*, 13 vols., 1865–76, and Collier, *History of English Dramatic Poetry*, new edition, 1879, are both somewhat out of date, though the latter contains much useful material. R. Pröloss, *Geschichte des neueren Dramas* (1881–83), and K. Mantzius, *The History of Theatric Art*, 3 vols. (1904), are slighter. The only rapid and readable survey of European drama is by Brander Matthews, *The Development of the Drama* (1906). For France, the authority for medieval drama is L. Petit de Julleville, *Histoire du Théâtre en France au Moyen Age*, 1880–86, 4 vols.; for Germany, R. Froning, *Das Drama des Mittelalters*, 1891; for Italy, A. Ancona, *Origini del Teatro italiano*, 1891, 2d edition. J. J. Jusserand, *Le Théâtre en Angleterre* (1881, 2d ed.); J. A. Symonds, *Shakespeare's Predecessors in the English Drama* (1884); G. Gregory Smith, *The Transition Period* (1900, in *Periods of European Literature*); Gayley, *Plays of Our Forefathers* (1907), are of value. Dealing more specifically with matters discussed in this chapter are the volumes of Cloetta and Spingarn cited in the last chapter, C. H. Herford's *The Literary Relations of England and Germany in the Sixteenth Century*, Cambridge, 1886, J. W. Cunliffe's *The Influence of Seneca on Elizabethan Tragedy*, Manchester, 1893, and R. Fischer's *Zur Kunstentwickelung der Englischen Tragödie von ihren ersten Anfangen bis zu Shakespeare*, 1893. The Elizabethan translations of Seneca have been reprinted by the Spenser Society (1887). Within the last few years three new translations have appeared: by Watson Bradshaw, in prose (1902); by Miss E. A. Harris, in verse, two tragedies 1899, the remaining eight 1904; by F. J. Miller, in verse, with introduction on Seneca's Influence on English Drama by J. M. Manly (Chicago, 1907). Text and discussions of plays are presented by A. W. Pollard, *English Miracle Plays*, Oxford, 4th ed., 1904; A. Brandl, *Quellen des weltlichen Dramas in England*, 1898; J. M. Manly, *Specimens of the Pre-Shakespearean Drama*, 1897 (2 vols., the third to contain notes and discussion). Dodsley's *Old Plays*, ed. W. C. Hazlitt, 15 vols., 1874–76, also contains texts. The matter of this and subsequent chapters also receives treatment in the general histories of literature. J. J. Jusserand, *Literary History of the English People*, 2 vols., 1895–, is especially valuable in its account of the drama. The new *Cambridge History of English Literature* (now in progress) will contain valuable monographs on the matter of this and subsequent chapters. *The Dictionary of National Biography* is, of course, most valuable for individual writers. F. E. Schelling's *Elizabethan Drama*, 1558–1642, which appears as this volume is passing the press, is a general history of the drama of the period stated, with special reference to the development of dramatic species. It contains an extremely useful Bibliographical Essay and "A List of Plays" written, acted, or published in England, 1558–1642.

CHAPTER III

THE BEGINNINGS OF TRAGEDY

N this chapter the development of tragedy is to be traced from 1562, the year of the production of "Gorboduc," to about 1587, the beginning of Marlowe's career. Our knowledge of the drama during this period is scanty, and there are few extant tragedies or plays resembling tragedy. Before examining these plays with the detail which their historical position demands, it will be necessary first to glance at the theatrical conditions. Reference has been made to some of the changes that had been working a transformation from the conditions of the popular performance of the religious drama in the fourteenth and fifteenth centuries. Through these, the drama had already to a large extent passed from the control of the guilds to that of small companies of amateur or professional actors; from the open air into the halls of noblemen or of the schools; from the large stage with its fixed stations for the different actors or the procession of pageants, to the small and perhaps improvised platform. Long plays with hosts of actors had given place to short plays with few parts, or many parts divisible among few actors, and constructed with a clear distinction between "on the stage" and "off the stage." Performances indoors, no specially prepared stage, few actors, and short plays represent the prevailing theatrical practice of the early sixteenth century.

From 1562 on, however, theatrical conditions were various and shifting, and not always easily discernible by the modern student. While miracles were still performed after the old popular fashion, the traveling professional companies were growing in importance and tending to monopolize the acting of interludes. Amateur actors, however, at court, school, university, inns of court, or, indeed, among the Bottoms and mechanics of the villages, still contended with the professional for the control and maintenance of the drama. So far as tragedy is concerned, it will be convenient to keep in mind at least four distinct kinds of performance. First, the Gentlemen of the Inns of Court, who throughout the Elizabethan period showed themselves liberal patrons of the drama, occasionally gave plays, usually in connection with special festivities. Second, there were performances at the schools and universities which continued to exert an important dramatic influence, as they had for the preceding sixty years. Plays at the universities were generally in Latin, but there were English plays at both schools and universities, and companies from the Merchant Tailors and Westminster schools acted at court; these last performances falling properly in the third group. Third, companies of children were trained for performance at court; and these were in the course of time restricted to the choir boys of St. Paul's and of the Queen's chapel. Fourth, the traveling professional companies, numerous at the beginning of the period, acted in the inn-yards of London, at court, in the halls of noblemen, on the village greens, in the guild halls, even in the churches of the towns, or wherever else they could obtain an opportunity, until the most important of them found homes in the London theatres. On all four of these classes of actors the influence of the court was considerable, for it was the highest gratification of either amateur or professional to be engaged in a court performance, and performances at court were subject to greater preparation than those in public.

Such were the conditions governing the presentation of tragedies in this period, but in the course of its twenty-five years the professional companies constantly grew in importance and in the end practically monopolized the business of giving plays. Schools, universities, and companies of amateurs became of decreasing moment in the development of the drama, while the choir boys were permitted to act plays publicly in their own theatres and thus became formidable professional rivals of the men's companies. In 1572 the statute compelling the common players to obtain the license of some nobleman reduced the number of the adult companies, but strengthened those that survived, which now became known as Lord Leicester's men, Lord Howard's men, and so on. In London they were able with the assistance of the court to establish and maintain themselves despite the active and constant opposition of the city authorities. The

Theatre, built outside the city proper in 1576, was soon followed by other playhouses, and in 1583 a company was licensed under the Queen's personal patronage. Henceforth the history of the Elizabethan drama is in the main confined to four or five companies of men and one or two of children, acting regularly in their established theatres and occasionally in the provinces, or at court, or elsewhere.

The character of a tragedy naturally varied with the circumstances of its presentation. A Latin play at one of the universities was much more dignified and scholarly than the performance of a few traveling actors for the delectation of a provincial audience; and a play by the Gentlemen of the Inner Temple was given with an elaborateness not to be expected in those by the choir boys, which were likely to be brief and to include a good deal of singing. The extant tragedies can consequently be best classified according to their methods of presentation. Before all audiences, it should be remembered, moralities of divers sorts were performed, but we are now concerned only with those that most closely approach tragedy. All the extant Latin plays were presented at the universities. Of English plays, "Gorboduc," "Tancred and Gismunda," "Jocasta," and "The Misfortunes of Arthur" were acted by gentlemen of the Inner Temple or Gray's Inn, and are all Senecan tragedies. "Damon and Pithias" and "Appius and Virginia" were acted at court by children, and show little Senecan influence, but are medleys of tragedy, comedy, and music. No performance by an adult company of any extant tragedy is recorded, but "Horestes" and "Cambyses," both of which may have originally been intended for children, bear some evident marks of popular presentation, and both are mixtures of morality, farce, and tragedy. These plays, with the exception of "The Misfortunes of Arthur," acted in 1588 at the very end of the period, were all written and performed in the sixties. With the addition of "Promus and Cassandra" (1578), apparently not acted, they comprise all extant plays acted before 1586–87 which can be classed as tragedies or tragicomedies. Our knowledge of the professional drama may be supplemented from the titles of non-extant plays and from the Revels Accounts of performances at court; but it should be observed that our information in regard to the development of popular tragedy is very meagre, especially for the important period after 1570, and that the group of Senecan plays, which we are to examine first, owed their existence to no popular favor, but to amateur performances under special conditions.

"Gorboduc," or "Ferrex and Porrex," printed surreptitiously in 1565 and with an authoritative text about 1570, was written by Thomas Norton and Thomas Sackville, the author of "The Complaint of Buckingham" and "The Induction" in "The Mirror for Magistrates," and afterwards Lord Buckhurst, Lord High Treasurer. It was performed before the Queen as a part of the elaborate Christmas entertainment of the Inner Temple in 1561–62. The plot is taken from a British

legend that was introduced into literature by Geoffrey
of Monmouth, and relates the division of the kingdom
by Gorboduc between his two sons, Ferrex and Porrex,
the murder of the elder by the younger, the murder of
the younger by his mother, the murder of both father and
mother by their subjects, the slaughter of the people by
the nobles, and the resulting civil wars. The story, evidently chosen because of its likeness to Seneca's "The-
bais," is treated in Senecan manner, each of the first four
acts being followed by a chorus of "Foure auncient and
sage men of Brittaine." The murders are not enacted
but are related by messengers, but the unities of time and
place are violated, as Sir Philip Sidney noted with disap-
proval. There is little characterization, much political
moralizing, which delighted Sidney, and an abundance
of long declamations, about eight hundred lines, nearly
half of the play, being comprised in ten speeches. The
play is written in blank verse, already used in Surrey's
translation from the Æneid, and perhaps adopted in
imitation of the unrhymed verse of the Italian tragedies.
After the Italian fashion, each act is preceded by a dumb
show, symbolizing the following action, and these dumb
shows seem to have been utilized to provide the spectacle
that was entirely wanting in the play proper. Supernatural visitants appear in the three furies before act iv; and
before the last act the dumb show consists of a battle-
scene, similar to those which later became the invariable
accompaniments of the chronicle history play: "there
came forth upon the stage a company of hargabusiers and

of armed men all in order of battaile," who discharged their pieces and marched three times about the stage.

In spite of the close adherence to the Senecan model, there is little direct borrowing from Seneca, and medieval elements are not lacking. The debates between the good and bad counselors are very like those of the moralities, and the structure is essentially that of a chronicle of a whole story rather than that of a classical tragedy. The first two acts are occupied by the interminable debates, and the last three by the catastrophe, or rather the succession of catastrophes, though the final scene of the fifth act is a sort of epilogue after Senecan fashion. The play has little literary value, though Marcella's recital is not without power and the disquisitions on discord and disloyalty in the state have the merit of earnestness; but it is clearly the beginning of a new species. It abandons current dramatic forms, and endeavors to depict the fall of English princes in accordance with the models of classical tragedy.

"Jocasta," by Gascoigne and Kinwelmarsh, acted 1566 by the Gentlemen of Gray's Inn, demands little attention. It is a translation in blank verse of Lodovico Dolce's "Giocasta," itself an adaptation of the "Phœnissæ" of Euripides. It thus furnishes additional evidence of the influence of Italian tragedy on English. The chorus numbers four, as in "Gorboduc," and the dumb shows, apparently of Gascoigne's invention, are notably elaborate and spectacular.[1]

[1] Before the first act, "there came in upon the stage a king with an

"Tancred and Gismunda," acted before the queen at the Inner Temple in 1568, under the title "Gismond of Salerne," was written in rhymed quatrains by five gentlemen of the Temple, and afterwards revised and put into blank verse by the author of the fifth act, Robert Wilmot, and first published in 1591.[1] In both versions Cupid appears before the first and third acts as the director of the action, and Magæra comes on before the fourth act to superintend the revenge and murder. The play is based on Painter's version of Boccaccio's *novella*, which is followed closely, but the base-born lover becomes a count according to the prevailing theory of tragedy. The story itself has an obvious dramatic power and a certain dramatic structure which it imposes on the play.

Imperiall Crowne upon his head . . . sitting in a chariot very richely furnished, drawne in by foure kinges in their dublettes and hosen, with crownes upon their heades, representing unto us ambition," etc. And before the fifth act there is a similar exhibition of a woman in a chariot driving kings and slaves. These shows may have suggested to Marlowe the famous business of Tamburlaine and his chariot. The show before act ii introduces the paraphernalia of coffins and a grave, afterwards so frequent in popular tragedy.

[1] The earlier version also survives in MS. and has been published by Professor Brandl in his *Quellen des Weltlichen Dramas*. The revised version is the result of elaborate care and reflects more highly developed dramatic conditions than existed in the sixties, but in some respects it may be closer to the original performance than is the manuscript. The songs of the chorus, now four maids of Gismunda's instead of four gentlemen of Salerne, and the dumb shows must have had some equivalents in the presentation before the Queen, though both are wanting in the earlier version. The dumb shows are noteworthy because, unlike those in *Gorboduc* and *Jocasta*, they are not allegorical, but represent important actions described or referred to in the text.

Gismunda's passion for the Count Palurin runs counter to her father's wishes; at the end of the third act love is triumphant, but in the fourth is defeated, and the gruesome catastrophe follows, Tancred and Gismunda dying on the stage. This is the earliest extant English play based on an Italian *novella*, and the first tragedy to adopt a romantic love story and to make the passion of love its central motive; and the authors accomplished their experiment with evident enthusiasm and some gracefulness and force of diction. They were, however, very conscious of their models. Seneca's "Thyestes," and "Phædra," itself presenting a story of passionate love, were perhaps their chief inspirations; but Buchanan's "Jephthes" and Beza's "Abraham," translated into English in 1577, are mentioned in Wilmot's dedication, and, together with other plays, supplied precedents for the treatment of the favorite tragic theme, the sacrifice of a child by a father. Moreover, Italian tragedies had, since Giraldi's "Orbecche," been turning to romantic fiction for their subjects instead of to history and mythology; and some of these, "Orbecche" itself, and, as Professor Creizenach notes,[1] Dolce's "Dido," doubtless influenced the young templars. There had, indeed, already been Italian tragedies based on Boccaccio's *novella*, and one by Frederigo Asinari (1576) had added an Œdipean horror by making Tancred put out his eyes before killing himself, an augmentation adopted by Wilmot in his revision. The play was thus not only thoroughly Senecan, but the result of a

[1] *Geschichte des neueren Dramas*, ii, 471.

tangle of derivative Senecan influences. The authors were probably unconscious of the incongruity so obvious to us between the classical form and the romantic material. They were interested in their story and were eager to give it all the advantages that erudition could discover; their intentions were doubtless perfectly reflected in the praise which William Webbe gave them for a play that "all men generally desired, as a work, either in stateliness of show, depth of conceit, or true ornaments of poetical art, inferior to none of the best in that kind : no, were the Roman Seneca the censurer."

"The Misfortunes of Arthur," by Thomas Hughes, was acted and published in 1588. The story from " The Morte D'Arthur " was suggested by its likeness to Senecan plots; and the play was an ambitious attempt to use British legend as Seneca had treated classical myth. The strife between father and son, with its accompaniments of adultery and incest, is viewed as constituting a Nemesis for the crimes of Arthur's father, Pendragon; and the ghost of the wronged Gorlois appears in the first scene to promise revenge, and in the final scene to triumph over its fulfillment. The author knew his models by heart, borrowed much, availed himself of all the particulars of the Senecan technic, and imitated everywhere with a good deal of spirit and success. The play has dramatic and poetic merits beyond its predecessors, but its late date makes it of small importance in our effort to trace the beginnings of English tragedy. Acted twenty-six years after "Gorboduc," it testifies less to the progress of dra-

matic art than to the conventionalizing effect of Senecan
models. Though perhaps the most successful of English
imitations of Seneca, it marks the failure of amateur
actors and courtly audiences to revive the classical drama
on the English stage. On the occasion of its performance
before the Queen at Greenwich, its actors and authors
may very likely have thought it full of significance for
the future of the drama; but "Tamburlaine" had already
been acted, and poetry had taken up its abode in the
despised public theatres. The chief interest for us in
"The Misfortunes of Arthur" is that it furnishes further
illustration of the use of English history and of stories of
revenge.

To understand the full importance of the attempt to
domicile Seneca in England, we must turn to the universities. Two English plays, which would be of interest, have not been preserved, "Ezechias," a tragedy
by Udall, acted in 1564 at Cambridge, and "Palamon
and Arcyte" by Edwards, the author of "Damon and
Pithias," acted 1566. These are the only English plays
at all tragical that are recorded; but the practice of giving Latin plays continued and grew in popularity.[1] We
hear of "Dido" and an "Ajax Flagellifer," apparently
a translation of Sophocles, both in 1564, and a "Progne"

---

[1] For a list of Latin plays acted at the universities, see Fleay, *Biographical Chronicle of the English Drama*, vol. ii, 347–366. This list must
be corrected in many particulars by an article, "Die Lateinischen Uni-
versitäts-Dramen in der Zeit der Königin Elisabeth," by George B.
Churchill and Wolfgang Keller, *Jahrbuch der Deutschen Shakespeare-
Gesellschaft*, xxxiv, 220–323.

in 1566. The extant Latin tragedies are of a later date. Gager's "Meleager," "Œdipus," and "Dido," all acted in the early eighties, are modeled strictly on Seneca, the first two showing direct borrowings. In the fragment which we possess of the third, the ghost of Sichæus appears to warn Dido, and is followed by the storm, represented, we learn, by sugar for snow, sweetmeats for hail, and rose-water for rain. Gager's "Ulysses Redux," acted in 1591, a little beyond the limits of our period, presents a somewhat freer treatment of the Senecan form, the number of characters and of scenes being larger than in the earlier plays. Of uncertain date are a "Herodes," which takes the form of a revenge play introduced by the ghost of Mariemma, and "Solymannidæ" and "Tonumbeius," which apply Senecan methods to Eastern instead of to classical atrocities. "Roxana " (1632), acted before 1592, is a translation of "La Dalida" of Luigi Groto, and won some contemporary distinction and the praise of Dr. Johnson two centuries later. It is a revenge play with a ghost, combining Senecan gruesomeness with the motives of romantic comedy.

More famous than any of these in its own day was "Richardus Tertius," a tragedy in three parts, each part acted on a separate night in 1579 at St. John's, Cambridge, the work of Thomas Legge, Master of Caius and afterwards Vice-Chancellor of the university. Legge seems to have felt the incongruity between the material of the chronicles, which he followed closely, and a strict Senecan form, and to have striven to overcome this by the mechanical expedient of prolonging the action over three plays. But the problem of presenting on the stage the events of a whole reign could not be solved in the terms of the Senecan formula. Legge copied the Senecan rhetoric, interpreted historical events and persons under the guidance of the formula, and retained much of its technic, the narration of deaths instead of their presentation, counsel scenes between hero and advisers, frequent use of the nuntius, and a vestige of a chorus. But the play departs as widely as popular dramas from the unities of time and place, contains many scenes with more than three speakers, is full of dramatic action, and presents processions, pageants, and battle scenes after the fashion of later chronicle plays in the public theatres. Its influence on popular drama may well have been considerable; though, on the other hand, its adherence to sources and its looseness of structure may have been reflections from the public stage. Whether the first chronicle play or not, it is the earliest extant play to indicate the result of the inevitable conflict between a narrow and stereotyped dramatic form and the wide range of material which the chronicles afforded.[1]

In these university Latin plays there is evident a

[1] Far more novel than any of the plays discussed in its departures from Senecan precedent, is *Perfidus Hetruscus*. So far as can be judged from the outline (*Jahrbuch*, xxxiv, 250–252), it offers no semblance of Senecan structure. There is no chorus, but there are six ghosts, a villain, two accomplices, — one a Capuchin, the other a Jesuit, — and an elaborate plot, as full of surprises as of poisonings. It seems to be a popular revenge play turned into Latin, and can hardly come within our period.

development similar to that traced in the English Senecan drama. Biblical themes disappear; close imitations of Seneca on classical themes give way to freer treatment of romantic or historical material. Revenge and the ghost are ever prominent; and English history introduces a host of events, varied, incongruous, panoramic, and bursting the bounds of the traditional structure. Nash, Marlowe, and others of the later dramatists were university men, and saw some of these plays performed, and perhaps took part in them. Their scenic spectacle, choices of themes, handling of situation, and general effect must have had an appreciable influence upon the subsequent course of the drama. To the various influences which we have denominated humanistic, and especially to the derivative influences reinforcing that of Seneca, we must add this of the Latin plays at Oxford and Cambridge. Latin tragedies continued to be acted at the universities for many years, but their influence on the popular drama can have been potent only during its formative period.

When we turn from these academic and amateur productions to the more popular performances,[1] we have

[1] One play should be mentioned here as standing in some ways between the classical and popular plays. *Promus and Cassandra*, by George Whetstone, published 1578, cannot be placed in any of our four classes, for there is no evidence that it was ever acted. Like *Tancred and Gismunda*, it was based on an Italian *novella*, also the source of *Measure for Measure*, and it follows Latin comedy rather than tragedy. In its division into five acts, its frequent soliloquies, its attempted observance of decorum (especially vaunted in the preface), and in its serious purpose and moral sentiments, the play shows a pedantic clinging to

to deal with a very different class of plays. The four to be considered were all written by men of scholarly training, and all deal with classical themes, but the Senecan influence is slight and mainly discernible in the figurative and hyperbolic diction and the fondness for sententious maxims. None of the four are divided into acts; none have choruses or other characteristic marks of Senecan structure; all present action to the exclusion of reflection, and all are in rhymed verse, the favorite metre, at least in the serious portions, being doggerel. All admit comic and farcical scenes, and three are in a large measure moralities. In the tragic portions all admit violence and murders of all kinds on the stage; there is a beheading, a hanging, and, in the case of "Cambyses," a flaying, accomplished, the stage direction reassures us, "with a false skin."

"Damon and Pithias" (1571), by Richard Edwards, was acted by the Children of the Chapel at court in 1563–64, and, judging from the title-page, probably also in public. The prologue, which contains a discussion of "decorum," explains that the term "tragicall comedy" is used because

classicism. In the main, however, it belongs with *Damon and Pithias* and *Appius and Virginia*, and seems to have been intended for performance by children. It is a mixture of tragedy, comedy, farce, and songs; and this abundance of incongruous material seems to have led to its division into two plays, as Whetstone says, for the purpose of decorum. Here, as elsewhere in the period, the experiment of putting new material into old dramatic structures burst the bottles. Clowns, parasites, tyrants, prostitutes, hangmen, Egyptians, and girls in boys' clothing make up a pageant which is a sort of tragicomedy but which the learned author called by the more popular title, "a history."

the story is a matter "mixed up with mirth and care."
The serious portion of the play presents the tyrant Diony-
sius as well as the two faithful friends, and shows evidence
of a study of Seneca; but it is intermixed with comedy,
where the influence of Plautus is noticeable, and indeed
with scenes of broadest farce. Carisophus, the parasite,
is hardly distinguishable from the vice of the moralities,
and is not only clown and mischief-maker, but the villain, whose infamy brings about the tragic entanglements. The play contains a number of songs, and this
mixture of tragedy, farce, and musical comedy seems
typical of the children's plays of this period.

"Appius and Virginia" (S. R. 1567–68), by an unknown
R. B., was also evidently acted by one of the children's
companies, perhaps, as Mr. Fleay plausibly conjectures,
by the boys of the Westminster school. It is much shorter
than "Damon and Pithias," but, like that play, is styled
a tragical comedy, is written in rhymed verse, mostly
doggerel, and contains farcical scenes and many songs.
The vice Haphazard is a clown and mischief-maker;
and, in addition, a number of personified abstractions,
Conscience, Justice, Comfort, Doctrina, etc., indicate the
close relation of the play to the moralities. The main
plot, however, is tragic and has no integral connection
with the comic scenes. It begins with the domestic happiness of the family of Virginius, and proceeds promptly
to the action. Virginia is beheaded, and the head is
afterwards exhibited; Appius Claudius and Haphazard
are executed out of the sight of the audience; and in

the closing scene the tomb of Virginia is shown upon the stage, Memory inscribes her renown, while Justice, Reward, Doctrine, and Fame apparently join in a song "around about the tomb in honor of her name."

"Horestes" (1567) by John Pickering was probably the "Orestes" acted at court 1567–68. It also seems to have been performed by children, but was very likely given public presentation by various companies. The title runs significantly, "A New Interlude of Vice, conteyninge the Historye of Horestes," etc. The vice, indeed, is hardly absent from the stage, and offers much that is new in his species. He is a clown, but apparently this is only a disguise, for he appears to Horestes as a messenger from the gods, urging him to revenge; later as Courage he is Horestes' faithful friend and supporter, then as Revenge he attends to the execution of Clytemnestra, and finally he appears as a beggar thrust out of court, since Revenge could not agree with the Amity dwelling there, and takes the opportunity to read a long lecture to women. The diversity of elements confused in this personage is typical of the play. It is in a large measure a morality; Nature appears to Horestes to dissuade him from including his mother in his vengeance, Fame appears as a judge and exempts him from guilt, and other abstractions are numerous and voluble. There are also a number of songs, Egisthus and Clytemnestra having just finished a love song when the messenger announces the avenger's approach. There are many scenes of sheer farce, where the humor lies wholly in fisticuffs and beatings; and the spectacular element suggests the later historical plays. Horestes is accompanied by an army which marches with drums about the stage and fights two pitched battles, one with the host of Egisthus and the other for the possession of the city. "Make your lively battel and let it be long," says the stage direction. Still further, the classical elements are curiously confused. Although there are a number of quotations from Ovid and frequent citations of other classical worthies, there is no mention of Seneca, though the plot of "a revenge for a father" here makes its first appearance in the English drama, and the authors appear to have been entirely ignorant of the Greek tragedies. The ultimate source is the sixth book of Dictys Cretensis. The author follows closely one of the popular versions of the Troy legend, retains the anachronisms of the romantic version, and imposes on that the structure of the morality, the vice taking the place of the oracle of Apollo, and abstractions mingling with the knights and dukes of the Trojan war. The play is thus interesting as marking another step in the translation of the morality into the "history" type of tragedy. The closing scenes, in particular, illustrate the adherence to sources with morality embellishments. The play by no means ends with the murders. Horestes is approved by Fame, accused by Menelaus, who arrives, defended by Nestor, who throws down his glove as a gage, then reconciled to Menelaus, married to Hermione, crowned by Duty and Truth, and applauded and advised by Commons and Nobelles.

"Cambyses" (S. R. 1569–70) was written by Thomas Preston, afterwards Master of Trinity Hall, and acted some time in the sixties. Perhaps originally intended for a school performance, it was later evidently acted in public, and seems more suited than even "Appius and Virginia" or "Horestes" to a performance by an ordinary professional adult company. The title-page sets forth the plot with a terse emphasis of its various elements: "A Lamentable Tragedie mixed full of pleasant mirth containing the Life of Cambises King of Persia from the beginning of his kingdome unto his Death, his one good deede of execution, after that, many wicked deedes and tyrannous murders committed by and through him, and last of all, his odious death by Gods Justice appointed." Like "Horestes," this is a combination of morality and history, and the chronicle or epical method is enforced by the fact that we have the whole story of "the life and death," as later titles ran, of a monarch. The chronicle structure is mixed full of pleasant mirth and pays a certain regard to climax. Cambyses begins by executing an unjust judge, and proceeds to murder the child of his minister, then his brother, then his bride, and finally himself. The comic scenes have a link of connection with the tragic ones in Ambidexter, the vice and accomplice of the villanous tyrant. Seneca is appealed to as an authority in the prologue, but there is little trace of his influence, unless it is found in the central figure of the wicked tyrant and his gory career, or in the highfalutin of Cambyses' vein. The extraordinary list of *dramatis personae* indicates sufficiently the hodge-podge of the action and the prominence of the morality influence. The deaths are managed by Cruelty or Murder; Commons Cry, Commons Complaint, Small Nobility, and Proof appeal against tyranny; the marriage feast is arranged by Preparation; the comic scenes are shared by Huf, Ruf, Snuf, Hob, and Lob; Venus and Cupid manage the love affairs; and Shame appears as a sort of tentative ghost:

"From among the grisly ghosts I come, from tyrants' testy train."

The fall of the Prince Cambyses, it should be added, is accidentally or providentially upon his own sword; and only the exit of Ambidexter and a few words from the three lords, who pronounce the accident a just reward from heaven and promise princely burial, are required to bring the play to a close.

In these plays we may trace the gradual emergence of tragedy in the popular drama in response to a growing knowledge of its functions and methods. It appears still mixed with farce and morality, but it has themes like those of Seneca, bloody, revolting, and sensational, and its freedom in stage presentation permits an emphasis on crime and death even greater than in the Senecan imitations. Notably, it introduces the stories of the downfall of a tyrant and the revenge of a son for a father. The structure has none of the Senecan characteristics, and consists merely in linking together, or rather in interrupting by extraneous comedy, a few scenes illustrating a story; but it is like that of the English Senecan plays in the space it gives to catastrophe. In general the plays begin conventionally with the depiction of peaceful and prosperous circumstances, and proceed at once to the disasters and deaths, with very little attention to the events or motives that lead to these results. The element of conflict is as yet hardly translated out of the abstract terms of the morality into those of actual life. The conflict of motives never leads to a dramatic crisis but keeps to the form of a medieval debate, as between Nature and Horestes, or, indeed, between the bad and good counselors in "Gorboduc." Characterization likewise depends mostly on the form of arguing abstractions, though certain types of importance later are already noticeable. The faithful friend and the aged counselor are ever at hand, and the part, if not the character, of the tragic hero is provided in Horestes and Virginius. The villain receives considerable attention. The English dramatists were puzzled to follow the classical tragedies in placing the source of evil in Fate or the decrees of the gods; and even when their stories provided them with persons sufficiently iniquitous to cause all the tragic trouble, they seem to have felt the need for a visible and special representative of the devil. Evil in "Gorboduc" may be said to arise from the counsels of the parasites as well as from the folly of the king and the envy of the princes. In "Tancred and Gismunda" it is due, after classical imitation, to the intervention of Cupid. In the popular plays the vice is borrowed from the moralities, and, in all except "Horestes," is made a mischief-maker, a source of evil, and the special representative of the devil. Questions in regard to the origin of the vice and his relationship to the devil of the medieval drama have not been freed from doubt by recent investigation, but it seems clear that in the early tragedies he was given some of the work later accomplished by the stage-villain and his accomplices. The part that women play in these early tragedies should also be noticed. Women and love, as Professor Creizenach has observed, receive far more attention in Renaissance tragedy than in Greek or Senecan. "Tancred and Gismunda" and "Promus and Cassandra" deal with stories of romantic love; Virginia and the queen in "Cambyses" present noteworthy though slight examples of the idealization of women so important in later drama. The purpose of all these plays, Senecan or popular, is superficially didactic, as is witnessed not only by the abundant moralizing in the Senecan imitations, but also in the popular plays by the emphasis in the closing scenes on the reward of virtue and the punishment of vice. In the last act of "Appius and Virginia" the lesson of the play is written on the tomb, and in "Horestes" the conduct of the hero is discussed by Nestor and Fame and finally rewarded by Hermione, Truth, and Duty. "Cambyses" is more in line with later tragedy in presenting the protagonist as a monster and in closing promptly after his punishment by death.

The most certain accomplishment, however, in the development of the drama up to 1570 had been in the widening of its range of material. The bible narrative

and moral allegory had been superseded by classical
myth and history, and these in turn were being en-
croached upon by the romantic fiction of the Italian
novelle and by the chronicles of English history. Italian
novelle were open to dramatists mainly through a series
of collections of translations, of which "Painter's Palace
of Pleasure" (1566) was the chief. The interest in English history was stimulated and fed by "The Mirror for
Magistrates" and the various editions of the chronicles;
Grafton, Stowe, and the third edition of Fabyan appearing in the sixties, and Holinshed in 1577; while interest
in the classics was maintained by numerous translations
as well as by an increasing knowledge of Latin. Translation, indeed, had brought the stories of the world to the
English mart, and the dramatic industry was now eager
in its demand for material.

Of the continued development of popular tragedy after
1570, and particularly of the sources drawn upon for
dramatic material, we can get a few hints from the titles
of non-extant plays. The incomplete Revels Accounts
of performances at court preserve the names of over
sixty plays acted between 1570 and 1585, and about
thirty are derived from other sources. Of the court plays,
none had biblical subjects; a number were moralities, a
few were drawn from old romances; but the majority
were from classical or Italian sources. Many of these
must have contained tragic incidents,[1] though probably

---

[1] *Ariodante and Genevra* (*Orlando Furioso*), *Ajax and Ulysses, Aga-
memnon and Ulysses, Cæsar and Pompey, Cloridon and Radimanta,*

they were not much more classical in form than "Appius and Virginia" or "Horestes." Only one title drawn from national history presents itself, "The King of Scots." The English chronicle play had evidently not yet made any stir at court; but many of the classical plays were drawn from Livy. Two other titles, "The Cruelty of a Stepmother" and "Murderous Michael" (Sussex's men, '78, '79), and a third of a play at Bristol in 1578, "What Mischief Worketh in the Mind of Man," may possibly have had for sources accounts of contemporary murders, and thus have instituted the species of domestic tragedy. A few titles, suggestive of tragedy, with accompanying comments, have been preserved by Gosson, who praises: "The Jew," "representing the greediness of worldly chusers and bloody minds of usurers," apparently a forerunner of "The Merchant of Venice"; "Ptolemy," "describing the overthrow of seditious estates and rebellious commons"; "The Blacksmith's Daughter," "contayning the treachery of the Turkes, the honourable bountye of a noble mind, and the shining of virtue in distress"; and his own play, "Catilin's Conspiracy," "showing the reward of traitors."

Some further information concerning the emergence of popular tragedy can be derived from the criticisms of

Duke of Milan, Effigenia (Iphigenia), Four Sons of Fabius, Mutius Scævola, Quintus Fabius, Perseus and Andromeda, Sarpedon, Scipio Africanus, Timoclea at the Siege of Thebes, Telemo, Twelve Labors of Hercules. Some titles suggesting medieval romance are: Knight of the Burning Bush, Red Knight, Paris and Vienna, Solitary Knight.

the period. Gosson in his "Plays Confuted" (1582), declares:—

"For the poets drive it most commonly unto such points as may best show the majesty of their pen in tragical speeches, or set their hearers agog with discourses of love; or paint a few antics to fit their own humours with scoffs and taunts or wring in a show to furnish forth the stage when it is too bare; when the matter itself comes short of this, they follow the practice of the cobbler, and set their teeth to the leather to pull it out. . . . So," he adds, "was the history of Cæsar and Pompey and the play of the Fabii at the theatre, both amplified where the drums might walk or the pen ruffle."

A similar criticism is made by Whetstone in his dedication of "Promus and Cassandra" (1578): "The Englishman in this qualitie, is most vaine, indiscreete, and out of order: he first groundes his work on impossibilities: then in three howers ronnes he throwe the worlde: marryes, gets Children, makes Children men, men to conquer kingdomes, murder monsters, and bringeth Gods from Heaven and fetcheth Divels from Hel." Sidney in the well-known passage on the contemporary drama in his "Apologie for Poetrie" (1595, but written about 1580) amplified these same criticisms, deploring the lack of "noble moralitie," the violation of the unities, and the admixture of farce in current tragedies, and especially animadverting on the histories and the "mongrel Tragy-comedie." He asks scornfully: "And doe they not knowe, that a Tragedie is tied to the lawes of Poesie, and not of Historie? not bound to follow the storie, but having liberty either to faine a quite new matter, or to frame the history to the most tragicall conveniencie. Againe, many things may be told, which cannot be shewed, if they knewe the difference betwixt reporting and representing," — and he goes on to illustrate. Evidently the medieval methods were still potent rather than those of Sidney's models, Euripides, Seneca, and "Gorboduc"; and the tragedies in the theatres followed their sources without recognition of the difference between a narrative and a dramatic structure, and with an appeal to vulgar taste by means of hideous monsters, pitched fields, scurrility, or "some extreme shew of doltishness." From these critical comments we may infer that the popular drama had before 1585 triumphed over the Senecan. The few extant tragedies before that date have shown little which was not paralleled in the contemporary drama of western Europe; but in the popularization of a professional drama that rejected Senecan technic but still delighted in the presentation of tragic fact we have the first clear differentiation of English tragedy from that of other nations. Unfortunately we have only this indirect evidence that such differentiation was well under way before Marlowe.

On the basis of such evidence, however, we may draw a few inferences in regard to the course of popular tragedy from 1570 to 1585. We may infer that Senecan imitations in the hands of amateurs did not multiply, and were not readily accepted even as object lessons by writers for the public theatres, who, whatever inspiration they may have received from amateur or academic plays, must have felt

the increasing force of the demand from the public for
amusement and sensation. While undoubtedly many
traces of Senecan influence continued, and while classical
themes persisted, the prevalent type of drama became
neither right comedy nor right tragedy but the so-called
"history." Whether based on history or fiction, its main
purpose was the presentation of a story, the more marvelous the better; and, even if it ended in deaths, it was
likely to contain a mixture of farce, romantic love, stage
spectacle, and, as time went on, a diminishing inculcation
of morality. Throughout the period, popular tragedy
probably remained commingled with other species of
drama. As it forsook the morality, it found itself wedded
with farce or spectacle; or, perhaps more extensively,
with history and romantic comedy. What course the
popular drama farthest removed from court or academic
influence may have taken, we can only surmise, though
the presentation of contemporary murders, which found
favor even at court, must presumably have flourished
with less cultivated audiences. And it is impossible to
resist the conjecture that English history must have received crude presentation in the public theatres much
earlier than we have any record of.

We may also surmise that in the quarter of a century
from "Cambyses" to "Tamburlaine" there must have
been some considerable development in the power to
depict tragic fact, in the traditions of tragic acting, and
in the cultivation of the taste of both audiences and
authors for the genuinely terrible, pathetic, and heroic,

but we must assume that tragedy still awaited the service of both literary and dramatic genius. The genius of Marlowe, however, had its way prepared by twenty-five years of extraordinary dramatic activity, during which the functions of comedy and tragedy had become known if not observed, comedy had attained a considerable development in Lyly and Peele, and tragedy had gained sufficient vigor to extend its themes, and to decide against a development imitative and scholarly, and in favor of one original and popular.

NOTE ON BIBLIOGRAPHY

Most of the books in the list for the last chapter are useful in connection with the matter of this. Creizenach and Ward are the chief authorities; Collier, Symonds, and Jusserand deal with the period. Spingarn, Cunliffe, and Fischer are valuable for their special fields. Texts are to be found in Manly, Dodsley, Brandl, and discussions in the latter. For the stage history of the Elizabethan drama, the works of F. G. Fleay are very valuable, though marred by much unsupported conjecture: *A Biographical Chronicle of the English Drama, 1559–1642*, 2 vols. (1891); *A Chronicle History of the London Stage, 1559–1642* (1890); *A Chronicle History of the Life and Work of William Shakespeare* (1886). The first-named is the most reliable and useful of the three. Original documents and records are printed in part in Collier and Fleay; and in Halliwell-Phillipps's *Outlines of the Life of Shakespeare* (6th ed., 1886); Malone's *Variorum* ed. of Shakespeare, 1821; Cunningham's *Extracts from the Annals of the Revels at Court*, Shakespeare Society, 1842; Nichols's *The Progresses and Public Processions of Queen Elizabeth*, 3 vols., 1823; *Aussere Geschichte der englischen Theatertruppen*, 1559–1642, by Hermann Maas (Materialien zur Kunde des älteren Englischen Dramas, 1907); Hazlitt's *English Drama and Stage* (1869); Chambers's *Notes on the Revels Office* (1906). The essays of Gosson, Sidney, Webbe, Puttenham, which supply most of the dramatic criticism of the period, are in Arber's Reprints; selections from these and other critical works with an introduction are collected in

Elizabethan Critical Essays, G. Gregory Smith (1904). J. W. Cunliffe's edition of Gascoigne's *Posies* (1907) contains the plays, which he has also edited with an introduction in *The Belles-Lettres Series* (1906). A study of Legge's *Richardus Tertius* is found in G. B. Churchill's *Richard III up to Shakespeare* (Berlin, 1906); and an account of the Latin university plays in the article cited, by G. B. Churchill and W. Keller (*Shakspere Jahrbuch*, 1898). W. W. Greg's *A List of English Plays written before 1643 and printed before 1700* (London Bibliographical Society) is based on the title-pages of the original copies. Fleay's *Biographical Chronicle* includes all plays known, extant or not. Greg, Fleay, and Schelling supersede Halliwell-Phillipps's *Dictionary of Old English Plays* (1860), and W. C. Hazlitt's *Manual of Old English Plays* (1892). *English Drama, a Working Basis*, by K. L. Bates and L. B. Godfrey, Wellesley College (1895), is the only attempt at a directory to modern editions, and though very incomplete, is the most serviceable guide to the whole field of English drama.

CHAPTER IV

MARLOWE AND HIS CONTEMPORARIES

HE growing national consciousness that reached its triumphant culmination in the defeat of Spain made itself felt in the drama, specifically in efforts to present the glories of English history, and still more potently in an awakened responsiveness to the new fields and new incentives for artistic ambition. The beginning of the greatness of the national drama is significantly coincident with the victory over the Armada. By that time the spirit of noble endeavor had found lodgment in every worthy breast. It animated Marlowe no less than Drake, and the author of the least successful chronicle play as well as admiral or counselor. The extraordinary achievements that had been contributing to the might of England as a political power were, indeed, but one expression of the freedom and eagerness of individual initiative that characterized this English Renaissance and found other expression in the activities and accomplishments of literature. In comparison with the men of preceding generations, the Elizabethan Englishman faced a world of new horizons, new ideas, boundless opportunities, and alluring rewards. Every career was open and promised an untrod pathway and unworn laurels. He might win fame as a pirate, philosopher, or poet; or in the new excitement of living he might crowd not one but many careers into the span of life. The versatility of a Raleigh only typifies the excitement and energy of deed, the lively movement of thought which quickened mind and body, and resulted, now in a voyage to Virginia, now in a conspiracy, now in a sonnet, and now in a history of the universe. And this feverishness to make trial of thronging opportunities was symptomatic not only of vigor of intellect, celerity of emotion, and independence of will, but also of an imaginative idealism that enlightened the daily living of many a sorry citizen, and was destined to live resplendent in the verses of Spenser and Shakespeare. In the stir of free ideas, the surprise of discovery, and the glow of accomplishment, life grew heroic, attainment seemed easy, and no ideals too lofty for the scaling ladders of human aspiration. Men achieved much and they dreamt of more. The apprentice went to the theatre to don Fortunatus's cap or to triumph with Tamburlaine; every one had his El Dorado distant only a short voyage; and, with the new world before them, poets and playwrights set sail in blithe confidence of splendid discovery. Never before, or perhaps since, have so many new things seemed within grasp, whether in literature or in life; never has all living so throbbed with a sense of the nearness of the unattainable, the kinship of the real and the ideal.

In non-dramatic literature the incentives of the classics and of the Italians from Petrarch to Tasso had led on from translations and imitations to experiments and inventions. In the dozen years before the Armada, lyric poetry, criticism, and prose fiction had felt the stir of successful English innovation, and the time was almost ripe for the vast projects of Spenser, Hooker, and Bacon. In comedy the development had been earlier and more rapid than in tragedy, and had already in Peele and Lyly reached the stage of dexterous expression and varied innovation. Whether presenting a story of classical mythology or of medieval romance, whether farcical, Plautian, pastoral, sentimental, satirical, or spectacular, comedy was by the time of Marlowe ready with its examples to offer instruction to any writer attempting tragic themes. Tragedy could hardly remain longer in the stage of translation, imitation, and feeble experiment which we have been considering.

Still further, a stimulus for tragedy was exercised by the daily events of that active era. These stirred men's imagination and ambition, and must almost inevitably have directed artistic impulse toward the heroic, the passionate, and the terrible. The abundance of bloodshed in Elizabethan tragedy may find some interpretation in the fact that Ben Jonson killed his man in a duel and that Marlowe was stabbed in a tavern brawl. The time was one of bloodshed, violence, quick and brutal passion; a time in which the torture of a Gloster or the revenge of a Shylock was far closer to life, to the life at least of poets and dramatists, than such stories are to-day. Drake in his cabin drinking and praying with the unmoved lieutenant whom he was to hang the next day is a bit of fact

that rivals in horror the devilries of a Barabas. Even if
Seneca's example had not already approved themes
of adúltery, murder, blood-vengeance, the atrocities of
tyranny, and the deadly strife of father and son, such
themes must have stirred men's minds in the days of the
Massacre of St. Bartholemew and the career of Mary
Stuart. If tradition had not already selected the falls of
princes as the especial field for tragedy, the history of
monarchical Europe in the sixteenth century must have
given such stories a power of appeal hardly to be appreciated now. In that strenuous generation the dramatist
must have found artistic impulses from bloody and gruesome deeds, and no less from daring ambition, heroic
struggle, and indomitable greatness of mind.

The summons, however, which the tragic muse heeded
came directly from the public theatres and the professional actors. The university men who at this time were
writing for the theatre under the lash and loans of a
slave-driving theatrical manager may have been tempted
to forget that their sordid and Bohemian existence offered
a means for triumphant artistic expression. The London
theatres were now well established, patronized by the
courtiers, and secured in prosperity by the motley audiences that crowded their performances. They had become important centres in the social life of the time,
comparable to the newspaper offices of a twentieth-cen-
tury city in their close touch with the daily life about
them; and in their task of affording amusement and
information fulfilling in part the functions of periodicals

and novels as well as of the drama at present. The stage, without scenery, was still in a transition state between the medieval and modern, and, to our view, almost unrealizably crude. Places were sometimes indicated by signs; properties, beds, tables, or trees were brought on or off as occasion required; or, a heavier property, like a cave, might remain whether the scene was in caveland or a counting-room. There was no drop curtain; actors went off, others came on, and the place changed from a seacoast to the palace; or, the actors merely moved across the platform, and it transpired that they had passed from " a fair and pleasant green " to a room in the house of Faustus. At the close of a tragedy all the survivors might be needed to bear off the bodies of the dead. A balcony in the rear of the stage stood in stead of a castle wall or the deck of a ship, while a curtained space below might represent an inner room or a dungeon vault. A curtain extending across the stage seems at times to have been used in managing a change of scene. Spectacular elements were not lacking: fireworks, ascents and descents of gods, armies, coronations, and battles delighted the eye. On costume, anachronistic but elaborate, the manager lavished his money and ingenuity. Cleopatra tightly laced, Tamburlaine in scarlet copper breeches are recorded facts, but Venuses, Apollos, mermaids, devils, satyrs, and nymphs leave something for fancy to conceive, as does the " gown to go invisible in " which perhaps shielded Ariel or Puck. Of the acting we have little information. Female parts were played by boys; clowns with their jigs were great favorites, but a considerable skill in acting must be supposed, — less subtle, less occupied with stage business than to-day, more declamatory possibly, and more attentive to the spoken word. Any superiority in the appreciation possessed by the audiences over those of to-day must be attributed not to their superior intelligence, but to their long training in listening to plays. They probably differed from uneducated audiences in the cheaper theatres of to-day chiefly, if at all, in spontaneity of emotions, a desire for emotional incongruity, and a cultivated delight in verbal fireworks or felicities. It is certain that in the time of Marlowe they were gaping for sensation and joyed in a comedy of beatings, a tragedy of murders, and a mixture of jigging and villany. For such audiences, for such a stage, under stress of immediate demand requiring hasty and collaborative work, Marlowe and his contemporaries wrote. They were hack writers, and so viewed by the literati of their day. Every one of them, Shakespeare included, had in the first place to satisfy the demands of the public theatres. This needs to be remembered no less than the fact that the plays of nearly all, of the meanest hack as well as Shakespeare, seem to have felt the stir and thrill of the effort to express thought in enduring words.

In the course of the six or seven years ending with Marlowe's death in 1593, tragedy experienced a rapid and multiform development. The various influences already noticed in the last chapter as at work were developed by the ingenuity and innovation of a dozen writers, and translated into the expression of individual genius by Marlowe and Shakespeare. No theory of tragedy ruled the theatres; no school of dramatists adopted any code of principles; the plays which we class as tragedies were mostly known as histories and were written in violence to the accepted literary conception. Nevertheless, tragedy was establishing itself as a popular species of drama, was separating its themes and their treatment clearly from those of comedy, and was defining the course which it was to follow until the Puritan revolution.

The impossibility of determining a precise chronology of the stage history of the period renders the exact appraisal of indebtedness, or the tracing of any certain evolution, very insecure. The changes in the companies in 1594 and the consequent publication of a large number of plays in the same year enable us to fix on a number of tragedies acted before Marlowe's death, and we may safely add a few others as not later than 1595. Among these extant tragedies and in the names of those that have not survived there are representatives of various types, — biblical plays, tragedies dealing with romantic love, domestic tragedies telling stories of contemporary crimes. In any one of these plays, indeed, various types may be combined; the writers were concerned with telling stories, not with *l'évolution des genres*. But the most salient and pervasive forces working in tragedy may be roughly denominated as (1) the chronicle history play, (2) the revenge type of tragedy, (3) the type of tragedy created by Marlowe. To these should perhaps be added romantic comedy with its idealized love story and its element of averted tragedy. But the first three types, though overlapping and not distinct, were of marked importance in the history of tragedy and need especial consideration in connection with the most important dramatists of this period, Peele, Kyd, Marlowe, and Shakespeare.

The chronicle history play may claim attention first, not because it was demonstrably earlier in appearance than the others, but because it engaged the efforts of nearly every dramatic writer of the period, and because in its disregard of foreign influence or parallel in its methods and structure, and in its devotion to the demands of the London theatres, it is most typical of the drama of the period. The prime essential of a play was that it should tell a story. A playwright took his material from *novella*, poem, or chronicle, and strove to translate it into an interesting and varied series of scenes. In the chronicles he found material peculiarly suited to such translation. Everything was there, — battles, coronations, counsels, conspiracies, amours, speeches, characterization, and sentiments. No enlargement was necessary as in the case of a *novella*, no considerations of consistency of characterization, few incidents in addition to those in the highway or the byways of the narrative, and only a minimum of invention. The interest of a distinct plot was superseded by that of historical persons, events, and spectacles, and these compelled only such unity as might be secured by taking the reign of one monarch as the basis of a play, or sometimes of several plays. The presentation of history involved a large number of persons on the stage, many changes of place, a long stretch of time, and an incongruity of matter, all this loosely organized into scenes themselves often long and varied and admitting some change of place and lapse of time within their bounds. Though the scene, rather than the act, was the unit in popular drama, it had almost no structural value. A play was really a continuous performance, the actors coming and going, a battle intervening, and now and then a withdrawal of all the actors and the appearance of a new group presaging a marked change of place or the beginning of an entirely different action. In the arrangement of scenes, however, some attention to parallel, contrast, and climax soon became manifest; and some integration of the confused material from the chronicles, particularly in the separation from scenes abounding in action of those purely narrative or expository and those purely lyrical, chiefly lamentations. In spite of such beginnings of system, the early chronicle plays, "The Famous Victories of Henry V," "Jack Straw," "Leir," "Edward I," and "The Troublesome Reign" are less coherent in structure, more incongruous in material, and less regardful of any clear fable, tragic or comic, than are other contemporary plays.

To determine criteria to define these plays and their successors as a class is by no means easy. They were

usually based on the chronicles, but the method of composition just described was applied to legend or poem
with similar results, and there were also plays based on
chronicles of contemporary events. They had for their
main purpose the presentation of history, but this was
shared by plays on French and Roman as well as English
history, and there were historical plays that had no
marks of the chronicle method of structure. The English
chronicle plays usually show a pronounced patriotic temper, but this is often subsidiary and neglected in the desire
for farce or sensation. The spectacular features are a
characteristic element, a battle-scene being perhaps the
most indispensable element or ingredient of a chronicle
play, but this again fails to supply even more than a
superficial criterion. In the popularity of the presentations of historical facts, all kinds of stories were worked
over into a likeness to "true chronicle history," and the
genuine historical, legendary, and biographical plays are
hardly distinguishable from the pretenders. An illumin-
ating illustration of the characteristics of the national
drama about 1590 can be found in a comparison of two
dramatic versions of a romance in Cinthio's "Hecatom-
mithi," one by Cinthio himself, the other by Robert
Greene. The Italian play is a tragicomedy in strict Senecan form, in which Arrenopia (Greene's Dorothea) appears as a declamatory queen confiding her troubles to
the attendant nurse. Greene took the romantic comedy,
added some pseudo-historical events, patriotic sentiments,
and a pitched field for the finale, and called the whole

"The Scottish Historie of James IV, slaine at Flodden."
For our purpose the chronicle plays are to be regarded
less as a distinct type than as representing a set of practices in vogue at this period and widely influential on
the drama's development. They possessed the following
characteristics and imposed some or all of them on very
different forms of drama: subjects drawn from English history, the presentation of historical and political
events, an incongruous mixture of material, a narrative
structure almost as unorganized as the chronicles themselves, patriotic sentiments, and the stage pageantry of
court and camp.

From their earliest appearance, however, the chronicle
plays offered opportunities for developments later consummated by Shakespeare. Comic scenes were freely
interspersed to enliven the tedium of royal declamations, and in these lay the possibility of the combination
of history and comedy in the Falstaff plays. On the other
hand, the history of a doleful fall of a prince or the retribution visited on some tyrant gave the plays a tragic
tone and opened the way for "Macbeth" and "Lear."
"The Troublesome Reign of King John,"[1] the basis
of Shakespeare's play, is the best example of an early

[1] It consists of two parts published 1591, and acted, as the prologue
indicates, shortly after *Tamburlaine*, perhaps in 1588. Its scenes cover
about the same ground as Shakespeare's play, with the addition of a
ribald account of the sack of a monastery, an explanation of the poisoning of John in his treatment of the clergy, and a scene of some power in
which Philip obtains from his mother, Lady Fauconbridge, a confession
that his father was Richard.

chronicle play presenting undeveloped possibilities for tragedy. It is written partly in blank verse, partly in rhyme, and partly in prose. It does not follow the chronicles with any fidelity, but twists history, adds fiction, and proclaims throughout a vigorous protestant patriotism. Battles, embassies, farce, orations, death, and much else mingle together, each scene being treated like another and no discernible method being followed in their arrangement or proportion, except that of a loose adherence to the scheme of "a life and death." The first part closes with John crowned and assured of the miscarriage of his intended murder of Arthur; in the second part, as the address to the reader declares,

> "First scenes shows Arthur's death in infancie,
> And last concludes John's fatall tragedie."

"The Troublesome Reign" indicates what little advance had been made toward tragedy when Marlowe's first play appeared. The prologue to that play was a declaration of reform and innovation.

> "From jigging veins of rhyming mother wits,
> And such conceits as clownage keeps in pay,
> We'll lead you to the stately tent of war,
> Where you shall hear the Scythian Tamburlaine
> Threatening the world with high astounding terms,
> And scourging kingdoms with his conquering sword."

The doggerel rhyme favored in the popular drama was to give place to blank verse, and the jigging clowns to heroic themes and "high astounding terms." Marlowe

came to the theatre,[1] fresh from the university, his fancy
aflame with the beauty of Latin verse and story, his
mind storming with the problems and ambitions of
adolescent genius. He threw aside Senecan traditions
and devoted himself to meeting the demands of the professional stage. When a few years later he died, English
tragedy had been created anew largely through his
achievement.

His independence and initiative are shown in his
choice of subjects. Although in "Dido" he took a standard theme of humanistic tragedy, and in the Henry VI
plays and "Edward II" followed the prevailing taste
for English history, and in "The Massacre of Paris"
another fashion for the dramatization of current atrocities; yet in "Tamburlaine" he chose the story of a world
conqueror, in "Faustus" a legend that had just entered
print in the German "Volksbuch" of 1587, and in "The
Jew of Malta" he worked over unknown sources into
a tragedy of revenge with evident freedom of invention.
All three stories present notable contributions to tragic

[1] *Tamburlaine* in two parts, certainly acted as early as 1588, gained
an immediate and long-continued popularity, and was followed by a
number of plays, all tragedies or histories. Without reckoning the
numerous plays that have been assigned to Marlowe on no sufficient
grounds, he collaborated on the *Tragedy of Dido* (1594), perhaps an
early work, and on the three parts of *Henry VI;* and was the author
of *The Tragicall History of Dr. Faustus*, printed 1604, acted 1588 (?);
The Jew of Malta, acted about 1589, and long the most popular of
Henslow's repertoire; *The Troublesome Reign and Lamentable Death
of Edward II*, printed 1594, acted about 1591; and *The Massacre of
Paris*, of an unknown date of acting.

themes, and the last two disregard both the fashion for historical subjects and the requirement that tragedy deal only with princes. These new and varied themes gave a chance for a considerable revolution in the content of tragedy. Revenge, murders, battles, intrigue, physical horrors are still prominent; but the Senecan round of incest and adultery disappears, and the "Mirror for Magistrates" no longer represents the epitome of tragic action. Marlowe's choice and treatment of plots seem, indeed, dictated by a new conception of tragedy, as dealing not merely with a life and death, or a bloody crime, or a reversal of fortune, but with the heroic struggle of a great personality, doomed to inevitable defeat. "Tamburlaine" is scarcely a tragedy at all, but rather a chronicle of the hero's greatness; but in "Faustus" and "The Jew" heroes with ambitions boundless and passionate like Tamburlaine's are overwhelmed in the end by the inexorable destiny of human weakness. In "Edward II," where the hero is less dominant over the action, the study of historical facts results in a more restrained, more human presentation of the same theme, a ruling passion drawing the protagonist to pitiful defeat.

In the structure of his plots Marlowe forsook the Senecan models and began with the methods of the chronicle play. "Tamburlaine" is a chronicle history, presenting the story of the events of a life and ending with death. Originally the play contained comic scenes, omitted in the published form and evidently of no value in structure or conception. Without these there is enough of a medley, though the amazing succession of conquests, defiances, murders, harangues, battles, funerals, wooings, and horrors is arranged with considerable skill. There is manifest regard for contrast in the alternating exhibitions of Tamburlaine's power and his enemies' weakness; his love for Zenocrate, an addition to the source, is integrated with the main story of conquest; and in Part I the climactical arrangement is emphasized by the division into acts. Each act comprises an important stage in Tamburlaine's career, act v presenting the culmination in the suicide of the Turkish emperor and empress, the conquest of Arabia, Zenocrate's former betrothed, and the submission of her conquered father to her marriage with Tamburlaine. Part II, the prologue implies, was an afterthought due to the popularity of Part I. The climax is carried on somewhat loosely up to the harnessing of the jades of Asia; but the reversal of fortune, though developed in the death of Zenocrate, the unworthiness of the eldest son, and the approach of death to Tamburlaine, is not given effective emphasis. Tamburlaine's death is merely the end of the play, not a tragic catastrophe. Epical and crude though their structure is, the two plays possess a firmer organization and a greater unity than any preceding popular tragedy. Everything centres in the protagonist; he keeps the middle of the stage; his towering passion and incessant declamation fix one's attention; episodes like the deaths of the Turks or of Olympia hardly divert the mind from his titanic personality.

A similar unity governs the structure of "Faustus" and "The Jew." In each there are many actions, some comic, instead of one serious action, and the history of a lifetime instead of a great emotional crisis; but in each the dominant figure and the course of his controlling passion impose a certain unity of structure. Both begin with soliloquies, revealing the protagonists at the height of fortune and about to face crises in their careers; and it is significant of the increased importance given to inner conflict that reflective soliloquies, neglected in "Tamburlaine," play a considerable part, especially in "Faustus." In both plays there is also advance in the clear conception of catastrophe, which now controls the structure. In "The Jew" his thwarted lust for gold drives him through a series of villanous triumphs over difficulties until he is melodramatically hoist with his own petard. In "Faustus" the choice of the devilish magic leads through apparent success, past opportunities for repentance, to final remorse and damnation. In both plays, the domination of the protagonist by a passion, its conflicting joys and sorrows, and its final failure become points for emphasis. The history of a life thus becomes organized into a tragedy.

In "Edward II," Marlowe's masterpiece in structure as in other respects, there is an absence of comedy, for which he seems to have had no aptitude, and adherence to the chronicles is governed by his maturing sense of the structural principles which should proportion the tragic story. Twenty years of confusion are condensed into five

acts which attain dramatic organization not only under
the direction of the central personality and the inevitable
catastrophe, but also from the skillful handling of the
counter-force. The play begins with a salient manifesta-
tion in the recall of Gaveston of the passion which is to be
the king's downfall. The hazardous combination of the
two similar careers of Gaveston and Spenser is adroitly
managed; it develops the central theme of Edward's
weakness and brings into active conflict the counter-force
of the barons under the leadership of Mortimer. The
alternating triumph and discomfiture of the king in his
struggle with the barons leads to the climax of their
humiliation at the end of act iii; and thus the turning-
point of the action is given an emphasis not found
in earlier plays. Henceforth the counter-force is in the
ascendant, and the catastrophe is realized with a tremendous power that justifies Lamb's extravagance: "the
death scene of Marlowe's king moves pity and terror
beyond any scene ancient or modern with which I am
acquainted." The play, to be sure, has many faults of
structure. It is the product of an immature period of the
drama and of crude theatrical conditions; but it indicates
clearly how Marlowe was developing tragic movement
out of the confused narratives of the chronicles, and was
giving to a presentation of diverse and crowded actions
principles not altogether unlike those that Aristotle had
found in the Attic drama.

It should be added that the manifest excellences of
the dramatic treatment lie less in the structure of any one

play as a whole than in the handling of the separate scenes. These have, of course, the peculiarities of the popular stage and the chronicle plays. Events are sometimes reported by an intercalary narrative like scene ii, act i, of "Edward II," which consists of four lines by Gaveston, announcing that the nobles have gone to Lambeth, and four words of reply by Kent. Soliloquies are often used to explain action or character. In the task of translating incident into dramatic situation, however, Marlowe had the advantages of centuries of dramatic practice and the traditions of tragic acting, and his genius often worked with facility and power. These qualities are most manifest in the death scenes. Olympia, Bajazeth, Zabina, Zenocrate, all die with at least stage effectiveness; and in the deaths of Faustus and Edward, Marlowe's dramatic power reached its highest mark. Death, synonymous with tragic catastrophe, was revealed to future dramatists as something more than physical horror or the end of existence. Death became the loss of active and glorious living, the negation of individual power, the expiring struggle of the drama of life, its last defiance and its most irresistible appeal to pity and terror.

Characterization, like conception and structure, in Marlowe's tragedy is largely an affair of the protagonist. Minor figures are for the most part mere sketches without any sustained and consistent delineation. Only in "Edward II" does the antagonist receive much attention, and only in that play is the character of the tragic hero free from lapses into caricature and absurdity. The protagonists, as in many tragedies before and since, are evil men intent on evil deeds. They appeal to our sympathy only in misfortune and disaster; in more fortunate circumstances they run counter to moral laws and excite a mixture of admiration, horror, and even contempt. Tamburlaine the atheist and Faust the dealer in magic invited a greater condemnation in every Christian then than now. Barabas is conceived, under the inspiration of Machiavelli and perhaps also of stage practice, as an intriguing villain with all the accompaniments ever since familiar in drama and fiction. He is the source of all evil and utterly without conscience; he avows his villany to the audience and he works by crafty intrigue with the aid of an equally conscienceless accomplice. Edward II, on the other hand, is of the type of tyrants, weak, vacillating, and self-indulgent, and he offers the difficult dramatic problem of a protagonist who is sometimes contemptible and must sometimes be heroic and pitiful. Marlowe's conception of a tragic hero, however, transcended any outlines furnished by his sources or any stage types such as villain and tyrant. He conceived his heroes first of all as men capable of great passions, consumed by their desires, abandoned to the pursuit of their lusts, whether they led to glory, butchery, loss of kingdom, or eternal damnation. This intensity of emotion gives them an elevation and a heroic interest that outlasts contemptibility or pathos. Nor are they without representational value. They linger in the mind as men, absurd, exaggerated, monstrous at times, but appealingly human in moments when their passion rings true, and impressively typical of the eternal struggle of passion and desire against the fixed limits of human attainment. It is in the realization of their emotions that the plays secure their great impressiveness. Tragedy has become not the presentation of history, myth, or events of any sort, but the presentation of the passionate struggle and pitiful defeat of an extraordinary human being.

Genuine human passion and a vital conception of life's tragedy found expression in verse, sometimes inspired, sometimes absurd, but always spontaneous and unfaltering. Blank verse, borrowed from Italy and adopted in English Senecan plays, now became a new instrument, and its preëminent adaptability for tragic poetry henceforth long remained unquestioned. If it has had many greater masters since, it had none comparable before, and, in spite of stiffness, monotony, and great unevenness, it rises now and again to remarkable technical excellence. It is *sui generis*, without known models, though it gathers to itself many of the prevailing characteristics of Renaissance poetry. It has plenty of Senecan hyperbole, but curiously little of Senecan antithesis or aphorism; it abounds in rant and bombast; it is overadorned with classical allusion; it delights in ornament and sonority; and in the main it is declamatory and lyrical rather than dramatically suited to character and situation. Again, it is mannered and often monotonous, especially in "Tamburlaine," where the repetition of

names and the recurrence of polysyllabic words at the
ends of lines give the familiar swing: —

"To ride in triumph through Persepolis " . . .
"Soft ye, my lords, and sweet Zenocrate " . . .
"Then shall my native city, Samarcanda."

Yet the lover of romantic poetry will find delight in the
very impetuosity of the rant, the thunder of the declamation, the roll of the proper names, the color and
pageantry of the descriptions, the occasional loveliness of
the luxurious classicism, and yet more in the splendid
surges of the verse to reveal the turmoil and anguish of passionate death. From the first moment Marlowe was an
undoubted poet; and to his tremendous facility of words
and rhythm he was adding, as "Edward II" reveals, a
moderation of ornament, an evenness of power, and a
dramatic consistency, while still retaining the potentiality
of dazzling dramatic flash. He brought not only blank
verse but poetry to the English drama, and the greatness
of its style dates from his achievement.

We must not, however, in the poet forget the playwright,
or lose sight of Marlowe's contributions to the purely
theatrical side of the drama. "Tamburlaine" set a standard in stage effects as well as in poetry. Kings and sultans
appear in droves, crowns are handed about like toys,
treaties are torn, cities stormed, battles fought. Frequently
eight or ten chieftains crowd the stage with their trains.
The tents of the conqueror are pitched and changed from
white to red and then to black as the beleaguered city con-

tinues to withstand his power. An emperor and empress dash out their brains against the bars of their cages. Tamburlaine drives the bridled monarchs harnessed to his chariot. Two bodies are burnt; there are murders by the dozen; and there is a solemn funeral scene where the hearse advances in the light of a burning town. The popular stage had probably never seen such a spectacle before. In "Faustus" new and even more surprising stage effects are supplied to illustrate the wonders of magic. In "The Jew of Malta" there is a display of plots and atrocities which the plays of the next thirty years strove in vain to surpass. Apart from these spectacular elements, it is obvious that the characterization and declamation, in fact the very structure of the plays, were designed to supply full opportunity for the acting of Edward Alleyn. He was nearly seven feet tall, we are told, the greatest actor of his day, and especially skilled in majestic parts. So to him, perhaps, as well as to Marlowe's conception of tragedy, was due the one-part play, the sonorous lines, and the passionate protagonists.

Such considerations recall the double purpose, hardly separable from the drama and particularly manifest in the Elizabethan dramatists, the two desires, to please their audiences and to create literature. The spectacle, bombast, and horrors, the new and startling stories of Marlowe's plays were certainly intended to win his public, and they probably caused no twinges to his artistic conscience. On the other hand, while hardly an element of the dramas is without the influence of theatrical conditions, and while of deliberate artistic theories there is little evidence, yet the study of character, the underlying conceptions, the maturing power of structure, as well as the beauty and wisdom of separate passages, reveal a mind of intellectual and emotional profundity seeking to give noble expression to the things in life that impressed him most vividly. In the traffic of the stage the young poet found a chance to study men and their motives, to seek " the immortal flowers of poetry," and to utter something of his own experience and view of life. Into the rapid translation of stories for the stage he threw his own conception of the rewards and defeats of an overmastering passion, of the glory of struggle, and the pity and terror of failure. In the further development of the drama, his influence continued not only in his series of tragedies forming a fairly definite type, but also as that of an inspiring personality.

> "Next Marlowe, bathed in the Thespian springs,
> Had in him those brave translunary things
> That the first poets had; his raptures were
> All air and fire, which made his verses clere;
> For that fine madnes still he did retaine,
> Which rightly should possess a poet's braine."
>   DRAYTON: *Epistle to Henry Reynolds.*

The influence upon the drama of Marlowe's whilom friend, Thomas Kyd, was not due to his personality, concerning which recently discovered documents create no very favorable impression, or to any remarkable poetic genius, but to a single play and the type of tragedy which

it fathered. "The Spanish Tragedy," [1] entered in the
Stationers' Register, 1592, and probably acted at about
the same time as "Tamburlaine," and earlier than Marlowe's other plays, was the first representative of this type
of revenge tragedies, and it gained an immediate and
lasting popularity, though 'after a time encountering the
ridicule of Jonson and later dramatists. The story of
revenge had already appeared in "Horestes" and in
Latin plays at the universities; and theme, ghost, treatment, and structure were derived from Seneca by Kyd
and adapted with great originality to the popular drama.
At least, no other dramatist has as good a claim to be
considered the creator of a species of tragedy that had a
long series of representatives even after its culmination
in Shakespeare's "Hamlet."

The main theme of the play is revenge of a father for
a son, superintended by a ghost; and this theme attaches
to itself other motives important both here and in their
later developments. The revenge is delayed by hesitation
on the part of Hieronimo, who finds his task a difficult
one and requires much proof and superabundant de-
liberation to spur his irresolution into activity. Madness

[1] The only other play certainly by Kyd is a translation of Garnier's
Cornelia, 1595, which was doubtless never acted. His authorship of
the *First Part of Jeronimo*, 1605, is denied by recent critics, and at
most the text represents a very corrupt abridgment of his work. *Soliman and Perseda*, S. R. 1592, is attributed to him solely on internal
evidence, and may have been by an imitator. The non-extant *Hamlet*,
alluded to by Nash in 1589, and not until twelve years later used by
Shakespeare as the basis of his play, is now generally assigned to Kyd.

is another accompaniment of the main theme; the second title of the 1602 quarto, "Old Hieronimo mad againe," indicating how important it was in the stage presentation. Hieronimo pretends madness, and his pretended madness often passes into real melancholy and distraction. Isabella, his wife, is driven by insanity to suicide. Intrigue used both against and by the avenger is another important element; the villain is a machinator and Hieronimo finally accomplishes his revenge by means of dissimulation and trickery. According to both Senecan and national precedents, vengeance moves in a pathway of blood; ten of the *dramatis personae*, innocent and guilty alike, pass to "the loathsome pool of Acheron," and the final slaughter leaves five bodies to be borne from the stage. Intrigue and slaughter characterize most of the tragedies of this period, notably "The Jew of Malta," but the ghost-directed revenge, hesitation, insanity, and the meditative soliloquies distinguished more specifically the Kydian species. In spite of the medley of intrigue and carnage, there is introduced, after Senecan fashion, much philosophizing and introspection. Meditations on fate, revenge, suicide, and similar subjects play a large part in the development of the story and are most frequently given the form of soliloquies. Hieronimo's inner struggle is revealed in lonely communings, now in defense, now in bitter condemnation of his delay.

The structure is an interesting adaptation of Senecan and popular characteristics. The play does not confine itself to the last phase of an action, and it introduces

various actions introductory or subsidiary to that of the
revenge, and a mixture of comedy. Moreover, everything is represented on the stage with the freedom established in the popular drama. On the other hand, there
is much exposition by means of narrative, and Revenge
and the ghost of Andrea appear, after Senecan fashion,
as a prologue, and after each act as a sort of vestigial
chorus. While there is a surplus of violent and external
action, the epic, lyric, and reflective scenes picture an
inner conflict and supply both aphorisms and a searching
psychology. When late in the play Hieronimo's revenge
for his son is finally started, it has to contend with both
his own hesitation and the intrigues of the villain. Its
development, in comparison with "Hamlet," is absurdly
faulty because of Kyd's failure to make clear from the
start the character of the avenger; but, if it is studied as
a first attempt to give structure to a complex theme, the
vicissitudes of Hieronimo's irresolution and frenzy will
seem carefully designed and strikingly prophetic of the
course of Hamlet's struggle.

Kyd's skill in devising stage situations is shown by the
dramatic value and lasting effect on the public of the
scene in which Hieronimo is called from his naked bed
to discover the body of his son hanging in the arbor, or
of the scene in which, offering a handkerchief to the
weeping Senex, he draws forth the bloody napkin which
he has kept as a reminder of his son's death. The play
within the play, used here as a means of revenge; the
scenes in which Isabella "runs lunatick"; the laments

and final exultation of the ghost; the exhibition of the body
of Horatio after the mock play, found later imitators
and became usual accessories of revenge tragedies. Indeed, minor bits of stage business, as the wearing of black,
the swearing by the cross of the sword, the capture of the
accomplice by the watch, the reading of a book before
a soliloquy, the falling on the ground as an expression of
grief, though not the inventions of Kyd, were given their
later vogue partly through the popularity of this play.

Some of the types of character represented also appear
again and again in later plays. Lorenzo is the villain *par
excellence;* his accomplice is grotesque as well as evil;
and Bel Imperia, both prettily sentimental and desper-
ately revengeful, is of a type not uncommon in later tragedy. The character of Hieronimo, rudely as it is drawn,
is not without subtlety of conception. This type of tragic
hero, very different from Marlowe's, naturally good and
noble, meditative by temperament, driven to melancholy
and madness by the responsibility forced on him by crime,
and at length accomplishing direful revenge through
trickery and irony, is manifestly a precursor of Hamlet.
Kyd's style justifies Nash's description, "whole handfulls
of tragical speeches" and "a blank verse bodged up with
ifs and ands." It displays the rhetorician rather than
the poet and, like his conception and structure, gives evidence of an ingenious innovator adapting Seneca. It
abounds in artificial balance, parallelism, antitheses,
word-play, strained figures, and it harrows hell for its
tragic vocabulary; but its love scenes have a verbal

prettiness and its tirades and soliloquies helped to confer
on subsequent tragic style sententiousness and elevation
as well as rant. Far inferior to "Tamburlaine" as an
artistic achievement, "The Spanish Tragedy" can no
more than that play be pushed aside as a mere blood and
thunder tirade. Beneath its absurdities there lies the
conception of an inner struggle against overwhelming
responsibility, and of the conflict of the individual against
evil and fate.

From the success of such a play Kyd may very naturally
have turned to the similar story of revenge embodied in
Belleforest's "Historie of Hamblet." From contemporary
references we infer that the old "Hamlet" was a tragedy
of blood, written under Senecan influence, and containing a ghost that cried "revenge." If, as seems undoubted,
it was used by Shakespeare, traces of it must be found in
the German version of Hamlet, in the corrupt first quarto,
and even in Shakespeare's final version; but there is as
yet no agreement among scholars as to what can be attributed to Shakespeare's borrowing rather than to his
invention and transformation. It seems entirely probable, however, that the early play was a companion-piece
to "The Spanish Tragedy," containing the motives of
revenge, hesitation, insanity, intrigue, and slaughter, with
the addition of the murderer's passion for the wife of
the murdered. On the now established theory that the
play was by Kyd, we may infer a protagonist like Hieronimo, much meditating and soliloquizing, a dramatic
structure like that of "The Spanish Tragedy," a play

within a play, a mad Ophelia, and an intrigue culminating in slaughter. There are evidences in Marston and later contributors to the revenge type that the original "Hamlet," fully as much as "The Spanish Tragedy," served as their model; while doubtless like "The Spanish Tragedy," Kyd's "Hamlet" must have borne a much closer resemblance than even that play to Shakespeare's masterpiece.

"Soliman and Perseda," if not by Kyd, at least shows many evidences of his influence and is itself an interesting combination of the tragedy of revenge and romantic comedy. Love, Fortune, and Death make up a Kydian chorus and debate for supremacy until the close, when Death, like the Ghost, exults in an enumeration of the dead. The love story furnishes a clearly defined plot. The course of true love, despite the heroine's jealousy, an unintended murder by the hero, his banishment, the sack of Rhodes by the Turks, and the Sultan's passion for the heroine, ascends through the first four acts to the reunion and prospective happiness of the lovers. The fifth act proceeds to their separation and death through the Sultan's wickedness. Some of the incidents are those of romantic comedy, such as the use of the chain as a symbol of loyal love, its loss, the resulting jealousy, and the donning of boy's clothes by the heroine in order to receive death from the sword of the hated suitor. The fun of the piece is furnished by a *miles gloriosus*, Basilisco, and the extraordinary merit of his characterization furnishes the chief reason for doubting Kyd's authorship.

Over lyric love, fortune, and fun, however, Death reigns
supreme. This is his favorite tragedy, for eighteen persons are actually killed on the stage, and at the close not
one of the *dramatis personae* is left to bear off the bodies
of the slain.

The successes of Marlowe and Kyd gave tragic stories
a new popularity with actors and audiences, and the stage
was occupied with fiercely declaiming Asiatic conquerors,
deep-dyed villains, and shrieking ghosts. Marlowe's
themes, characters, and blank verse found many imitators, while Kyd's plays encouraged the presentation of
stories of ghosts and revenge similar to those in Seneca
and his English imitators. Direct imitations of Seneca
in technic and language are also common. The abundance
of bloodshed is invariable. A wide range of material was
drawn upon, including Asiatic story, Italian *novelle*,
Plutarch, Xenophon, and the Bible, although the English
chronicles remained the favorite source, and the majority have at least the semblance of a historical setting.
Many have a mixture of comic material, but they show
in general a preponderance of tragic events and emotions
far greater than in the early popular tragedies. There
seems to have been a general effort in conformity with an
address to the audience placed in the second act of " The
Wars of Cyrus," acted by the Children of the Revels,
which announces that they have " exiled from our tragicke
stage " " needlesse antickes," and promises " mournfull
plaints writ sad, and tragicke tearmes." The gentle reader
will not linger long over any of these plays or discover in

them signs of nascent genius, but they have a considerable interest in illustrating further the development of chronicle history toward tragedy, the influence of the Senecan tradition, and the dominating power of Marlowe's example. They also inform us of the conditions governing tragedy when Shakespeare began his career. In their many resemblances one to another we have evidence not so much of direct borrowings as of the close relations then existing among the few theatrical playwrights and companies. Any successful innovation was bound to have its immediate imitations, and on the other hand the keen rivalry for success was likely to result in innovation and novelty.

Of these plays perhaps "Locrine"[1] has the most diverse indebtedness. It presents a story of a bloody family feud, but it is also of the chronicle history order, with a mixture of battles, patriotism, and farce. It exhibits borrowings from Spenser, imitations of "Tamburlaine," Ate as a chorus, dumb shows requiring a menagerie, two ghosts, one of whom takes part in the action, and a story of double revenge. The hero is occupied with revenge number one until the fourth act, when his infidelity makes him the object of a return revenge that culminates in his death. Among the plays mainly indebted to Marlowe are: Greene's "Alphonsus of Aragon," a comedy that is almost a travesty on the first part of "Tamburlaine";

[1] Printed 1594, "as newly set forth, overseen, and corrected by W. S.," sometimes assigned to Peele, and in an earlier form perhaps acted about 1590.

"Selimus," ascribed to Greene, which also shows Senecan structure and philosophy; "The Wounds of Civil War, or the Tragedies of Marius and Sylla," the first extant play based on Plutarch; "The Wars of Cyrus," in part romantic comedy; and Peele's "Battle of Alcazar," which has a presenter, dumb shows, three ghosts, and a Moorish villain of the same class as Marlowe's Barabas and Aaron in "Titus Andronicus."

The English chronicle plays also felt Marlowe's influence, most notably in Shakespeare's early historical plays, to be considered in a moment, but also in several plays almost contemporary with "Edward II" and the first versions of "Henry VI." "The True Tragedy of Richard III" (1594), by an unknown author or authors, seems to have preceded Shakespeare's play and to have followed the third part of "Henry VI." It presents a combination of chronicle play with Marlowesque protagonist and a Kydian apparatus of revenge. The ghost of Clarence appears at the beginning crying, "Vindicta," and Truth and Poetry supply the necessary exposition. The revenge element becomes prominent toward the end of the play, when the ghosts of Richard's victims appear to him in a dream, not visible as in Shakespeare, and the remorseful villain declares that not merely his victims but all the forces of nature, sun, moon, and planets, cry revenge: —

> "The birds sing not, but sorrow for revenge.
> The silly lambs sit bleating for revenge."

Richard is a man of powerful will carried away by ambi-

tion and evidently modeled on Tamburlaine; but unlike
the Scythian and like Faustus, he is conscience-smitten,
and his punishment comes in remorse as well as death.
This conception, based on the chronicle, is treated with
power, but in the main the play is a hodge-podge. More
worthy examples of chronicle history are "Edward III,"
often ascribed to Marlowe and not unworthy of him, and
the anonymous "Tragedy of Woodstock." [1] The latter
shows frequent resemblances to "Edward II" and apparently preceded Shakespeare's "Richard II," leaving
off at the point where that play begins. The events of
half a reign are focused about the central personalities
of Richard and Woodstock, a weak king beset by flatterers
and an honorable and patriotic leader of the nobles.
The construction is skillful in its integration of comedy
with the main action and its alternation of tragic and
comic, action and counsel, force and counter-force; and
the characterization is remarkably well individualized.
Woodstock, especially, has human appeal and is notable
as a tragic hero, or at least the central figure of a history,
who meets misfortune and death through no fault of his
own but solely through the wickedness of others.

Holinshed's chronicle is also the source of "Arden of
Feversham" (1592), sometimes ascribed on very insuf-
ficient grounds to Shakespeare, the earliest extant domestic tragedy. The play deals with a notorious murder of
some forty years before, and follows the crude drama-

[1] Preserved in MS. and first printed in the *Shakespeare Jahrbuch*
in 1899.

turgy of the earliest chronicle plays. The stage presentation of notably brutal murders is common to-day and was to be expected on the Elizabethan stage, but the play seems also to represent reaction from the royalties, marvels, and unrealities of the contemporary tragedy. The epilogue, indeed, offers a defiance of romanticism and the since well-worn creed of the realist.

> "Gentlemen, we hope youle pardon this naked tragedy,
> Wherein no filed points are foisted in
> To make it gratious to the eare or eye;
> For simple truth is gratious enough,
> And needes no other points of glosing stuffe."

Notwithstanding this protestation, occasional monologues reveal the common stylistic decorations. The play is tediously detailed and artlessly realistic, though it has some vigorous blank verse and several powerful scenes; the most powerful, when Michael in the middle of the night is awaiting the murderers of his master, recalling a well-known passage in " The Spanish Tragedy." But the greatest merit of the play lies in the portrait of Alice Arden, absorbed in a despicable passion, but cunning and unabashed, incomparably the most lifelike evil woman up to this time depicted in the drama.

Peele's " The Love of King David and Fair Bethsabe, with the Tragedie of Absalon," acted about 1591, has, unlike " Arden," many " filed points to make it gratious to the eare and eye." It gains a unique interest as the only extant tragedy of this period based on the biblical narrative. The bible story is treated just as a historical

chronicle would have been; and the play, divided by
choruses into three "discourses," offers no advance in
conception, structure, or characterization on the average
tragedy of the period. Yet it is the masterpiece of one of
the most active among Shakespeare's predecessors and
illustrates his most distinctive contribution to the drama's
development. As the author of "Alcazar," "Edward I,"
and possibly "Locrine," as well as "David and Bethsabe,"
Peele's contribution deserves some note. His dramatic
career began at Oxford, where he made a version of one
of the "Iphigenias" of Euripides, which was acted at
Christ Church, and where he also aided in the production
of Dr. Gager's Latin plays. In London he became the
friend of Nash, Greene, and Marlowe, and the versatile
adopter of the latest dramatic modes, whether in comedy,
pastoral, history, or tragedy. In his best work, however,
and especially in "David and Bethsabe," there are graces
of style which justify Nash's eulogy of his friend as
"primus verborum artifex." The great innovation of
this early drama was, after all, in poetic style; and in
furthering this Peele may claim a place only second to
Marlowe. If Marlowe gave sweep and grandeur to blank
verse, Peele brought a sweetness of cadence and, as
Professor Ward observes, "a vivacity of fancy and a
variety of imagery." As Marlowe turned everything into
sonorous phrase, now bombastic, now superb, so Peele
turned every thought to music and fancy, sometimes
banal, sometimes lovely. "David and Bethsabe," with
its oriental setting, though treated with careless dramatic

art, proved an inspiration to the stylist. The excess of
verbalism, indeed, gives the play a sugary and monotonous effect, and its poetry loses connection with character
or situation. Absalon plays with conceits for twenty-five
lines while hanging by his hair, and laments melodiously
for fifteen lines more after being stabbed. But there is
charm and gracefulness everywhere, in the choruses, in
the defense of Hamon, and in the parables, and now and
again the very allurement and luxury of words, as in the
famous,

> "Now comes my lover tripping like the roe
> And brings my longings tangled in her hair."

While this operatic verbalism with its faults and merits
cannot of course be assigned wholly to Peele, he seems
to have been in the drama one of its earliest and most
influential purveyors.

The dozen plays just noticed furnish departures from,
as well as adaptations of, the Kydian and Marlowean
types of tragedy, but they reveal no marked advance in
conception or structure. In characterization, however,
there is a development in various ways; thus, a hack play
like "The True Tragedy" has considerable power in its
conception of a conscience-smitten villain, in "Woodstock" there is clear individualization, and in Alice Arden
and the Countess of "Edward III" female character becomes lifelike and impressive. Still more salient is the
attention paid to style. The Elizabethan theatregoer
was used to the spoken and not to the written word, and
expected at the theatre to be delighted by verbal display.

Dramatic style then had functions which have since been relegated to other arts. It was to be declamative, taking the place of oratory; descriptive, supplying in part the place of scenery; and operatic in its word-play and decorative phrasing, and in its lyric interludes and laments. Moreover, medieval tradition and Senecan models alike enforced the necessity in tragedy of a heightened style; and many dramatists doubtless agreed with Gosson in placing first among dramatic requirements "sweetness of words, fitness of epithets with metaphors, allegories." Still further, along with the excesses resultant from this delight in words, there was manifest a growing mastery of language to represent truthfully situation and character. "Arden" gave crude expression to this reaction toward realism in style; "Woodstock" much more effectively; and colloquial directness was mingled with the artificialities of "The Spanish Tragedy" and the beauties of "Edward II." Henceforth the Elizabethan drama exhibits a conflict between dramatic suitability of language and its declamatory, operatic, or aphoristic decorativeness, promoting on the one hand a realistic presentation of life, and on the other fantastic absurdity and imaginative idealism.

The preceding discussion of Marlowe and his contemporaries must have made it apparent that Shakespeare cannot be treated as outside of the circle, although his plays have for convenience been reserved until now. The young actor and poet learned to meet successfully the demands of the stage through an apprenticeship of hack-work, collaboration, and revision, and progressed in his art by means of adaptation and imitation. He wrote in association and rivalry with his fellow playwrights, responding like them to theatrical fashions, and feeling like them the spur of current artistic impulses. The dramatic activity that we have been discussing bears at every point upon his early work. He shared both the limitations and the incentives, bowed to the commanding influences, and rose to the opportunities for initiative which characterize this period. His dramatic career probably began two or three years later than Marlowe's, and of the plays now to be considered several were probably not written until the years following Marlowe's death. "Titus Andronicus" and the three parts of "Henry VI" belong to the early nineties and should be classed with the tragedies of blood and the chronicle histories of those years. "King John," "Richard III," and "Richard II" came somewhat later and form a part of the more advanced development of chronicle history variously represented by "Edward III," "Woodstock," and Marlowe's "Edward II." "Romeo and Juliet," in its final form perhaps still later, is a great and original masterpiece, but one still very characteristic of the dramatic period of which it is the crown and flower.

How much of "Titus Andronicus" is to be regarded as Shakespeare's remains a debated question, a recent and plausible theory being that it was his revision and combination of two old plays.[1] The play, which was

[1] Harold DeW. Fuller, *Publ. Mod. Lang. Assn.* 1901.

coupled by Jonson with "The Spanish Tragedy" as popular twenty years after its first appearance, is mainly an imitation of Kyd, though the phrasing and rhythm frequently show an advance over that author's work. In situations and various specific passages the imitation is pronounced and the motives of the Kydian type are in the main repeated. The revenge of a father for his son is opposed by villanous intrigue, involves a play within the play, and leads the hero into madness. Kyd's finer conception of a tragic hero hesitating in the face of fearful responsibility is, however, lacking; the combination of the two revenge stories — Tamora for her child murdered by Titus, and Titus in return for the murder of his children — resembles "Locrine"; and the black Aaron is, like the negro-Moor in "Alcazar," one of the many Marlowesque villains. The play surpasses current revenge plays chiefly in its unapproached orgy of mutilation, murder, and horror.

The three parts of "Henry VI"[1] are certainly only in part Shakespeare's and represent the complex form of collaboration not infrequently found in the drama. It is likely that Marlowe and Greene were concerned in the

[1] The collaborators on Part I (1623) are unknown, and Shakespeare's contribution to the present form seems likely to have been written later than the bulk of the play, a not very impressive example of chronicle history. Parts II and III (1623) exist also in the abridged and altered forms of the two quartos of 1594, *The First Part of The Contention* and *The True Tragedy of Richard Duke of York*. The problems of the relations of these two quarto plays to the folio texts are among the most puzzling encountered by Shakespearean scholars.

plays, and that Shakespeare's share was mainly in revision.
The three plays were at all events very popular and occupy
an important place among the early chronicle histories.
The contention between the houses of York and Lancaster becomes an epic theme, uniting the three parts,
and affords manifold opportunity for battles, defiances,
coronations, usurpations, and patriotism. The structure
as well as the material is of the chronicle, without any
approach to tragic unity or coherence; but the plays do
in some ways invade the field of tragedy. Comedy is
practically excluded except in the Cade scenes; and the
last two parts, as their titles indicate, present a series of
"falls of princes" — "the death of the good Duke Hum-
phrey; And the banishment and death of the Duke of
Suffolke, and the tragicall end of the proud cardinall of
Winchester" and "The true Tragedie of Richard Duke
of Yorke, and the death of good King Henry the Sixt."
With themes of bloodshed and battle, material at least
full of tragical possibilities, and under the schooling of
Marlowe, Shakespeare served his apprenticeship for historical tragedy.

In "King John" Shakespeare still followed chronicle
history methods without any clear advance toward tragedy.
He was engaged in rewriting the old "Troublesome
Reign," and he followed its plot with great closeness,
scene after scene with entrances and exits being the same
in both plays. But here his indebtedness practically stops.
He seems to have made out a careful scenario, following
the old play with only such alterations and omissions as

were necessary for the condensation of its two parts into a single play, and then to have thrown aside the old text and almost forgotten it. His improvements consequently coincide with the developments which we have found common in the tragedies of the period in that they concern characterization and style. Faulconbridge and Constance become incomparably more vital and impressive than in the old play and win our interest away from the battles and arguments of the rapid scenes. The style, almost never reminiscent of the early play, is mainly rhetorical, though always vigorous and usually surpassing the models which it frequently recalls. It often displays the conflict between the ornamental and naturalistic tendencies; as, for example, when Arthur, facing the murderer, quibbles for ten lines over the red-hot iron which is to put out his eyes, and then, as the attendants enter, forgets his rhetoric in words whose sincerity and simplicity have touched every reader.

"Richard III" and "Richard II," though possibly earlier than "King John," show the imitator and adapter rather than the reviser, and represent independent efforts to give tragic unity to the material of the English chronicles. While all the tragedies and histories so far considered have long since proved unfitted for the stage, "Richard III" has maintained its first popularity and continued to attract the greatest actors and to win the liking of the patrons of the theatre of each generation. Yet, though it has for three centuries exercised a profound impression on the popular imagination, it shows in the opinion of all critics a great indebtedness to Marlowe, and is so evidently imitative of current models that critics writing from such different points of view as Mr. Fleay and James Russell Lowell have been led to doubt Shakespeare's authorship. External and internal evidence both contradict such doubts emphatically, but the close relationship of the play to " Henry VI " makes it improbable that Shakespeare turned to the theme solely of his own initiative. "Richard III " is the fourth play of a tetralogy manifestly planned before the earlier members were completed. Margaret appears in all four plays; the character of Shakespeare's Richard is distinctly outlined in Part III; and it was evidently meant to end the contention of York and Lancaster with the triumph of the Tudor dynasty, and the long series of falls of princes with the tragedy of the villanous Gloster. The chronicle of Richard's reign had indeed been given a tragic unity in the history by Sir Thomas More and in a long saga of chronicle and literature which had developed still further the conception of this masterful and dreadful villain. The suitability of this material to current forms of tragedy was obvious. Dr. Legge had found in this saga the material for a Senecan play; the unknown author of "The True Tragedy" had discovered there a ready-made tragedy of blood and revenge; and there are indications of non-extant plays on the same theme. For either Marlowe or for Shakespeare working with him on the history of the struggle between York and Lancaster, the opportunity for a tragedy with a central hero of the type of Tamburlaine, Faustus, or Barabas must have been apparent.

Shakespeare found in the chronicles a full-length portrait of Richard and a detailed outline of the events of his career, while "The True Tragedy" supplied a few hints. His most notable omission of matter in the chronicle is his neglect of the pangs of conscience, dwelt on in More's history and made salient in "The True Tragedy," and suggesting such a dramatic presentation of remorse as he later created in "Macbeth." His most notable addition is the wooing of Anne, the betrothed but not the wife of Prince Edward, which has no historical foundation and is somewhat extraneous to the main action, though dramatically one of the most effective scenes in the play.[1] In dramatizing the chronicle he manifestly followed Marlowe, making the protagonist the dominating force everywhere in the action, and the other persons foils to set off the hero's villany. But he adopted only with skillful and essential modifications the prevailing methods of the tragedies of blood and revenge. The idea of Nemesis, made clear in Polydore Virgil's account of Richard, must have suggested a Senecan tragedy, or at least a ghost overseeing the course of the villain and finally triumphing in his defeat. Shakespeare, however, personified Nemesis in Margaret, and gave her the various functions of a supervising ghost and of a chorus, — curses, laments, and exul-

---

[1] Somewhat similar situations between Lycus and Megæra in *Hercules Furens*, Locrine and Estrile in *Locrine*, and Tamburlaine and Zenocrate in *Tamburlaine* must have been known to Shakespeare.

tations. Moreover, with a tact unique at that time and not displayed by him in "Titus Andronicus," he perceived that the presentation of many murders on the stage would detract from rather than add to the terror and horror centred in Richard, and so removed all the murders from view excepting that of Clarence. To compensate in a way for this lack of stage sensation, he developed Richard's dream of ghosts into the highly spectacular presentation of the spirits of the eleven victims in their nocturnal appearance between the two opposing camps.

An abundance of theatrical effects, already familiar on the stage, is indeed supplied. The murder of Clarence, with its prolonged dialogue between the murderers, the victims led away to execution, the orations before the battle, the funeral cortège, the battle scenes, the laments and curses, now multiplied and expanded beyond the verge of absurdity, all reflect current stage practices. The structure, still over-dependent on the chronicle sources, indulges after the current fashion in the retention and prolongation of undramatic material: such as the feeble forebodings of the citizens (ii, 3), the prolongation of Hastings's warning of death (iii, 2), and the useless soliloquy of the scrivener (iii, 6). Yet, in comparison with contemporary plays, there is great superiority both in dramatic construction and theatrical effectiveness. The main action progresses with rapidity and coherence to the moment of Richard's reversal of fortune (iv, 4), thirteen years being condensed into a few days; and the interest from this climax to the catastrophe is maintained by

startling melodramatic effects. But the great dramatic
merit of the play lies in the use of contrast, surprise, and
particularly of dramatic irony in the separate scenes and
in their masterly integration to display the character of
Richard himself.

Following closely the character outlined in the chronicle, borrowing conception and treatment from Marlowe's
protagonists, and mindful of the host of stage villains
that had proved so popular in tragedy, Shakespeare constructed a cacodemon who remains not only a great stage
figure but also alive and human in our imaginations. That
he is the source of all evil in the play; that he is absurdly
and impossibly diabolic; that he informs the audience
of all his nefarious schemes; that he has a Machiavellian
skill in intrigue; that he is in intellect and will easily the
superior of all whom he encounters; that he is possessed
by an egoism superhuman in its audacity; that he is an
accomplished and ironical hypocrite; that he is conscienceless except when half asleep and dreaming; that
from the beginning to the end he is a masterful and relent-
less pursuer of his ambition, uninfluenced by persons
or events, alike subjects of his contempt,— all this indicates a skillful adaptation and continuation of sources
and models. But Richard is more. He is dramatically
immensely effective; he is always at hand at the right
moment; he is never nonplussed; a murder is hardly
over when he appears smiling and ironically repentant;
he can ask for strawberries with murder in his heart, or
play with the children or woo the woman whom he has

already marked for doom. That these theatrical fascinatioñs were the results of a consistent conception based on a profound ethical and psychological study can hardly be maintained. It may indeed be doubted whether in this respect there is much advance over Marlowe's villains, or even those of his contemporaries, to say nothing of an approach to Macbeth and Iago. Richard is sometimes a human being, sometimes a monster, and always a stage villain. But the very fact that critics have delighted to analyze and moralize over his traits is proof that Shakespeare, in spite of the monstrosities of his conception, gave to its dramatic presentation not only a stage effectiveness but also plausibility.

This plausibility must be accredited largely to the vigorous colloquialism of his speeches. The play manifests the usual conflict of artificial and natural styles; the elaborate stichomythia and the wailing and cursing queens furnish examples of the common affectations of tragic style; and the rhetorical display appears not infrequently in Richard's speeches. But in the main he speaks with a naturalness and directness far greater than was usual in tragic heroes, and the natural-speaking Richard often makes plausible and convincing the theatrical and rhetorical villain. Thus, after the opening soliloquy he drops his rhetoric for the conversational tone of his conference with Clarence; and thus, the procession of ghosts remains still impressive on our stage because it is followed by a soliloquy that surpasses all except a few of Marlowe's in power and naturalness.

Throughout the play, while others declaim, wail, and curse, the most impossible figure of them all becomes the only convincing human being, very largely because of the realism of his speech.

In " Richard II," written at about the time of "Richard III," Shakespeare was also writing under the influence of Marlowe, but now in direct imitation and rivalry of "Edward II." The first part of the reign of Richard II had already received treatment in " Jack Straw" and "Woodstock," and the theme of a weak king forced to abdicate had been presented in "Henry VI" as well as "Edward II." Shakespeare followed, as always hitherto, his source, Holinshed, very closely, and the historical material determined the plot and characterization, but Marlowe's example led him to an interpretation of the fifteen years' history as the tragedy of the reversal of fortune of a king whose temperament made him contemptible in prosperity but pitiable in adversity. Along with the story of the rise and progress of the conflict between Richard and the barons under Bolingbroke, there runs the story of "the reluctant pangs of abdicating royalty," which give a new pathos to that favorite theme of medieval tragedy and Elizabethan history, the vanquishment of a prince by scornful Fortune. The struggle within Richard's own heart, even more than in the case of Edward II, absorbs the interest and points the moral, the hollowness and uncertainty of earthly grandeur.

Structurally there is no advance on "Edward II" in exposition, integration of action, or catastrophe. Ad-

herence to the chronicle results in a long drawn out and
iterative first act, a virtual repetition of Richard's
struggle over the relinquishment of the crown in iii, 3,
and iv, 1, and a slight and melodramatic treatment of the
catastrophe. On the other hand, there are some changes
from Marlowe's method of interest in connection with
later tragedy. Elegiac scenes with their lamenting women, also conspicuous in "Richard III," are an addition
to the historical source and an important factor in the
structure; their distribution through the play indicating
that they were employed to supply a relief from the
scenes of much action and high tension, more suitable
to tragedy than the relief of comic scenes, and also to
take, as in "Richard III," the place of a chorus through
their lyrical reinforcement of the tragic emotions excited
by the action. Again, as the theme is Richard's reversal
of fortune rather than his death, so the emotional crisis
receives a structural prominence not unlike that given
to Hamlet's, and the catastrophe of death is relegated to
a postscript. The passage from crisis to catastrophe is
managed, as in "Hamlet," "Lear," and "Macbeth," by
the introduction of incidents extraneous to the main
action, here the episode of Aumerle's conspiracy.

The main departures from Marlowe, however, are to
be found in those elements of dramatic composition to
which in this period the genius of Shakespeare as well as
the talent of his contemporaries most readily responded,
the characterization and the style. Not only the king
himself but many other persons in the play, and notably

Bolingbroke, are presented with consistency and subtlety. The historical narrative is transformed into a gallery of full-length historical portraits that lead us to forget history and drama in our study of their personalities. The euphuistic and sentimental Richard gives a fair field for the stylist, but his example is infectious, and the Queen, Gaunt, York, Bolingbroke, the gardener, and in fact all the persons of the drama, employ word-play, periphrasis, and the various flourishes of Elizabethan rhetorical style. If one accepts the theory that tragedy is a game for rhetorical display, and further accepts the conventionalities of Elizabethan style, there must be unmeasured admiration for the extraordinary verbal skill displayed. Shakespeare employs the current artificialities of diction with abounding facility and zest, and often suits them skillfully to the delineation of character; while his constant attention to expression results in a sustained eloquence, which, if it blurs the outlines of reality, substitutes a haze of fancy, and sometimes the glory of magnificent beauty. The miserable years of Richard's downfall are forever associated in our minds with the picturesqueness of the two entries into London and with the splendor of the apostrophe to England and the recital of Norfolk's death.

In the three chronicle histories just considered, although the historical material largely determines structure, tragic conception, and characterization, and although all these are obviously under Marlowe's influence, yet Shakespeare had reached a stage far more advanced than that of mere imitator or adapter. In " Richard III " he had added his

own impress to the Marlowean type of tragedy, and in
"Richard II" he had introduced innovations foreshadow-
ing his later conceptions. As a playwright he had equaled
any of his contemporaries in immediate popularity and
outdone them in permanent theatrical effectiveness. He
had acquired a complete mastery over the conditions and
conventions of the stage, and had frequently, if not always,
outdone the best of his rivals in dramatic ingenuity and
power. Like his contemporaries, however, he was hampered by theatrical conditions and intractable historical
material; and his chief interest was in the opportunities
furnished by the chronicles for the delineation of character and the exercise of his gift of tongues. In range and
verisimilitude his characters already far surpassed Marlowe's; and as a poet, whether in lyric, descriptive, or
purely dramatic passages, whether in sustained treatment
of situation or in splendid purple patches, he had shown
himself the peer of his master.

In "Romeo and Juliet" the same dramatic and poetic
qualities are exhibited as in the historical plays, but the
happy choice of the already well-known love story led
Shakespeare outside of the direct range of Marlowe's
example, freed him from the limits of the historical material, and gave his genius full scope. The importance of
love as a motive in the Italian drama of the Renaissance
is one of the traits that distinguish it from its classical
models, and the influence of Italian drama and fiction
was important in turning Elizabethan dramatists to stories
of romantic passion. These had already been widely

adopted in comedy and had formed the principle plots of
"Tancred and Gismunda" and "Soliman and Perseda,"
as well as minor parts in other tragedies of the period.
The story of Romeo and Juliet, which Brooke speaks of
having seen "lately (1562) set forth on the stage with more
commendation than I can look for," may have been made
into an English play before Shakespeare was born.[1] It
had at least been dramatized in France and Italy, where
Luigi Groto's "Adriana" (1578) surpassed all contemporary plays in the number of its editions.

Brooke's poem, "Romeus and Juliet" (1562), was the
main source of the play and provided a story eminently
adapted to dramatic representation. The plot, with its
conflict between love and hate, the brief triumph of love,
the interference of feud and family authority, the separation and death of the lovers, has been repeated in its
essentials in thousands of stories, and has played an enormous part in the imaginations of four centuries; but it has
hardly found a more effective scenario than that which
lay imbedded in Brooke's long-spun narrative. A lesser
genius than Shakespeare might have discovered it, but
his powers of invention and construction are amply apparent, especially up to the turning-point of the play. The
brawl and the love-sick Romeo of the first scene, dramatically expository and symbolic of the whole action, the
meeting of the lovers at the dance, the balcony scene,
the embassy and return of the nurse, the fatal fight with

---

[1] See H. DeW. Fuller, "Romeo and Julietta," *Modern Philology*, 1906.
It seems clear, however, that Shakespeare drew directly from Brooke.

Tybalt, are all executed with a wealth of incidental invention, a sureness of technic, and a rapidity and directness of dramatic movement that relied but little on Brooke's narrative or contemporary example. The second half of the play, though skillfully condensed, follows the source more closely and, perhaps for this reason, impresses the modern reader less vividly. Shakespeare's dramatic skill is manifest in his departure from the current methods of the tragedy of blood as well as in his treatment of the narrative. What imitators of Seneca and of Kyd did with similar love stories we have seen in "Tancred and Gismunda" and "Soliman and Perseda"; and "Romeo and Juliet" had an equal chance for ghosts, villany, and physical horrors. Some traces of the prevailing fashion do survive, as in the addition to Brooke of the murder of Paris and in the attention paid to the horrors of the tomb. But many of the best scenes are of the sort that occur in romantic comedy, — the repartee of gallants, the preparations for a feast, the dance, the street affray, the meetings and partings of the lovers, — and there is no villain, no figure of Nemesis, no ghost, no warring armies, and no pomp of courts. No tragedy had yet appeared with less theatrical sensationalism, and none which maintained the interest of the spectators upon the story with comparable dramatic intensity.

The extraordinary advance over the historical plays in dramatic technic is, however, overshadowed in our appreciation of the play by the irresistible appeal made by the persons of the story. They are more closely realized for us than the friends and foes of our daily life, yet they dwell forever in the enchantment of idealized romance. To analyze Shakespeare's power to portray and at the same time to exalt human nature would be to unlock the very key to Shakespeare's heart; we may well be content to wonder and exclaim. Yet, we may note that, while characterization, which had been increasing in range and individualization in the historical plays, is here triumphant, the means and methods are not unlike those already noticed. The brilliant translation of prose narrative into monologue and dialogue gives us the nurse; the vivacious amplification of a type familiar in comedy — the garrulous old man — results in Capulet; and even the greatest creations naturally retain traces of contemporary influences. Mercutio is the prince of a throng of quick-witted quibblers, and Juliet is sometimes declamatory, sometimes fantastic, like Brooke's heroine. But they are Shakespeare's own, and the first representatives of two ways in which his imagination characteristically and supremely manifested itself in later plays. Mercutio is the first of those imaginative achievements that concentrate into a few lines of blank verse the complete individualization of a human being; Juliet is perhaps the first of the amazing series of idealized women. If one considers how often the young girl in love has been the theme of genius, and recalls Fielding, Scott, Browning, and Meredith, one may secure some measure of Shakespeare's achievement. When one seeks comparison with the naïve and likable young animal of Brooke's doggerel, or the women of preceding drama, even the charming heroines of Greene's comedies, the art that produced Juliet must seem miraculous. The idealization of woman was, to be sure, common in Renaissance art; and the union in her of wit and beauty, power and charm, passion and purity, innocence and wisdom, was not solely Shakespeare's conception; but the power to conceive such a being with truth and to realize her dramatically, alive, human, and consistent, was his alone.

The conception and expression of character cannot be separated; there lies in the qualities of the poetic style some explanation of the impression we receive of idealized humanity. While colloquial directness is not wanting in the play, the prevailing style has the artificialities, the lyricism, and the exuberance we have found prevailing elsewhere. It exhibits about all the faults and affectations of the dramatic poetry of the time, but these are the defects of an art that finds poetry in everything and ever lingers to enjoy the beauty of words, whether over Queen Mab, or the apothecary's shop, or Friar Laurence's herbs. It stops to display its verbal ingenuity in a pun; it delights in lyric outbursts, sestette or sonnet, morning-song or epithalamium; it riots in the refrains on "banished," becomes grotesque in the wailing quartette, and finds its supreme opportunity in the fancy and music and passion of the lovers underneath the summer moon. It is this exuberance, this spontaneity, this carelessness of incongruity, this delight in ornamentation, this abandon to music and fancy that transfigures the

Verona of brawls, dinners, nurses, and deaths, and, forever ascendant over our fancies, like Romeo's blessed moon, "tips everything with silver."

It is in part this poetic style which distinguishes the play from the later tragedies, but the difference is everywhere manifest to our impressions. The evil and gloom and pessimism that help to make up the tragic fact in "Lear" and "Macbeth" are here scarcely felt. To joy comes sorrow, because of evil and through accident, — this is the tragic theme. In the course of its presentation one may find it suggestive of the passing of youth to age or of passionate love to oblivion, but surely no one comes from the poem with a dominant impression of the wickedness of family feuds, or of the inevitable brevity of romantic passion, or of the dangers of youthful precipitousness, — rather the mind glows with the beauty and joy revealed in life.

In this impression the play has a kinship with the tragedies, even the poor and the maimed, that had preceded it. Tragedies so far have been strangely free from Christian teaching or sentiment. Compared with the medieval drama, early Elizabethan tragedy seems not only secular but pagan. This is partly because it followed its sources and treated of Romans, Moors, Scythians, and heroes of myths and legends; partly because it derived stoic and fatalistic sentiments from Seneca and other classical writers; but it also represents an entire departure from the medieval point of view, a departure necessarily emphasized in tragedy. In the medieval drama, death had been a translation to final reward or punishment, — the portals of heaven and hell were open on the stage. In the Renaissance conception of tragedy death was the point and pith of tragic fact. Faith, forgiveness, reliance on Providence, assurance of immortality are rarely alluded to. Chance, mysterious fate, the emissaries of the devil, the powers of evil in the mind of man are the forces to which tragedy must attend; and they lead to a death terrible and pitiful, to be met bravely and defiantly, it may be, but not peacefully and hopefully. And this emphasis of the gloom of death required an equal emphasis on the glory and beauty of life. Tragedy was the passing into darkness from under this majestic roof fretted with golden fire, the loss of noble reason and infinite faculty; and it must needs proclaim the beauty of the world as well as the quintessence of dust.

And so, although writers of tragedy dwelt on the horrors of death and its accompaniments of blood and atrocity, and though they symbolized in their villains their sense of the reign of evil, yet, in Marlowe's treatment of an Asiatic conqueror or the ignoble fascination of Edward II, or in Peele's fancy that made musical the amours of David; everywhere indeed, in the Pantheas and Persedas, the Marii and Selimi, they were presenting human life as removed from the commonplace, the sordid, the usual, and as the abode of heroisms, splendors, and aspirations. Even evil deeds and villains, even death itself sometimes partook of this glorification; and tragic theory, moral purpose, and theological dogma were alike forgotten in the fascination of human character, passion, and achievement. This idealization of life was, as we noted at the beginning of the chapter, characteristic of the national temper and of the artistic impulses in every field of literature during its brief breathing spell between the Protestant and Puritan revolutions. Its power is curiously illustrated in the effect of the story of Romeo and Juliet upon Brooke in the course of his by no means despicable attempt to turn it into a tragic poem. In his Address to the Reader, he dilates with medieval propriety on the moral of the poem " to raise in the reader an hatefull lothyng of so filthy beastlynes." "And to this ende (good Reader) is this tragicall matter written to describe unto thee a coople of unfortunate lovers thralling themselves to unhonest desire, neglecting the authorite and advice of parents and frendes, conferring their principall counsels with dronken gossyppes, and superstitious friers (the naturally fitte instrumentes of unchastitie" — and so on through all their evil doings until " finallye, by all meanes of unhonest lyfe hastyng to most unhappye death." So wrote the conscious Puritan; but the story charmed the artist. It enticed his meagre art to a share in the joys of the lovers, it led him to a delight in unhonest life, it dissolved his sermon into romance. and poetry, and left him enamored even of his "superstitious frier."

And so the tragedy of the lovers became for Shakespeare as for Brooke and as other stories had become for Marlowe, Peele, and Greene, the spur and the means to an idealization of life. It is not in the reconciliation of the families, still less in the sense of a deserved punishment, that we find an antidote for death and evil; but in the assurance that human passion may be so lovely, human nature so full of strength and beauty. "The sun for sorrow will not show his head," says Prince Escalus at the end, but we believe with Romeo that

> "Jocund day
> Stands tiptoe on the misty mountain tops."

NOTE ON BIBLIOGRAPHY

Ward, Fleay, and Schelling are the best general guides for this period. The books already mentioned by Collier, Symonds, Jusserand, Cunliffe, Fischer, and Churchill bear directly on the matter of this chapter. The sources for documents and records are the same as for chapter iii, with the important addition of *Henslowe's Diary*, vol. i, 1904, ed. by W. W. Greg. The sources for lists of plays and bibliography are the same as in chapter ii, — Greg, Fleay, Hazlitt, Schelling, and Bates. There is no satisfactory and comprehensive treatment of Marlowe's work; J. H. Ingram's *Christopher Marlowe and his Associates* (1904) supplies a full bibliography. Marlowe has been well edited by Dyce and by A. H. Bullen. Dyce's editions of Greene and Peele have long been standard. Bullen has also a good edition of Peele. The recent Clarendon Press editions of Greene, Lyly, Kyd supply careful texts and full introductions. My article, *The Relations of "Hamlet" to Contemporary Revenge Plays* (Publ. Mod. Lang. Assn. 1902), has been drawn upon for the discussion of Kyd; it furnishes references to the various critical discussions of Kyd's work. Texts of the plays by minor writers are to be found in Dodsley; W. C. Hazlitt's *Shakespeare's Library* (6 vols., 1875), containing old plays and other sources for Shakespeare's plays; Delius, *Pseudo-Shakspere'sche Dramen* (1874); the Tauchnitz edition of *Doubtful Plays of Shakespeare*; and in the editions of several of the pseudo-Shakespearean plays by K. Warncke and L. Proescholdt, Halle. This last edition of *Arden of Feversham* contains a valuable introduction. For direction to the bibliography of Shakespeare, see chapter v. On the Henry VI plays,

Miss Jane Lee's paper, *New Shaks. Soc. Transactions*, 1875–76, still offers the most exhaustive treatment of the question of authorship. On *Titus Andronicus*, Mr. Harold DeW. Fuller's article, *Mod. Lang. Publ.* (1901), and Mr. J. M. Robertson's *Did Shakespeare write Titus Andronicus?* (1905) are among the latest discussions. My review of Mr. Robertson's book, *Journal of Eng. and Germ. Philology* (1907), treats in detail some of the discussion of this chapter. The latest studies of the Elizabethan theatre are C. Brodmeier's *Die Shakespeare-Buhne* (Weimar, 1904), which reduces the "alternation" theory to an absurdity, and G. F. Reynold's *Some Principles of Elizabethan Staging* (Chicago, 1905), which disposes of Brodmeier's theories, but goes a little too far in the other direction. See, also, Baker's *Shakespeare as a Dramatic Artist* for a careful and detailed account of the London theatres. Miss V. C. Gildersleeve's *Governmental Regulation of the Shakespearean Drama* (Columbia Univ. Studies in English, in press) is an exhaustive treatment of its subject and incidentally throws light on theatrical matters. Volume iv of Courthope's *History of English Poetry* is on the "Development and Decline of the Poetic Drama," from Marlowe to 1642. Schelling's *The English Chronicle Play* (1902) is the best discussion of this species. W. Bang's series, *Materialien zur Kunde des älteren englischen Dramas*, includes reprints and studies of interest in connection with this and the three following chapters.

CHAPTER V

SHAKESPEARE AND HIS CONTEMPORARIES

FTER "Richard II" and "King John," Shakespeare turned aside from tragedy, and within the next half-dozen years produced his masterpieces of romantic comedy and non-tragical history. With the exception of "Titus Andronicus" and "Romeo and Juliet," the first half of his dramatic career was devoted entirely to comedy and history. With "Julius Cæsar," about 1600, began the period of tragedies and bitter comedies, which lasted until about 1608, when he turned again to romantic comedy and tragicomedy. In these main divisions and turning-points of his dramatic activity there is a correspondence with the development of the contemporary drama which we are able to mark with an approach to definiteness. Both romantic comedy and chronicle history had their heyday during the dozen years that he was devoting to those species. Then at the close of the century various influences produced an abandonment of those forms, a revival of tragedy, and an extensive production of satirical and domestic comedy. About 1608, again, the plays of Beaumont and Fletcher led a return to romance. The Shakespearean period of tragedy may thus be separated from the Marlowean by an interval, during which few tragedies of importance appeared; and its beginning was coincident with new and important developments in the drama.

The leading force in initiating these changes was apparently Ben Jonson, whose prologue to "Every Man in His Humour" (acted 1598) avowed the principles which that play exemplified, and proclaimed the establishment of a comedy of humors. This change was heralded as the result of a more critical and conscious art, of a desire to free the drama from the absurdities and lawlessness of the past, and to supply it with literary standards and artistic aims. His practice, which during the next ten years was mostly in accord with his preaching, was followed or paralleled in many respects by most of the other dramatists. At the date of "Every Man in His Humour" Shakespeare was proclaiming in the choruses of "Henry V" his sense of the incongruities of the chronicle history play and bidding farewell to a form of drama that he had made preëminently his own; and Chapman and Middleton were forsaking romantic comedy for realistic comedies of London life. Perhaps a little earlier, the satires of Donne, Hall, and Marston had created considerable stir and doubtless had a share in turning literary endeavor from sentiment to satire. This satire and exposure of the follies and evils of society also received encouragement from the moral and social change that was working in England and especially in London. The healthy and aspiring national life that had found expression in the sound morality and the imaginative idealism of the earlier drama was now giving place to the moral corruption, social laxity, and lack of national pride that render the reign of James I notorious. At all events, whatever the causes, the comedy of the next seven or eight years was prevailingly realistic, domestic, or satirical.

In tragedy the changes were similar, though less distinct. The protest against the lawlessness of the early drama was manifested in the infrequency of chronicle plays and the appearance of tragedies presenting foreign, and especially Roman, history with due regard for both historical truth and tragic structure. Realism appeared just at the beginning of the century in a number of domestic tragedies that violated the established conventions by dealing with actual events, contemporary society, and humble persons. Satire of contemporary manners became frequent in tragedy, and satirical comedies often dealt with tragic events and exercised an influence on pure tragedy similar to that exercised by romantic comedy in the earlier period. Up to this time popular tragedy had hardly received critical consideration even from the dramatists themselves. Marlowe, Kyd, Shakespeare, and others had been mainly concerned in telling stories on the stage without much consciousness of theory or of the types of drama which they were creating. In this period, however, the demarcation between tragedy and comedy and the definition of a conception of tragedy became positive both in occasional critical comment and in the practice of the dramatists. The old types, how-

ever, survived. Medleys of various kinds of tragedy and
comedy, such as "Old Fortunatus" or "The Downfall
and Death of Robert, Earl of Huntingdon," are not found
much after the beginning of the century; but the revenge
tragedy received a remarkable development by Marston,
Chettle, Tourneur, Chapman, and Jonson, to say nothing
of Shakespeare.

Practically synchronous with the period of Shakespeare's great tragedies are these several interesting
developments: the domestic tragedies, and especially
the allied work of Heywood; the Roman historical tragedies, especially the two by Jonson; the French historical
tragedies by Chapman; and the various revenge plays,
beginning with Marston's "Antonio and Mellida." These
dramatists, however, were mainly occupied with comedy,
and no one of them devoted himself as exclusively to
tragedy as did Shakespeare. Nor did any of them equal
him in immediate popularity. The imitative methods
of his artistic apprenticeship had given place to a
maturity and independence of art that at once won a
supremacy in tragedy even greater than that already
attained in comedy. Yet in themes and treatment there
is no divorce from the practice of his fellow dramatists.
His genius continued responsive to the demands of the
stage of the day, and it felt the changes in dramatic conditions, of which we have been noticing some symptoms,
and which made the tragedies of others as well as his
own more satirical and realistic than those of Marlowe's
time, more concerned with the problem of evil, more

conscious and critical in their art, and in their style less
lyrical and descriptive, more reflective and sententious.

Of the domestic tragedies, very much in fashion from
1597 to 1603, the few survivors show little advance over
"Arden of Feversham." These presentations of hideous
contemporary crimes maintain the protest initiated by
that play against the conventionalities of "the ghost and
revenge" drama, and echo its demand for realism. The
satirical description of Tragedy in the induction to "A
Warning for Fair Women" (1599) is particularly noteworthy as indicating the definiteness which the current
conception of tragedy had assumed. The epilogue reiter-
ates the cry of the realist in an era of romanticism:—

> "Perhaps it may seem strange unto you all,
> That one hath not avenged another's death
> After the observation of such course:
> The reason is that now of truth I sing."

A second of these plays, "Two Lamentable Tragedies"
(1601), is a curious combination of the story of the babes
in the wood and that of the recent murder of one Beech.
A third, "A Yorkshire Tragedy," acted by Shakespeare's
company about 1605, and published with his name (1608),
is remarkable for its naked realism and the vividness and
rapidity of some of its prose.

With these plays may be grouped Heywood's "A
Woman Killed with Kindness" (1607, acted 1603), for,
although it does not deal with real events, it lacks the
usual accompaniments of tragedy, courts, kings, ghosts,
and battles, and presents a story of current English life.

Its themes are the common ones of adultery and revenge,
but it gives them an entirely novel treatment, the husband
refusing to take vengeance on his guilty wife, who dies
repentant and forgiven. After a fashion soon to become
general, there is an underplot which, like the main plot,
presents a problem of social ethics, the question of the
sacrifice of chastity to save a brother's honor. Similar
problems are common in contemporary comedy, and
the play might be classed indifferently as a domestic
tragedy or a tearful comedy. It is Heywood's masterpiece
and exemplifies the qualities that won him the affection
of Lamb, "generosity, courtesy, temperance in the depth
of passion, sweetness, in a word, and gentleness." The
wife falls too easily and repents too sentimentally to be
of much interest, but the character of Frankfort is finely
conceived and, especially in the great scene of the discovery, executed with a power and truth of feeling rarely
combined outside of Shakespeare. In a very similar play,
"The English Traveller," written long afterwards, Heywood speaks of two hundred and twenty plays in which
he had a main finger. Some of these lost plays must
have further exemplified the method of "A Woman
Killed with Kindness"; but his success failed to en-
courage other dramatists to attempt domestic themes
and to abandon the tragic conventions. Such realism
as his was left to comedy, and tragedy continued to seek
its stories in romance or history.

Ben Jonson's two tragedies, "Sejanus" and "Catiline,"
reveal an effort to treat Roman history with accuracy

and dignity, and to enforce on the public stage what he regarded as the essential rules of tragedy. Such representations of Roman history as "The Wounds of Civil War" or the still more incongruous medley of Heywood's "Lucrece" must have excited in him still greater condemnation than did the English chronicle plays. Even Shakespeare's "Julius Cæsar" provoked a sneer, though its dramatization of Plutarch's portraits of the great conspirators apparently excited his emulation and suggested much in his treatment of Sejanus and Catiline. Incongruous spectacle and farce disappear from these plays, and the events are treated upon a well thought out theory of historical tragedy. Jonson strove to present the main events and characters with accurate fidelity to authorities, and even minor persons and deeds in constant harmony with the historical narrative. But the scholar overtopped the dramatist. "Sejanus" has a paraphernalia of notes like a doctor's dissertation; and "Catiline" long excerpts from Cicero's orations.

His plays, however, were intended for the public stage, and are by no means to be classed with closet dramas like Daniel's "Philotas," the tragedies of Fulke Greville and Alexander, or the earlier translations of Kyd and the Countess of Pembroke. Jonson started with current popular forms, with "Julius Cæsar" rather than the Senecan models for a basis. His purpose was to rebuild these, not without some recognition of current dramatic method, but with his main reliance upon classical rules. His cardinal error was his acceptance of the current classical theory of tragedy, the belief that the essential difference between epic and dramatic fable lay in the observance of the three unities and similar proprieties. As he was forced to confess, the ambitious careers of Sejanus and Catiline and the style of action demanded by the audiences of the day did not lend themselves easily to such limitations. But he persevered in his doughty fashion. If in "Sejanus" he gave up the unity of time, he maintained the unity of place; if he retained the comic scenes of the courtesan, he avoided any grotesque mixture of the comic and tragic; he omitted battles, jigs, and spectacles, and secured a coherent development of the main action. In "Catiline," which he boldly proclaimed a "dramatic poem," he adopted the Senecan technic of an introductory ghost and a segregated chorus. But though the action be one, perfect and entire, according to Jonson's understanding of those terms, he never learned Shakespeare's art of focusing events about a spiritual conflict.

Yet in characterization Jonson's interest, like that of his contemporaries, largely centres. Catiline, Cicero, Sejanus, and Tiberius are thoughtfully conceived and faithfully represented. The representation, indeed, is that of exposition, each scene illustrating and emphasizing some trait without securing much illusion of life. The style, especially in the long speeches, is too often rhetorical, and rarely displays great beauty or dramatic power. Yet it is masterly in its way, careful and competent to its purposes, and free from obscurity or over-richness.

His plays mark another failure to turn popular tragedy back into the classical mould. They contributed, perhaps, to a greater regularity of action on the part of his contemporaries and to a more serious consideration of the functions of drama, but the scholarly student of history failed to make it live, the author of " Bartholomew Fair " did not find his best opportunity in the acceptance of classicist theory.

Chapman's tragedies attempted a field hitherto untried except in Marlowe's " Massacre," that of contemporary French history. While treating historical events with freedom of invention, he dealt with real persons and careers familiar to his audience. In the long-popular tragedy of "The Death of Bussy D'Ambois" (1607, acted 1600–1604) he turned to the court of Henry III and centred a story of treasonable ambition, conspiracy, and adultery about the interesting personality of the insolent and indomitable D'Ambois. After the fashion of Kyd and Marston, he followed " The Death " with a " Revenge of Bussy D'Ambois," which adopted the established technic of the revenge plays, with less alteration than might have been expected after Shakespeare's transformation in "Hamlet." The avenger, Clermont, is a " Senecal man," and his sententious and rhetorical philosophizing was doubtless incited by "Hamlet," though it followed a long-established precedent. The " Conspiracy and Tragedy of Byron " (two parts, 1608, acted 1607) dealt with important affairs in the reign of Henry IV that were still fresh in the memory of the audience,

Biron having been executed in 1602. In the original form of the play, in fact, Queen Elizabeth was represented, and the French queen boxed the ears of her husband's mistress, but the protest of the French ambassador made a revision necessary.

The new material of these plays did not lead Chapman to attempt any variations in form from the current drama, nor did it result in any advance in method; his fondness for long speeches and narrations resulting rather in a treatment more epical and less dramatic than is found in any of his contemporaries. Nor did his study of contemporary memoirs for his sources and his interest in political philosophy result in any advance in reality or vividness of characterization, though here he is often very felicitous, as in his portrait of Henry IV, and though his arrogant protagonists are interesting and original variations of the Marlowean tragic hero, not without successors in the later drama. But for Chapman, tragedy was in the main, as for the writers whom Gosson derided, an opportunity "to show the majesty of his pen in tragical speeches." The abundance, ingenuity, and beauty of his figurative language are simply amazing. Every person, deed, or sentiment calls for illustration and lets loose a flood of similes. Finished verse, a highly picturesque sense of the value of words, a remarkable union of pregnant sententiousness with vividness of description, have made his plays the delight of many a reader, though perhaps most of his admirers have experienced a fatigue that found satisfaction in Dryden's perverse criticism, "dwarfish thought dressed up in gigantic words, repetition in abundance, looseness of expression, and gross hyperboles." For, though the thought is by no means dwarfish, the dress is often too big for it. We are wearied by the constant effort to write up to the tragic opportunity for a heightened and sententious eloquence. In this respect, Chapman's style partakes of the faults of his day. It has not the spontaneity and ease of Marlowe, Peele, and "Romeo and Juliet"; it is difficult, involved, pretentious, and self-conscious, yet its splendors remain. Its abundance of resource, its imaginative condensation, its suggestive power again and again compel comparison with Shakespeare himself.

Revenge directed by a ghost found favor with both Jonson and Chapman, but they were preceded in the use of this popular motive by John Marston. In 1598, at the age of twenty-three, he made something of a sensation by his satires and immediately proceeded to carry his censoriousness of human frailties into the drama. His earliest play, "Antonio and Mellida" (two parts, 1602, acted 1599–1600), reveals in Part I the still dominant influence of romantic comedy, despite its tragic trend; but Part II, "Antonio's Revenge," is a tragedy of the Kydian type. The play was followed by a number of comedies, all outspoken in satire of contemporary manners and in the exposure of social immorality. Several dealt with tragic material, and one, "The Malcontent," is a notable combination of a tragedy of blood and a satirical comedy. Its protagonist is of a type represented in the other comedies and not without influence on contemporary dramatists. Marston's malcontents are men of virtue and honor "who hate not man but man's lewd qualities"; in disfavor and out of joint with the world; given to melancholy and a showy pessimism that finds fitting expression only in images of filth and putrefaction. His tragedy "Sophonisba" (1606), which he seems to have deemed the most important of his plays, treats history with great freedom, and unites melodramatic horrors with his usual unflinching fondness for rankness of thought and imagery. The horrible realism of the Erichtho scenes comes in strange contrast with the songs, dances, and musical accompaniment suited to a performance by the child actors for whom all of Marston's plays were written.

"Antonio's Revenge" is the earliest representative in this period of the Kydian type of revenge tragedy. The satirical passages in "A Warning for Fair Women" indicate the popularity of ghosts and revenge, and there are many evidences of the continued vogue of "The Spanish Tragedy" from 1597 to 1602. Marston's play was evidently modeled on "The Spanish Tragedy," and probably still more directly on the Kydian "Hamlet." The story is the revenge of a son for a father murdered by a villanous duke who seeks to wed the hero's mother; the revenge is directed by the ghost of the father; the hero is driven to hesitation, irresolution, and the verge of madness; he pretends to be a fool; intrigue and trickery are indulged in by both hero and villain,

and the revenge is accomplished with an abundance of
bloodshed. There is a minor story of revenge, enforcing
the main situation as does the Laertes story in "Hamlet" and the scene with the Senex in "The Spanish
Tragedy"; and, doubtless as in the early "Hamlet,"
the passion of the murderer for the widow of his victim
now becomes an important motive in the action. Moreover, the play abounds in psychological introspection
and meditative philosophy set forth for the most part
through the soliloquies of the hero.

The indebtedness to the earlier revenge plays extends
to details of the stage presentation. Revenge is accomplished much as in "The Spanish Tragedy," though by
means of a masque instead of a play, and without the
death of the hero. From similar scenes in the old "Hamlet" were probably derived the appearance of the ghost
at midnight, the cry "Antonio, revenge!" and the second
appearance of the ghost to the hero and his mother.
The dumb show exhibiting the wooing of Maria, the
use of the churchyard, the banquets, carousals, funerals,
exhibition of the dead bodies, and the oaths of the
conspirators were perhaps already conventional accompaniments of a revenge play. "Antonio's Revenge,"
however, is not wanting in inventiveness; its abundant
horrors and its melodramatically ingenious stage effects
were probably recognized as an advance upon the old
favorites, and they excited the emulation of succeeding
dramatists.

The hero, too, is of the Kydian type. Like both Hiero-

nimo and Hamlet, he is a scholar, interested in philosophy and also in theatrical performances. Like them he
is distinguished by a tendency to reflection, and struggles in solitary meditation at each crisis in his career.
Like them he is driven to the verge of madness by the
pressure of his heavy responsibility and by his awakened
sense of evil in the universe. Though he does not seek
further proof, yet, like Hamlet after the revelations of
the play, he becomes frantic and irresolute, neglects an
opportunity to kill the duke, and wastes his vengeance
upon an innocent child. Like Hieronimo and Hamlet,
he is tricky, wild, and ranting. With all his overdrawn
passion, however, his mental struggle occasionally attains
intellectual depth and tragic power. As he tells us, it was
"the stings of anguish," "the bruising stroke of chance"
which made him run mad "as one confounded in a maze
of mischief."

Several years, then, before Shakespeare's "Hamlet,"
we have a play dealing with the old story of a revenge of
a son for a father, following closely the methods introduced by Kyd, appealing to a taste that delighted in
extravagant violence and melodramatic sensationalism,
but also striving to simulate profundity of thought and
a passionate sense of evil. It is difficult to-day to take
Marston seriously. His plays have little merit, while his
bombastic sententiousness gives an air of insincerity to
everything that he wrote; yet a serious purpose and a considerable influence on later drama cannot be denied to
his efforts in tragedy. Like so many others, he deserves

to be remembered for what he attempted rather than
for what he did. Absurd though "Antonio's Revenge"
be as an artistic achievement, it is historically of importance as indicating an ambitious attempt to give
poetical expression to the spiritual conflict of a mind
brought to face dreadful evil. The prologue that he
addressed to his London audience testifies sufficiently to
his serious and ambitious intentions, and to the clear
separation of tragedy from other forms of drama, which
he and other poets were trying to force upon the theatre.

> "Therefore we proclaim,
> If any spirit breathes within this round
> Uncapable of weighty passion,
> (As from his birth being hugged in the arms
> And nuzled 'twixt the breasts of Happiness,)
> Who winks and shuts his apprehension up
> From common sense of what men were, and are;
> Who would not know what men must be: let such
> Hurry amain from our black-visaged shows;
> We shall affright their eyes. But if a breast,
> Nail'd to the earth with grief; if any heart,
> Pierced through with anguish, pant within this ring;
> If there be any blood, whose heat is choked
> And stifled with true sense of misery:
> If aught of these strains fill this consort up,
> They arrive most welcome."

A number of plays dealing with "revenge for a father"
followed. In 1602 "The Revenge of Hamlet" was entered
in the Stationers' Register; and the first quarto, a pirated
and very corrupt edition, appeared in the following year.
This quarto, in the opinion of a majority of critics, represents Shakespeare's partial revision of the old play,

which was put on the stage by Burbage's company in
1601–02. In the same years Ben Jonson was receiving
pay from Henslowe of the rival company for two sets of
additions to "The Spanish Tragedy," and these were
published in 1602. In that year Henslowe also paid Chettle for a tragedy, "Hoffman" (1631); and in 1602–03
Tourneur's "Atheist's Tragedy" (1611) was probably
acted.[1] By 1603 Shakespeare had given "Hamlet" its
final form as represented by the second quarto (1604).
The almost simultaneous appearance of these various
plays is sufficient testimony to the popularity of the old
revenge story with both audiences and authors. Dealing
with similar plots, they naturally have many elements in
common, but they exhibit few or no signs of servile imitation of one another. They represent independent developments of the type that Kyd had introduced a dozen
years before and that Marston had revived, each retaining many of the old conventions, and each adding
much that was new.

Jonson's additions to "The Spanish Tragedy" are
distinct from the rest of the play and affect the proportion and movement of the action rather for the worse.
They deal in the main with Hieronimo; his irony is
increased and made more effective; his reflections become more elaborate and pregnant; above all, his madness gains enormously in reality and intensity. His

---

[1] Mr. Elmer Stoll's argument against this early date does not seem
to me convincing. See the Appendix to his *John Webster*, Cambridge,
1904.

madness, indeed, receives a disproportionate development. Throughout the additions Jonson is picturing a mind diseased by grief, sometimes conscious of life's unrelaxing pain and again lost in frenzied delirium. Thus, the imaginative impulses that responded to the demand for revenge plays here stirred a great poet to a rehabilitation of the crude ravings of the old Hieronimo in a form more intellectual, more vitally human, and of immensely greater imaginative range.

"Hoffman" is a sensational melodrama by a hack writer not unskillful in using prevailing conventions with theatrical effectiveness. The story is again the revenge of a son for a father, but there is no ghost, only the skeleton to excite him to vengeance. He banishes "clouds of melancholy" at the start and shows no hesitation in carrying out the revenge until turned from his purpose by his passion for the mother of his chief victim. Intrigue and slaughter reign supreme; and, as in "Locrine," there are two plots of revenge — Hoffman seeking revenge for his father and every one else seeking revenge on Hoffman. In the pathetic situation of Lucibella, driven insane by grief, Chettle made use of a character and a situation familiar on the stage in much the same fashion as they must have been presented in the old "Hamlet." Lucibella's madness, however, is made the instrument of some telling hits at the villain and the means of discovering his iniquity. While Ophelia's madness has no influence on the main action, that of Lucibella leads directly to the *dénouement*. Dramatically this is a very important difference and seems due to Chettle's invention. Unlike Marston or Jonson, he made little effort to give the story either imaginative intensity or philosophical significance. He took common theatrical motives and situations, added much and changed much, and constructed a good acting play not without some grace of verse. A play that was popular thirty years after it was written must have successfully met the stage demand.

Tourneur's "Atheist's Tragedy" differs in many respects from all preceding revenge plays. The revenge is for a father murdered by an uncle and directed by a ghost. The revenge, however, is left to Providence; the ghost is Christian; the avenging son not only hesitates, but after a little irresolution overcomes his inclinations to revenge, and, obeying the ghost's behests, resignedly awaits the judgment of heaven. In stage presentation the play also shows a wide departure from Kyd, especially in the indescribable comic underplot. There are, however, three appearances of the ghost, — one to soldiers on watch, — churchyard scenes, banquets, sword fights, suicides, scaffolds, and death's-heads. In the accumulation of horrors, in the development of the villain's character, in the emphasis on new sensational motives at the expense of revenge, and in the more elaborate handling of the intrigue, it may be said to carry the general development of the revenge tragedy a step farther than Marston or Chettle, and a step nearer to Webster. On the other hand, in its definite attempt to present an intellectual conception not lacking in moral grandeur, it sometimes, more closely than any of the other plays considered, approaches "Hamlet." The change in the revenge motive is especially manifest in the soliloquies and reflective passages, which unite in a fairly well connected argument that points the moral of the action, the omnipotence of God's providence.

When, after an interval of some half dozen years, Shakespeare returned to tragedy, evidently both the demands of the theatres and the artistic impulses of the poets were different from those of Marlowe's day. The plays of Marlowe and Kyd were still active forces in the drama, but in 1600–01, when Shakespeare was perhaps writing both "Julius Cæsar" and the first revision of "Hamlet," the man of the hour in tragedy was Marston.

In "Julius Cæsar" Shakespeare availed himself of a theme already a favorite. The story of the overthrow of a tyrant, the progress of a conspiracy, the fall of a prince, and his revenge upon the murderers furnished material well approved for tragedy, while the greatness of the events and the actors both gave assurance of popular interest and incited the poet to his best. Shakespeare was not directed by scrupulous regard for historical accuracy, but his genius was stirred by that of Plutarch to give the events of the Roman civil war the interest and vitality he had given to the reigns of English kings. In dealing with a story that followed so closely the standard lines of tragedy, — the murder and the revenge,—Shakespeare adopted some of the methods current in contemporary plays. There is really no evidence to support Mr. Fleay's ingenious surmise that the play was originally in two parts, — I, The Death, and II, The Revenge of Cæsar, — but the play seems to have separated itself naturally into those two divisions. The rise of the action traces the rise of the conspiracy to Cæsar's death; the return of the action proceeds to the failure and deaths of the conspirators. But from the beginning Shakespeare must have found his interest engaged less by the story of conspiracy or revenge, or even by the presentation of the turmoil of an empire, than by the delineation of the character of Brutus. There, for him, lay the kernel of the tragedy, in the struggle of a highly gifted nature with a task unfit for his accomplishment. The play became not a tragedy of overreaching ambition, as Marlowe might have made "The Tragedy of Cæsar," nor the tragedy of supernaturally ordained revenge, as Kyd might have made "Cæsar's Revenge," but the tragedy of Brutus, — the fateful struggle of a noble mind against counter actors and against chance, and also against an incurable deficiency in his own temperament.

Similarly, in revising the old "Hamlet," Shakespeare must have been attracted by the possibilities in the character of the hesitating avenger. Here, however, as we have seen, the influence of his contemporaries was considerable and complex. The plot, situations, types of character, and leading motives of the old "Hamlet" were already familiar to the stage in several plays. Revenge, directed by a ghost, hesitation on the part of the hero, insanity real or feigned, intrigue, copious bloodshed, a secondary revenge plot, meditative philosophizing in the form of soliloquies, were all essential elements probably of the Kydian "Hamlet," certainly of several other revenge plays. The refusal of an opportunity to kill the villain, the songs and wild talk of a mad woman, the murder of an innocent intruder, scenes in a churchyard, the appearance of the ghost to soldiers of the watch, the play within the play, — all these as well as many more minor conventionalities, such as the swearing on the sword hilt, or the voice of the ghost in the cellar, had appeared in other plays than the old "Hamlet." And Hamlet himself, wild and ranting at times, crafty and dissimulating at others, cynical and ironical, given to melancholy and meditation, hesitating in bewilderment, harassed by the unavoidable "whips and scorns of time," — so far as we can analyze the tragic hero, his characteristics had been already used by contemporary dramatists. Dramatic ingenuity was all that was required to make a new play out of this abundance of old material. Chettle succeeded in doing just this. Marston, Jonson, and Tourneur, however, had been trying to give the old story philosophical significance and a highly imaginative phrasing. They had glimpses of the dramatic and poetic possibilities that lay in the situation of the hesitating revenger, and at moments they succeeded in realizing these. Shakespeare set himself to their task, and naturally enough he was in many ways limited and directed by their efforts. It was perfectly possible for him to change the plot completely, or to omit the ghost in the cellar, or to remove the bloodthirsty and intriguing elements from the part of Hamlet, or to give a more Christian interpretation to the revenge; but in these and other matters he followed the practice of the earlier plays. There was no dramatic need of so many long soliloquies; the meditative avenger need not have been ironical; insanity might have received less elaboration; but in these respects Shakespeare was in agreement with his contemporaries. The themes which they took inspired him. He succeeded in doing what they vainly attempted.

He by no means neglected the external story or denied the theatrical demand for sensation. He, perhaps, did not radically change the course of events as depicted in the old play, but he unquestionably improved on any preceding tragedy in the mere effectiveness of the scenic presentation of a sensational story. How great this effectiveness is may be judged by the continued popularity of "Hamlet" as a stage performance even before unlettered auditors. We may surmise that had poetry and philosophy both perished, it would still draw its crowds as it does to-day on the remote borders of civilization. This theatrical triumph is due in part to dramatic excellence of structure and presentation. From the old play probably came a story restricted by semi-Senecan technic to a great emotional crisis; but Shake-

speare at least resisted the temptation, to which his contemporaries succumbed, of extending the action over
the events leading up to the murder. And assuredly to
him rather than to Kyd or another is due the recognition
of the dramatic values of the story's beginning, middle,
and end. Magnificent as is his development of the ghost
scenes at the beginning, still more important structurally is his realization of the value of the middle of the
tragedy and treatment of the play within the play and
its immediate sequences; and if the end is developed
with an Elizabethan looseness of coherence that will
not correspond to any logical scheme of structure, yet
the pathos of the Ophelia scenes and the wonderful
grotesquery of the graveyard excite and renew the
spectator's interest to the final catastrophe. The scenic
presentation, while telling a sensational story with pre-
eminent effectiveness, becomes as never before in English drama the means for exhibiting the inner struggle
of the protagonist. Parallel with the external conflict
between murderer and avenger, beginning with the ad-
vent of the ghost and ending with a holocaust, there
runs the story of a man's moods and thoughts; and this
story of doubt and melancholy overpowering resolution
imposes its unity of structure and emotional tone upon
the external conflict so full of visible action. The throng
of dreadful happenings becomes a foil to set off the inner
struggle of thought. Their climax is only the brink of
resolution from which Hamlet shrinks. Their catastrophe
is the end of irresolution in silence.

The reflections and moralizings and broodings over misfortunes inherited from Seneca, and long an essential element in the revenge plays, are also, like the sensational incidents, integrated and humanized by the conception of the hero's character. The soliloquies, though keeping to the themes and methods of contemporary drama, become landmarks in the depiction of the inner struggle and in the general progress of the action. The absurd convention of speaking aloud one's unformed and unbidden thoughts becomes theatrically exciting, dramatically essential, and, through the reach of Shakespeare's imaginative expression, representative of the eternal battle of human frailty against the mysteries of chance and evil.

Analysis might, indeed, continue to discover in the multiform impressiveness of the characterization and the poetry survivals of old conventions and hints of the method of Shakespeare's transformation. Taken apart, various passages seem overburdened with rhetoric, after the style of the day, and others over-sententious. Taken piece by piece, the sarcasm, the irony, the pessimism, the stoic philosophy, even the passionate protest against destiny, have much in common with the ideas then current in other plays. But here again the transformation accomplished through unrivaled powers of expression and knowledge of human nature seems to result from an absorbing interest in the meditating and hesitating temperament of the hero. The union of a drama of blood-vengeance with a drama of thought, a union that had been often attempted by others, is finally achieved, because here for the first time there is full recognition of the tragic interest, movement, and significance of a man's battle with himself. The tragic drama of character has been consummated.

In Shakespeare's conception of the tragic hero we find many characteristics and some incongruities that belong to the old avengers; but there is new penetration into the sources of human motive that results in an essentially new view of the functions and scope of the tragic drama. As in most tragedies since "Tamburlaine," the play is a one-part play, presenting a hero far above the average in mental and moral power, but for the time mainly under the sway of one dominating mood or emotion. Like the other heroes of revenge tragedies, Hamlet is a good man brought suddenly face to face with evil. Again, like the heroes of Seneca and of most tragedies dealing with a reversal of fortune, Hamlet is a strong man brought to face the enmity of chance. He is an individual forced to struggle against a hostile environment. Again, he is a man in a tragic crisis that requires the exercise of all possible powers on his part if he is to avoid disaster, who finds himself afflicted with a temperamental weakness that makes failure possible or indeed inevitable. Critics emphasize now one and now another element of his character as they emphasize one or another of these conflicts as the most important. Shakespeare here, as again in later plays, united in one hero all the varieties of conflict catalogued by the critics.

But if we ask which is most peculiarly Shakespearean, it must be said to be the conflict with his own temperamental unfitness, call that irresolution, melancholy, meditativeness, or what you will. Here lies Shakespeare's main differentiation from preceding tragedy, though one distinctly presaged in "Julius Cæsar." At all events, we have a conception of tragedy carried out in his succeeding plays. The hero, noble and righteous, is brought into conflict with the results of evil and circumstance, and he is crippled by his own inability or weakness. Tragedy becomes inherent in character, in the incompleteness that marks the best and mightiest of mankind.

Our consideration of "Hamlet" has been prolonged partly because its relations to contemporary drama can be traced more readily than those of Shakespeare's other tragedies, and partly because it is the first of his plays to afford a full definition of tragedy, a conception of prime importance both in the development of Shakespeare's art and in the future history of the drama. A sensational struggle is presented, and the abounding incidents are wrought into effective if loosely connected stage-scenes, dealing with material similar to that then current in the theatres, — villains, ghosts, murders, insanity, grim farce, meditations, aphorisms. But the scenic presentation and the dramatic structure are to express not only an external conflict between hero and counter-force, but an inner struggle of the hero himself. They are to be the effects and results, nay, the very mirror of the inner thought and feeling. And the disaster that falls upon the hero and those by him beloved comes home to us as due not merely to external forces or circumstances or to evil working within, but also to an inherent unfitness of his own.

This conception of tragedy found further exemplification in "Othello," [1] freer from Elizabethan methods than any of the other tragedies, and the most masterful of all as a play. The fable was found in an Italian *novella* that related, like so many of its class, a bald story of love, jealousy, and villany. The very baldness of the narrative in comparison with the fullness of incident and characterization of the chronicles or Plutarch, gave Shakespeare's imagination an untrammeled opportunity. The ingredients of the story, common in romantic comedy and already combined by Shakespeare in "Much Ado about Nothing," were also not unfamiliar in tragedy, but Shakespeare enlarged and interpreted them to fit the conception of his two preceding tragedies, the presentation of a spiritual struggle in which goodness is attacked by evil at its point of greatest vulnerability.

---

[1] *Troilus and Cressida* in some form was probably acted in 1602. The editors of the Folio apparently first intended to class it with the tragedies, but they changed their minds while the book was printing and placed *Troilus* without pagination between the histories and tragedies. The preface to one of the quartos of 1609 classes it with the comedies, and the prologue inclines that way. For an interesting though not always convincing discussion of the many difficulties offered by the play, the reader is referred to Mr. R. A. Small's *The Stage Quarrel between Ben Jonson and The So-called Poetasters* (1899), pp. 139–170. The play offers problems of importance in Shakespearean criticism, but in a history of tragedy it seems negligible. The concluding scenes (v, 7–10) are clearly not by Shakespeare, and the Prologue and v, 4–6 are doubtful.

The credulity of Othello, however, is assaulted by a more active agent of evil than in "Julius Cæsar" or "Hamlet." Malignant evil is embodied in Iago, and it is against his machinations that the nobly idealized characters of Othello and Desdemona prove incompetent and defenseless. He is the person who dominates the action and gives explanation and plausibility to the circumstances. He not only opposes the hero in the external action, he creates through his insinuations all the evil suspicions that struggle in Othello's mind. He might almost be considered the protagonist of the tragedy.

In structure there is a notable advance over preceding plays, accomplished apparently in part through deliberate intent. The first act with its account of Iago's craft and the marriage is a distinct introduction. The remaining four acts present a practically continuous action, confined to Cyprus and representing about thirty-six hours. Moreover, by a skillful ambiguity, which Christopher North called "the double clock," Shakespeare, while securing this rapid and uninterrupted process of time, has succeeded in conveying an impression of protracted intrigue and slowly-developing motives. Thus, without lessening the variety and importance of the events and emotions, he gains, by a closer observance of unity than in the other tragedies, a greater degree of theatrical illusion and of dramatic intensity. Again, "Othello" technically is noticeable among the tragedies for its relinquishment of many current methods. It is neither a chronicle history nor a Senecan tragedy.

There is no presentation of history and little of court ceremonies. There are no battles, no long exposition, no spectacles, no ghosts, no insanity, and almost no comedy. It has few persons and virtually a single action. The under-plot is subordinated and closely united to the main action, and there are no delays and new excitements between crisis and catastrophe as in "Hamlet" and "Lear." Nowhere else in Shakespeare is the progress of character, emotion, and deed toward the final event so consecutive and so uninterrupted. This advance in coherence and proportion seems due less to the contributing causes just enumerated than to the explanation of action by character. Accept the unbelievable malignity of Iago — and you do accept it before you have proceeded far — and every step of the appalling chain of intrigue seems a natural outcome of the motives of the persons before us.

In consequence of this integration of character and action, the characters are, more than in the other tragedies, distinct and unmistakable. As if to make stronger the contrast between good and evil, the good man is a Moor, apparently, as in the case of the Moors in "Titus Andronicus" and "Selimus," hardly distinguishable from a negro; and the bad man is deprived of the motive which in the *novella* rendered his wickedness intelligible. Yet nowhere, even in Shakespeare, are generosity and greatness of soul more admirable than in Othello, nowhere is villany more human than in Iago. The stage villain here receives his apotheosis as the

avenging hero did in "Hamlet." The source of all
the evil in the play, the Machiavellian machinator, the
subtle hypocrite whose every action is a pose to conceal
its purpose, the simulator of honesty and bluntness,
the shameless egoist who proudly avows his villany and
bawls it to the gallery, the intellectual master who plays
every one for a dupe, and especially his accomplice
— all this had been embodied in the villains of Kyd
and Marlowe. Although intelligible to Elizabethan psychology and theology, and credible in the light of Tudor
politics and feuds, such a type would seem to lack
enduring truth. While preserving all the attributes of
the stage type, Shakespeare made it the means for
that searching analysis of human depravity to which
his contemporaries were less successfully dedicating
their efforts. This soliloquizing devil becomes identified
with the suggestions and sinuosities of evil that partake
of the flux of our consciousness. Hypocrisy, cynicism,
cruelty, the absence of human sympathies, the pride and
malignity of intellectual superiority have henceforth
their symbol in Iago. Impossible, diabolical, inhuman
as Barabas or Richard III, he is never for a moment
unplausible, because he ever unearths a corresponding
potentiality in us.

The persons of the play, while unusually effective
on the stage, and while human and real in their discourse, have a universality of appeal essential in the
greatest works of art, desired by Aristotle and dimly
foreshadowed in Elizabethan efforts after greatness and

typicality. Othello, Desdemona, and Iago create fresh reflection and new impulse in every reader of every generation. And to each they are not only real persons but also symbols and ideals of the generosity, sweetness, and iniquity of the universe. This idealization of character is accomplished with wonderful clarity by means of an expression, splendidly eloquent, untroubled by conceit or obscurity, equally masterful in prose or verse, magnificently adapted to the representation of every mood or temperament. Shakespeare here realized the ideal toward which English tragedy under the leadership of Marlowe had been struggling, the presentation of human greatness in blank verse beautiful and dramatic.

If "Othello" is comparatively free from current conventions, "Lear" is in many respects the most Elizabethan of Shakespeare's tragedies. Story, themes, situations, stage effects constantly recall the plays of his predecessors; and if his creative imagination here attains the most astounding triumph in all literature, it cannot be said to free itself entirely from a confusion of archaisms and absurdities.

Returning to English history, Shakespeare selected a story that had outgrown the chronicles and been narrated by several poets and in one drama. From the early "Leir" he took a few important hints, but he treated the material of the chronicles with a freedom which both its obviously legendary character and its remoulding by other poets permitted. He was only slightly concerned with the presentation of history and hurried over the battles and the shows, the still indispensable accompaniment of historical plays. He was concerned solely with the tragic entanglements of character, with the devastations of evil and folly.

The kernel of the story, Lear's trick and Cordelia's unsatisfactory reply, though possessing a kind of objectivity suitable for the stage, is of itself so absurd and childish as to impede illusion of truth. Its development is full of inconsistency, and the interwoven themes of madness, villany, lust, ambition, family feud, and ideal virtue suggest no break from the Elizabethan canon of tragedy. To the story of Lear and his daughters, Shakespeare added the still more childish parallel story of Gloster and his sons. This common device of a reinforcing subplot is here extended to every situation and motive. Even the devoted Kent is balanced by Goneril's faithful creature, Oswald; the inhuman sisters are supported by the machinating Edmund; and, most extraordinary of all, the assumed madness of Edgar becomes an accompaniment for the real madness of Lear. The elaboration of the sub-plot causes an unprecedented complexity of persons and events, and it dislocates the structure. The intense interest which is absorbed in the sufferings of Lear finds itself distracted and dissipated in a medley of incidents so incongruous and so confusing that one wonders how a rational mind could have selected them. The crowded scenes which separate the climax of the third act from the catastrophe assuredly form one of the least happy instances of the Elizabethan habit of intro-

ducing a change of interest and a variety of incident
in the fourth and fifth acts. Yet the structure of the
play, if far from faultless, reveals amazing mastery.
The development of the action in the first three acts
with the constantly increasing tension of feeling, and the
final gathering of all the different actions in the won-
derfully condensed catastrophe, are among the greatest
achievements of dramatic plotting. Moreover, in spite
of his zest for crowded and diversified action, Shakespeare's feeling for unity of emotional effect caused him
to omit one motive that modern renovators have never
been able to forego. He found a place for battles, villany, childish intrigue, the clown's songs and jests, the
plucking out of Gloster's eyes, and the protracted foolery
between Edgar and his helpless father, but he refused
to admit romantic love into this drama of the madness
that separates father and child.

Though Shakespeare chose to involve himself in these
manifold difficulties of story and structure, he hardly
felt his fetters. No play depends less on mere incident
and event. The inconsistencies and confusion of the
action are forgotten in the wild turmoil of human passions. Wild, terrible, elementary, brutal, grotesque, or
sublime, — everything in the play is touched with the
imaginative truth that gives it limitless range of suggestion, applicable to any discord of parents and children
or to the most dreadful spiritual torture. Insanity, long
a favorite theme of Elizabethan tragedy, and fantastic
grotesqueness, often its bane, summon his imagination

to its most wonderful creation when the feigning Bedlam counters the mad king mid the jests of the fool
and the havoc of the storm. Such a conception could
have been attempted only in an age which took its emotions strong and mixed, which found insanity a subject
for laughter as well as horror, and which refused to limit
the imagination by reason or rule. In that age a lesser
than Shakespeare might have formed the bare design of
making his audience laugh at the fool and poor Tom,
and shudder at the eyeless Gloster and the raving Ancient.
Something akin to it may be found in many scenes, in
that in which Marlowe's emperor and empress dash out
their brains against the bars of their cage in a frenzy of
humiliation, or that in which Webster's duchess stands
undazzled amid the dancing ring of obscene maniacs.
The Elizabethan drama had prepared the opportunity
for the full and terrible presentation of the discords and
agony of a breaking mind. The London audience was
ready for the scenes on the heath.

Madness is only one element that contributes to the
overwhelming effect of the play. Its so-called pessimism
is the only other on which our meagre survey may dwell.
English tragedy had from the beginning concerned itself
mainly with heinous crime and sin; and during the years
immediately preceding and following "Lear" there was
a distinct conception of tragedy as the representation
not only of the depths of iniquity but of the moral confusion and blackness that beset us all. In "Hamlet,"
"Othello," and "Measure for Measure" the sense of

evil is ever present. In "Lear" it grips the reader like the rack. As in "Othello," evil, here represented by the two fiendish daughters as well as by an intriguing villain, dominates the action, and carries all that is good along with it to destruction. But evil is only one of the forces that cause suffering and ruin. Lear and Cordelia contend against their own imperfections and against chance and circumstance so hostile that they seem directed by gods who sport with men as with flies and loose the fury of the elements to torment their victims. Where else in tragedy are the forces that make for ruin so appalling and so irresistible; and where else are suffering and ruin so dreadful and so complete? The sufferers are powerless. Suffering does not here arouse a Promethean defiance, but it discovers and purifies human virtue. If evil is dominant over the action, Cordelia, Kent, the Fool, and the chastened and purified Lear are dominant in our reflections. The end is not the fall and cessation of all that is good. Even in our dismay at the convulsion which evil may cause, there remains the memory of the perfection of human devotion and love. The final impression must, however, partake of confusion and horror at the blackness and ruthlessness of a moral order that can sacrifice perfect virtue in an effort to free itself from the hideous enormity of evil. This is the tragedy of life as Shakespeare saw it, and the cry of bewilderment and agony seems to come from the poet's own heart. The language, sometimes crowded and difficult, has hardly a trace of artifice. Rarely as perfectly mastered as in

"Hamlet" and "Othello," it surpasses even those plays in the tremendous sincerity of its passion. If passionate despair at things human has a language, it is the speech of Lear.

"Macbeth" offers a marked contrast to "Lear" in its brevity and rapidity. In spite of a few probable interpolations, the text is so short that it may likely represent a condensation of the original version. In none of the tragedies is the story told with more breathless directness, or with more effective presentation of the externals of the action. The play is more dependent on the chronicle than "Lear," and pays more attention to the representation of history. In "Lear" the political and national importance of the events is forgotten, but in "Macbeth" the convulsion of the kingdom is kept in mind, and the battles, political intrigue, and the prophecies of future dynasties recall the early chronicle plays. The story in Holinshed's chronicle, however, conforms to the current ideas of tragedy, so closely indeed that one wonders that some writer had not earlier attempted its dramatization.[1] Apparently it awaited a Scottish king and a general interest in Scottish affairs. The story is one of crime and retribution with a rather striking likeness to some of the classical dramas. It coincides with the Senecan plan of a crime committed and then revenged through the accompaniment of supernatural agencies. It is the story, familiar to both humanistic and popular tragedy,

[1] There is in fact a reference in Kempe's *Nine Days Wonder* (1600) to the story, which may possibly indicate an earlier play.

of a usurper who becomes a bloody tyrant and is over-
thrown after a reign of increasing crime. Macbeth's
inordinate and fatal ambition also offers an obvious
chance for a development akin to that of Marlowe's
protagonists. Again, as in most English tragedies from
"Cambyses" to "Sejanus," the story presents the punishment of evil rather than the suffering of the good,
and, except for the absence of lust as a motive, might
have found favor with any contemporary dramatist. All
these possibilities in the story were seized upon by Shakespeare and adapted to his purpose. "Macbeth" might
be studied as the complement of "Lear" in the reflection
and summarizing of all preceding essays at tragedy.

Shakespeare's use of these various potentialities of the
story and the definiteness of his unifying purpose may
both be seen by a comparison with his treatment of the
very similar materials furnished by the chronicles for
"Richard III." There, following closely the Marlowean
methods, he for some reason minimized the motive of
remorse emphasized in his sources, and left Richard
as conscienceless as Tamburlaine or Barabas. In "Macbeth" the story of ambition is also a story of the temptation, defeat, and remorse of conscience. As in the other
great tragedies, Shakespeare informed the old material
with the struggle of the human will. At the same time
he made the most of the hints in the chronicle that the
protagonist was driven by fate or some forces beyond
his control. He united with marvelous dramatic tact the
destiny tragedy of the Greeks and the villain tragedy of

the Elizabethans. As a result the character of Macbeth
has its paradoxes that are the despair of the analysts.
We do not quite know how far free-will and how far
superhuman agencies determined his course. But while
the superhuman agencies give his villany a mystery
and impressiveness, they never confuse for a moment
the distinctions of good and evil. The powers of right
and wrong are clearly marshaled, and the triumph of
evil leads to anguish as well as to ruin.

Shakespeare's transforming and vitalizing use of both
the suggestions of Holinshed and the established conventions of tragedy in order to suit this changed purpose
is manifest at every turn, but nowhere so transcendently
as in his treatment of the supernatural. The ghost that
interrupts the banquet is no shrieking revenger, hardly
more than a hallucination of the murderer. The invisi-
bility of the ghost to all but the one whom he would
frighten or admonish has other examples in the drama,
but by 1605 most of the playwrights made their ghosts
either melodramatically horrible or vulgarly familiar.
In "Macbeth" Shakespeare not only etherealizes the
ghost as in "Julius Cæsar" and "Hamlet," but makes
him a part of the very mood and temper of the murderer.
And similarly, the witches, drawn from Holinshed's
hints, represent a supernatural interference very different
from that of the furies, devils, or sorcerers usual in the
theatre. Some of their stage effects are archaic enough,
as the shows of the head, the bloody child, and the
monarchs; some, like their vanishing in air, may have

been novel on the stage of the Globe; certainly they were all intended to surpass in mere theatrical novelty and effectiveness any of the supernatural or magical creatures of the contemporary drama. Delighting the groundlings and appealing to the current interest in witchcraft, they are none the less essential to the drama, inwrapt in the conception of character. The foul hags of superstition, they seem also to have the attributes of the classical Fates. Novel and effective on the stage, they are the supervisors of Macbeth's destiny. They lay bare the path to his crimes, yet they seem to obey rather than to govern his inclinations. The embodiments of the desires hid in his bosom, they become, like the dagger in the air and the ghost of Banquo, the symptoms of his soul's disease.

The disease of the soul is the theme, and the attention is centred upon crime and its accompaniments, as in many contemporary plays, but with less relief than in any other of Shakespeare's tragedies. While the range of crime is confined, lust for instance never appearing as a motive, there is an unrelieved concentration on the evil course of ambition. The virtuous and noble have only minor parts. Lady Macbeth is an instigator and accomplice in crime. For the first time since Shakespeare's early plays, there is no idealized woman. The wickedness of Iago and the wolfish sisters was relieved by the lovableness of Desdemona and Cordelia, unavailing for the time but unforgettable in the sympathies of the reader. The eternal stars never glimmer through the blackness that broods over Macbeth.

Because of this concentration on one process of evil and the absence of any idealization of goodness, the play has a less intense appeal to our sympathies than the three preceding tragedies. Again, because of its concern with historical and political results, it removes itself from immediate relationship to common experience. In these respects it links itself with the two Roman historical tragedies that followed it.

"Antony and Cleopatra" and "Coriolanus," like "Julius Cæsar," are dramas of great historical characters already splendidly described in Plutarch. They are consequently far more limited by their sources than are the other tragedies. Shakespeare was circumscribed by the main historical facts of persons and events, and he was writing as the translator and interpreter of Plutarch; yet his conception and methods remained the same as in "Hamlet" or "Macbeth." An idealization of the tragic struggle of the protagonist is environed by a wealth of incidents and persons, and accomplished by a gathering and transformation of the methods and matters of current tragedy. The world of antiquity is not faithfully reproduced, but it is made alive and akin to our daily experience in the same fashion as are the Elsinore of Polonius and the grave-diggers, and the Britain of Osric and Kent. And the tragic conflicts that involve the great persons, if confused in the spectacles and actions of this varied stage, are the accompaniments of momentous national crises, themselves of hardly less imaginative appeal than the spiritual struggles which they parallel.

The mental battles of Macbeth and Lear are reflected
and magnified by the incantations of the weird sisters
and the turmoil of the elements; those of Coriolanus and
Antony by the battle of the powerful and the oppressed
and by the throes of a dying civilization.

In "Antony and Cleopatra," the subject of many Renaissance tragedies, Shakespeare chose for a theme an
ignoble infatuation that leads counter to duty and on to
destruction. The difficulties of the historical material
led to a remarkable reversion in dramatic structure to
the methods of the early chronicle plays, innumerable
and loosely connected scenes, constant shifting of place,
prolonged time, and an absence of tragic unity. The
problem of a confused and intricate action, voluntarily
imposed in "Lear," is here forced upon the dramatist
who will combine the wars of the triumvirs, the conflict
of East and West, and the story of an enchantress and
her victim. The tragic course of the conflict between
infatuation and ambition is incumbered by historical
details and stage spectacles, but in style and characterization few plays more greatly reveal Shakespeare's
genius. In no play is the idealization of character more
magnificent; no other dramatist has made Antony in
the lures of a strumpet still representative of what is
illustrious and magnanimous in mankind, no other has
made a woman with the manners and heart of a strumpet the rightful empress of the imagination. The interest
in the play is less centred than in the other tragedies.
It is divided between the spectacle of historical events

and the conflict of motives; it lies as much in the persons
as vitalizations of history as in their fate as human beings.
But this is the triumph of historical tragedy as Shakespeare conceived it. Its scenic presentation makes alive
the events and persons, and through a grandiose pano-
rama interprets the passions that ravished both empires
and the souls of their possessors.

The human drama in "Coriolanus" is involved not
only in historical circumstances, but also in the eternal
conflict between the upper and the lower classes, the
incurable disease of the body politic. While their pride
in class, their blindness to the rights of others, and
their failure in patriotism are made apparent, the patri-
cians are treated as the representatives of righteousness
and nobility. The plebeians, on the contrary, are depicted
without appreciation of their sufferings or rights, as
ignorant, imbecile, and the dupes of tricky demagogues.
Contempt for the mob was a common sentiment in Renaissance literature, and the people as a factor in history
held little place in the thoughts of the sixteenth century or in the historical drama. But here and in "Julius
Cæsar" Shakespeare treats them with far less consideration than does Fletcher or Massinger, with a contempt,
indeed, that can hardly have flattered his audiences and
that has often been taken as indicative of strong personal
feeling. Shakespeare must have foreseen at least some
of the political lessons which would be derived from the
play, but one may easily exaggerate its importance as an
exposition of his political theory. He was following Plu-

tarch closely, with an eye for interesting theatrical scenes
as in "Antony and Cleopatra," but with less than his
usual inspiration. The lack of individuality in the persons, a certain typicality in the characterization, and the
heaviness and complexity of the style may have been
caused less by an intrusion of political theory than by a
lapsing of that splendid power of characterization so long
maintained. Moreover, the political partisanship is in part
a dramatic necessity, almost compelled by Shakespeare's
conception of tragedy and his dramatic method. Coriolanus must be given resplendent virtues. The populace
as a foil and contrast must be made contemptible and
the ready tool of vice. Pride, the fatal defect of the hero,
must be exposed as was the sensuality of Antony, but
it must be made the flaw of an Achilles. The rôle of
villain is left for the demagogues, and that of the wit-
less accomplice for the people. Again, here, as in all his
histories, Shakespeare is blind to the importance of the
people, because for him, as for his contemporaries, the
dramatization of history was the dramatization of its great
personages, and their passions, vices, and ambitions.

The loss of power discernible in "Coriolanus" is conspicuous in "Timon." Its corrupt text and unfinished
condition and the certainty that only part of the play is
Shakespeare's render uncertain its importance among the
tragedies. Here, however, as in "Coriolanus," though
the interest in the causes that make man's misery is still
keen, the lack of inspiration results in an exaggerated
type for a protagonist and in an unconvincing exposition

of human baseness. If Coriolanus's politics were Shakespeare's, certainly Timon's misanthropy was not.

With these themes Shakespeare's interest in tragedy exhausted itself. Possibly influenced by the success of Beaumont and Fletcher's early romantic plays, he attempted in "Cymbeline," and perfected in "A Winter's Tale" and "The Tempest," a type of play combining tragic and idyllic elements, full of romantic variety of incident, and resulting in surprising and happy *dénouements*. The possibilities for tragedy are there; jealousy, villany, and intrigue abound; even death is introduced. But the main actions are not of suffering and ruin; love and forgiveness heal all ills; and the end is reconciliation and marriage. These romantic tragicomedies are not only departures from the established tragic forms, but from any consideration of tragic themes and problems comparable in seriousness or intensity with that of the plays which we have just discussed.

NOTE ON BIBLIOGRAPHY

Ward, Fleay, and Schelling continue to be the best general guides. Important critical discussions of Shakespeare's tragedies by Professors A. C. Bradley, Lounsbury, and Baker were noted in the Bibliographical Note to chapter i. Other recent books of special interest are: *Shakespeare*, Walter Raleigh (1907, English Men of Letters Series); *William Shakspere*, Barrett Wendell (1894); *Shakespeare and his Predecessors*, F. S. Boas (1896). For a general survey of the course of Shakespearean criticism, see Ward, vol. i, chap. iv; or Lounsbury, *Shakespeare as a Dramatic Artist*, and *Shakespeare and Voltaire;* or the bibliographical lists in the various volumes of Furness's Variorum edition. This edition, now in progress, and Malone's Variorum edition of 1821, are the most valuable in furnishing information. Nearly all recent editions of Shakespeare supply fairly adequate information in regard to critical conclusions on matters of date, sources, and text. Probably the most serviceable bibliography of Shakespearean editions and criticism up to 1870, and to a considerable extent for the Elizabethan drama, is to be found in the *Catalogue of the Barton Collection* of the Boston Public Library (1888), accessible in most large libraries in this country. A complete Shakespearean bibliography since 1865 is supplied by the bibliographies published in the *Jahrbuch der Deutschen Shakespeare-Gesellschaft.* These also comprise nearly all monographs of importance dealing with the drama from 1557 to 1642.

The present chapter borrows from my article on Hamlet and the Revenge Plays (*Publ. Mod. Lang. Assn.* 1902), referred to in chap. iv. E. E. Stoll's *John Webster* (Cambridge, Mass., 1905) gives a further discussion of the Revenge Plays, and especially of Marston. Bullen's edition of Marston is the standard. The editions of Heywood's Works (1874) and of Chapman's (1873–75) attempt no scholarly discussion. F. S. Boas's edition of the two Bussy D'Ambois plays in the *Belles-Lettres Series* (Boston, 1905) has a valuable introduction. Gifford's edition of Jonson (1816) is unfortunately not yet superseded. The careful editions of various of his plays in the *Yale Studies in English* as yet include none of his tragedies. *Ben Jonson, l'homme et l'œuvre* Paris, 1907, by Maurice Castelain is very elaborate, and contains a full bibliography with a preliminary descriptive note of editions. A new edition of Jonson edited by C. H. Herford and P. Simpson is announced.

CHAPTER VI

SHAKESPEARE

UR study has perhaps already made it evident that Shakespeare's tragedies were in many ways the product of a rapid and complex evolution. At the same time it is clear that, until Shakespeare, Elizabethan tragedy with all its genius and innovations had failed to attain finality of art, or to mark out any sure pathway thither. It was still in its formative period when he created out of it something new and immortal, and its development continued after his death mainly in response to forces not of his initiating. For the past two centuries, to a constantly increasing body of spectators and readers, his tragedies have had a life entirely unconnected with the works of his contemporaries, an existence that has dominated our theatres and our conceptions of tragedy, and become a part of the daily living and the permanent ideals of the race. It is therefore necessary to separate his plays from the mass of tragedies, and to review them for a moment as the creations of a genius that was the chief creator as well as the glory of English tragedy.

Two points of view that have been largely maintained in nineteenth century criticism of Shakespeare may, however, be neglected in our summary. His plays have been viewed as the reflection of his personal experiences and emotions; and his return to tragic themes about 1600 and his occupation with them for the next eight years have been connected with a supposed period of spiritual depression in his own life. Again, the generalization of experience and the abundant wisdom of his tragedies have been viewed as the result of a conscious and rather systematic philosophy of life. Much might be said for these attitudes of criticism. Any attempt to describe the plays in terms of our emotions as readers is likely to result in the attribution of those emotions to the author, an interesting process of analogy and one hardly to be disproved. Any attempt to survey his work as a whole and to relate its parts is likely to result in the systemization of his message and philosophy. But for students of the growth of his dramatic art under the peculiar conditions of the reigns of Elizabeth and James, these nineteenth century points of view involve dangerous critical anachronisms. Shakespeare does not seem to have been a lyric Shelley or Byron, making poetry out of his changing moods, or a Tennyson or Browning generalizing life in the persons of his men and women. There seems no reason for separating him from his companion poets and playwrights. Like them he was in the first place telling a story for the stage; like them he found in these plays opportunity for the expression of his knowledge of human motives in the guise of beautiful verse; and like them, when he chose tragic themes, he became absorbed in the presentation of the tragic facts and problems of life. Our attempt to determine his relations to them is not to discover indebtedness large or minute, but rather by the safest approach to arrive at a right appreciation of his genius and its transcendent contribution to tragedy.

For the purpose of our survey we may have the four great tragedies chiefly in mind. The early tragedies are manifestly the products of an experimental period and the precursors of the latter plays; and the three Roman histories have a subordinate and contributory rather than an essential and preëminent part in his achievement in tragedy. Whatever can be said of the four great tragedies applies in its essentials to all.

All these plays taken together illustrate the extraordinary amalgamation of the medieval and classical inheritances that English tragedy had received as a birthright. No play escapes from its narrative sources, and some are bound closely by them; yet the choice of sources often indicates the influence of the Senecan formula, sensational externals giving opportunity for an introspective analysis of emotional crises, notably in the stories of crime, revenge, and retribution. Their enormous variety of incident, their mingling of the comic and the tragic, their admission of physical horrors, deaths, and spectacles mark the survival of the medieval tradition, while the aphoristic and heightened style, the ghosts and the soliloquies are derivatives from Seneca. The freedom of the medieval stage to the presentation of all sorts of matters accounts in part for their splendid comprehensiveness, while classical theory is partly responsible for their restriction to momentous events and supernormal persons. Their structure remains epic and popular, but progress toward dramatic unity seems conditioned by the Senecan five-act scheme. The medieval idea of the pagan deity Fortune is preserved; and conceptions of good and evil, like those of the morality, stand side by side with classical conceptions of the struggle between the individual and fate. The union of these diverse elements has become too close for disentanglement. "Macbeth," based upon Holinshed's chronicle, comes nearest in conception and treatment to classical tragedy; "Antony and Cleopatra" in structure and method reverts the nearest to medieval models.

More distinct contemporary influences reappear similarly amalgamated and transformed. In "Hamlet" we have a play closely related to those of a particular species; but in the other plays of Shakespeare's maturity nothing like close relationship can be found to the great examples of Marlowe, to the peculiar type introduced by Kyd and developed by Marston, or to the contemporary efforts of Chapman and Jonson. Any one play doubtless responded to a tangle of influences not now to be separated. Current popular plays, practices on the stage, the personalities of the actors, Shakespeare's own preceding plays, contemporary non-dramatic literature, current events such as the Essex rebellion or the Gunpowder Plot, and hosts of other influences were at work directing the development of an old story into a tragedy. Taking the plays as a body, some of the more important of these limiting and directing influences still remain discernible in the transformed result.

All the tragedies but "Othello" and "Romeo and Juliet," only partial exceptions, relate the falls of princes and the revolutions of kingdoms. These stories of princes are of the same kind as in other Elizabethan tragedy. In a setting of court and camp they place sensational crimes, and trace the accompaniments and consequences. Their themes are revenge, madness, tyranny, conspiracy, lust, adultery, and jealousy. They abound in villany, intrigue, and slaughter. They avoid Senecan atrocities and the abnormal phases of lust; but the tearing out of Gloster's eyes recalls the horrors of the early plays; while revenge, conspiracy, and villany are as prominent as in the contemporary tragedies of Marston, Jonson, and Chapman. Three of the stories include ghosts, while in "Macbeth" the weird sisters offer an opportunity for a most original treatment of the supernatural. Comedy is always combined with tragedy, and the medieval tradition and the popular taste for an emotional contrast receive artistic vindication in the grotesqueness of "Hamlet" and "Lear." Each plot, like those of Marlowe's plays, centres about a great personality and illustrates a temperament dominated by passion. It traces the course of folly, mistake, or sin to the wages of death as in "Lear," "Othello," and "Antony and Cleopatra"; or it begins with a murder and records its progeny of crime and death as in "Julius Cæsar," "Hamlet," and "Macbeth."

Shakespeare's choice of stories was clearly determined by the Elizabethan conception of tragedy and by the current tastes of the theatre. And by these stories his imagination was directed and limited. However absorbed he became in character or ethics, he never neglected the plot or the theatre. Consequently the great revelation of tragic fact which he gave to posterity was limited by these stories of crime and hampered by their improbabilities and stage effects. The tragedy of ambition is limited to the story of a murderer who sees a ghost; and the tragedy of ingratitude is joined to a relation of senile folly, crime, and the humors of Tom of Bedlam. Even his interpretation of human motives suffers, for the bloodthirstiness of Hamlet and the perverse reticence of Cordelia belong to the old plots as much as to the characters. Yet Shakespeare's greatness of mind no less than his responsiveness to contemporary taste appears in his very choice of material. Whether he took the oft-told tragedies of Cæsar, Brutus, Antony and Cleopatra, or the old plays of Hamlet and Lear, or the neglected themes of Othello and Macbeth, he chose always stories of great dramatic interest and those that presented the range and vicissitudes of human passion. His attraction for each story was evidently in the emotional conflict that made each protagonist a great acting part and also a fascinating study of human motive.

Moreover, in his general treatment of this material

there is a uniformity that gives some hint of a Shakespearean definition of tragedy. In each play a man of great attainments is presented as involved in a moral conflict that results in his death. This conflict is twofold, internal between opposing desires, and external against some persons of the counter-actions. Conflicting forces contend for mastery in the hero's breast, and from their confusion he drives on to action that is disastrous. The unusual powers, the best potentialities, of his nature are opposed and thwarted by the forces of chance and circumstance beyond his control; by the force of evil, whether in his own breast or represented by the crime and intrigue of others; and still further, by a defect or deficiency in his own personality. The force of chance, equivalent to the Greek Fate, plays a part in all tragic story and drama; the power of evil without or within was the counter-force in medieval drama, and was the theme most powerfully dwelt upon by Shakespeare's immediate contemporaries. The fateful power of incompatibility of temperament with conditions of life seems to have been Shakespeare's own conception.

In Sophocles, arrogance and audacity are accounted evil; in Marlowe and Chapman, it is intensity of desire that drives to disaster; but in Shakespeare the melancholy and reflective temper of Hamlet and the generous and credulous magnanimity of Othello are the allies of untoward circumstance and designing villany in bringing suffering to the good and failure to the potent. The greatness of Shakespeare's conception, however,

results from the massing of all these combatants against
the hero. The conflict thus gains in the comprehensiveness of its presentation of life; and human nature in the
face of such odds becomes magnificent even in failure.
Hero wars with villain; human intrepidity and wisdom
with chance and destiny; conscience with sin; greatness
of purpose with crippling defects of temperament.

Such a conception of tragedy involves a recognition
of the blindness of chance that cannot be squared with
any theory of poetic justice or theological view of the
rewards due to virtue. But it also involves a recognition
of moral law that results in the punishment of its vio-
lators. The villains never escape as they do in comedy.
The wages of sin are always death, though the reward
of virtue is not happiness. The vastness of evil in the
world, its malignant influence, its temporary triumphs
are conceived in a manner not different from that of
contemporary thought. The doctrines of total depravity
and of moral responsibility go side by side as in medieval drama, theology, and psychology. In the depiction
of the waste of effort, the expense of spirit, the crippling
of greatness by weakness, the ineffectuality of virtue,
Shakespeare gave a far more comprehensive and a far
more penetrating representation of tragic fact than the
world had yet known, but without professing any solution of its mysteries.

Such a conception gives unity to the action of each
play, but not always a unity that governs details of
structure. The structure of a tragedy cannot be described

in terms of a system, for the dramatic presentation of each play differs from the others and conforms to the story it relates. There are many survivals of the early epic lawlessness, as in "Antony and Cleopatra" and "Lear"; and in no play is the main action kept entirely free from intruding incongruities. Neither act nor scene receives much regard as an integral unit of structure. The most noticeable structural division is due to an event of extraordinary importance reached somewhere in the middle of the play. This point, to which the terms climax or crisis are sometimes applicable, brings to an end one important development of the action, and thus divides the play into two parts. Cæsar's murder, Duncan's murder, Lear's madness complete one course of tragic incident and introduce us to another.

The effectiveness of Shakespeare's construction, however, was not due to a formulation of system or rule but to his intuition and experience. His sense of what parts of a narrative should be acted and what parts not, had developed beyond that of most of his contemporaries. In comparison with his own earlier plays the tragedies contain little, whether comic, spectacular, or essential to the main tragic action, which had not a manifest value on the stage. His ability to create great dramatic situations was also at its height, and the great scenes are prepared for and emphasized by what precedes, so that they gain all the effect possible from the dramatic construction. Thus, the appearance of the ghost, the play within the play, the funeral of Ophelia,

and the final slaughter are given a value in the mere
narration of the story for which there is no parallel in
the many other treatments of similar stories. Of far
more importance is his use of the developments of character as the determining factors of the progress of the
dramatic narrative. The rapidity with which the first
two acts of "Macbeth" hurry us to the murder of Duncan, the tremendous climactic pressure of the first three
acts of "Lear," are extraordinary examples of his power
to compel incidents to reveal the course of motive con-
vincingly. In each play the order of incidents becomes
a logical development from the characters of the actors;
each deed, thought, or speech has its sequence. There
are no tricks, no surprises, no sudden conversions of
character. Once admit the premises, a person of a
certain temperament, facing a certain situation, and
subject to a certain accident, mistake, or folly, and we
cannot escape the conclusion. The dramatic necessities
of character are never violated. From the clear exposition of the first scene, the progress is inevitable to the
end.

The persons of the plays spring from the old stories,
and by these the study of their motives is in many ways
limited. It is limited again by the types and conditions
of stage-land. The bloody tyrant, the hesitating avenger,
the Machiavellian villain come hence. The acts which
they commit, their moods, motives, their very language
depend in part on the representatives of these types
that had long been familiar to the audiences of the

theatres. Yet the host of individual personalities are the result of a most profound and fresh observation of an almost boundless range of life. That interest in characterization which distinguishes the early drama and finds its main illustration in Shakespeare's own practice in the preceding decade here comes to its culmination. Not only the main actor, but the most conventional part, the most absurd business, the merest supernumerary, receives its touch of truth. And something more than truth to life or knowledge of motive is manifest. The great characters are cast in large moulds. They represent the courses of the master passions. Smallness of horizon, triviality of design, feebleness of mind or body are absent. Momentous crises that try men's souls are the real subjects of the tragedies. The accidents of dress, or manner, or time, or race, the incidents of action, are forgotten as revenge, jealousy, irresolution, and lust seize their splendid prey. The greatness of human nature, the power of the human will, the responsibility of the individual remain. There is no belittling of reason even when it breaks under the crash of the storm. Iago is no mere stage villain, though he has all the characteristics of the type; nor is he merely a transcript from life, though he has all the variety and plausibility of a human being. He is the embodiment of our countless evil impulses, the incarnation of depravity. So with all the others. They are human in their truth; they are magnificent idealizations in the range and value of their manifold suggestiveness; they leave the stage to become the hab-

itants of our imaginations, contributing to our reflections
their embodiments of good and evil, folly and reason,
resolution and doubt.

They speak a language all their own, though with
resemblances to their kinsmen in the other Elizabethan
tragedies. The blank verse, far more flexible than in the
early plays, presents a triumphant union of the conflicting
tendencies toward decoration and naturalness observed in
the other dramatists; and it is freely mingled with hardly
less masterly prose. Marvelous in comparison with preceding verse is its extreme condensation in spite of its
opulence of figures and aphorisms. Although crowded
with thought and image, it is nevertheless, in its response
to the varying persons and moods, superbly dramatic.
A critic who is both a poet and a philosopher [1] objects
to Macbeth's dagger "unmannerly breech'd with gore"
as violent and crude in comparison with the historical
reminiscences with which Homer might have made
Achilles describe the weapon. But recall the scene. Macbeth has murdered the grooms and rushes from the
chamber to confront the fearful suspicions of Duncan's
sons and friends. Surely, his false and frenzied excuses
must be over-fanciful, violent, and crude.

> "Here lay Duncan,
> His silver skin laced with his golden blood,
> And his gash'd stabs look'd like a breach in nature
> For ruin's wasteful entrance: there, the murderers,
> Steep'd in the colours of their trade, their daggers
> Unmannerly breech'd with gore."

[1] George Santayana, *Reason in Art*, p. 113.

Such a style, however, does not readily give up opportunities for aphorism or beauty for the sake of absolute truth to situation or character. Still less does it mimic actual speech. It does give a potency to the stories, otherwise hardly conceivable; and it adds to truth of character the allurement of music and picture, and the idealization of a magnified suggestiveness. A father has reason to curse his daughter — gesture and incoherent words might correctly represent life; a plain sentence of Ibsen's might convey the tragedy of the situation — but it is the extravagant and terrible imprecation of Lear that has for centuries made men's imaginations shudder. Style such as this the drama will never recover. We shall sooner find another Shakespeare to blend its diverse elements than a host of dramatists, like the Elizabethans, fascinated by a newly discovered world of poetry and daringly adventurous in search of melody of verse, wealth of aphorism, luxury of fantasy, and truth to character.

The effect of Shakespeare's tragedies on spectator or reader is so complex as to defy analysis. Incidental wisdom, effective scene, immortal story all contribute; but the main sources of their abiding impressiveness have surely been the characterization and the poetic style. If we must continue to seek for a katharsis, do not they supply it? The great tragedies are full of disaster, wrong, and suffering. The world they reveal is not the abode of happiness, but of darkness and remorse. Though the bad are punished, the good are not rewarded. Sweetness and innocence suffer and perish along with foulness and malevolence. The noblest spirits are broken; the wages of mortal effort are failure. There are many "breaches in nature for ruin's wasteful entrance." Nor does the life hereafter offer a promise of compensation. Death ends all, — that is the great catastrophe toward which human endeavor precipitates itself. This is not Shakespeare's view of life, but it is his view of the tragedy of life, and its effect upon us is gloomy, overpowering, heartrending. But everywhere this tragedy of life is revealed in verse infinitely appealing to intellectual analysis and to imaginative exhilaration. Everywhere there are men and women, not dead but living, representative of much that is most intensely and universally interesting in life, and the permanent guests of our reflection. The old ethical adage that it does not so much matter what men do as what they are has a particular truth when applied to the people of Shakespeare. That they do this or that, love, murder, die, is in the story; what they are remains the possession of humanity. Our horror at the successful villany of Iago finds a certain relief in the intellectual pleasure and admiration at the creator's achievement; it accomplishes a certain purification in its application to the Iago in ourselves. Still more do the persons who most excite our sympathy survive the intolerable emotions that first greet their misfortunes. When we read "Othello" we feel an overwhelming pity, a fierce resentment, but we would not erase from our possession the memory of Desdemona and her Moor. The misery and

wrong and death go to make up in our reflection the
beings whom we love and cherish. It is Lear's fivefold
"never" that completes for us the loveliness of Cordelia.

A comparison of the tragedies with the masterpieces
of other national dramas might disclose their faults but
would not diminish their glories. Faults in plenty there
surely are, whether judgment be taken of classicists or
realists, or of the best standards of the Elizabethans.
There are many quibbles or fantasies of diction that
might be criticised, many bits of dialogue or stage spectacle that might be omitted without detracting from the
total impressiveness. How many minor inconsistencies
of plot or characterization might be corrected. How
complicated and bewildering is "Hamlet" in comparison
with the simpler harmony of "Antigone." How involved
and cumbrous, and how undignified in its appeal to the
emotions, is much of "Antony and Cleopatra" in comparison with "Phédre." How impossible and fantastic
is much of "Lear" in comparison with "Ghosts." But
Shakespeare's defects and deficiencies belong to his time
and to his methods. They are inseparable, indeed, from
the very means on which depend his consummate results.
Not in response to literary tradition, but to the public
theatre; not by a refined but by a daring art; not by
simplicity and unity, but by complexity and opulence of
effect; not by devotion to creed or science or fact, but
by the idealization and sublimation of man's emotional
nature, did Shakespeare give to his dramas their imper-
ishable wealth of life.

CHAPTER VII

THE LATER ELIZABETHANS [1]

HAKESPEARE'S great tragedies did not create a new epoch in the development of the drama. In themes and general treatment they made no marked departure from the past. Their translation of story and circumstance into the conflicts and processes of character was beyond the reach of imitation, and, indeed, not likely to gain full recognition from contemporaries. They were rather the consummation of the old than the heralds of a new era, though their influence on succeeding dramatists was wide and permeating, especially as time and publication brought a growing appreciation of their greatness as literature. Meanwhile, the old types of tragedy continued their sway, sometimes little touched by Shakespeare's influence. English history plays were rare; Roman history plays frequent; Senecan closet dramas continued; the Marlowean and Kydian traditions received further development. The revenge play, in particular, continued to be one of the most conspicuous types. Further, a most important innovating force appeared just at the close of Shakespeare's tragic period

---

[1] Elizabethan has been used to designate the whole period of the drama from 1559 to 1642.

in the heroic romances of Beaumont and Fletcher, which gained an immediate popularity and created new practices in both tragedy and tragicomedy.

The times were changing. The improved social status of the theatre, the support of the court, the vogue of private theatres like Blackfriars, the increasing interest in the stage on the part of the lettered and fashionable classes, supplied more intelligent and critical audiences; but the increasing Puritanism separated the drama more and more from sympathy with the main public. The drama became less national, more critical, and less moral. The corrupt society of the reign of James I supplied little of that imaginative idealism which had found expression at the time of the Armada. It offered the serious drama either objects for satire and cynicism or sophisticated and courtly ideals of conduct. In consequence, a more conscious art found itself less competent than in the early drama to depict greatness of mind, and resorted to the tracing of abnormal passion, the casuistical inquiry into moral problems, the exposure of evil, or to romance without moral intention.

Yet dramatic enterprise continued unabated. The theatre continued to attract poetic ambition. Scholars, men of letters, gentlemen of rank turned to the popular stage. There was as yet no suspicion of decadence. Rather the past seemed to offer, through a recognition of its merits and a pruning of its faults, encouragement for a greater achievement in the future. In spite of critical realization of the absurdities of the early drama, and of the necessity for a better regulated art, the integrity of the national tradition was recognized and maintained. In 1612, in a preface to his "White Devil," Webster, after explaining that he had departed from the classical standards "willingly, and not ignorantly," proceeds to extol his contemporaries and masters: —

> "Detraction is the sworne friend to ignorance: for mine owne part I have ever truly cherisht my good opinion of other mens worthy labours; especially of that full and haightened stile of Maister Chapman, the labor'd and understanding workes of Maister Johnson, the no lesse worthy composures of the both worthily excellent Maister Beamont & Maister Fletcher, and lastly (without wrong last to be named) the right happy and co-pious industry of M. Shake-speare, M. Decker, & M. Heywood; wishing that what I write may be read by their light; protesting that, in the strength of mine owne judgement, I know them so worthy, that though I rest silent in my owne worke, yet to most of theirs I dare (without flattery) fix that of Martiall:
>
> — non norunt haec monumenta mori."

After a time the greatness of the past masters proved rather an impediment than a stimulus. But in 1612 their work seemed to offer encouragement for even greater achievement in the immediate future.

For the historian this period offers less difficulties than the preceding ones. After 1610 comparatively few plays of importance are non-extant, and few of the ex-tant plays are anonymous. The bulk of the important plays was produced by a few dramatists, who dominated the theatres and whose careers determined the drama's development. After examining the revenge plays which

about 1612 gave a further extension to that species, and
the heroic romances of the Beaumont-Fletcher collaboration, which were produced within a few years before
that date, we may trace the succeeding developments
of tragedy mainly in the work of Fletcher, Massinger,
Middleton, Ford, and Shirley.

The main line of the development of the revenge
tragedy is represented by Tourneur's "Revenger's
Tragedy," the anonymous "Second Maiden's Tragedy,"
and Webster's "White Devil" and "Duchess of Malfi."
The four plays may be said to constitute a new species
whose differences from the old type seem clearly unconnected with Shakespeare's "Hamlet" but directly trace-
able to Marston's plays, especially his "Malcontent."

Revenge is no longer the main motive but is a subsidiary element in complicated stories of revolting lust
and depravity. Tragedy has become the representation
of vice and sin, with a proneness for their foulest entanglements. In one play a brother plays the part of
pandar to his sister; in another a father to his daughter;
and in a third a mother to her daughter. Nor is revenge,
even in its subordinate position, the simple blood-for-
blood requital that it is in Kyd. It may be for various
causes beside murder; it is born of malice rather than
duty; it may share in the moral turpitude of the rest of
the action. The ghost no longer directs the course of
revenge, and may disappear entirely. In "The Revenger's Tragedy" the skull of the betrothed, as the skeleton
in "Hoffman," takes the place of the apparition; and

in other plays the duties of the ghost are minimized
or farmed out among various supernatural agents, two
female ghosts appearing. Hesitation on the part of the
avenger does not appear. Indeed, his entire character
has changed. He may be a villain, as in "Hoffman,"
or the villain's accomplice, or one of Marston's "malcontents," or a combination of these parts. The other
leading elements in the Kydian type are preserved. Insanity of various forms, real and pretended, is prominent. Intrigue of a complicated kind abounds, but is
often dependent, after the fashion of current comedy,
largely on improbable disguises. Deaths are as frequent
as ever and more horrible. Much of the old stage effect
reappears, as in the masques, funerals, ghosts, and exhibition of dead bodies, but there is a great increase in the
number and ingenuity of melodramatic sensations. Each
play is a chamber of horrors. In one, a wife dies from
kissing the poisoned portrait of her husband; in another,
the lustful king sucks poison from the jaw of a skull; and
in a third, from the painted lips of a corpse. Comets blaze,
there are many portents, the time is ever midnight, the
scene the graveyard, the air smells of corruption, skulls
and corpses are the *dramatis personae*. Every means seems
to be employed to make theatrically effective the horrors
of death and decay. And once, at least, these means
are used with tremendous power in the riot of madness,
torture, and corruption that preludes the death of the
Duchess of Malfi.

All or nearly all of the active characters are black with

sin. The extraordinary exploitation of villany in Elizabethan tragedy here reaches its culmination. The archvillain as ruthlessly devoted to crime as Hoffman, the accomplice assiduous in revolting baseness, the villain touched by remorse, the malcontent reviling human life, — all these appear — sometimes all combined in one person — and play their parts along with unshrinking prostitutes and lustful monarchs. The study of villany, however, has gained intensity and plausibility over the earlier plays. If none of the villains take to themselves much individuality, most of them have moments of dramatic impressiveness, and they are intended to be realistic. They are drawn with an accumulation of detail, a fondness for probing into depravity, with a sense of the dramatic value of devilry, and with a bitterness and cynicism that often seem sincere and searching. It is this cynicism which gives character to the reflective elements of these plays. The Kydian soliloquy on fate has given way to the prevailing satirical and bitter tone that finds its favorite themes in the sensuality of women and the hypocrisy and greed of courts, and its favorite means of expression in the connotation of the obscene and bestial.

The qualities attributed to these four plays recall "Hoffman" and "The Atheist's Tragedy," and still more Marston's plays, and the satirical comedy of the preceding decade as well as the tragedy. Though the four plays are thus classed together, their differences are marked. "The Second Maiden's Tragedy" manifests

more than the others the influence of Beaumont and
Fletcher. Tourneur's "Revenger's Tragedy," far superior
to his earlier "Atheist's Tragedy," surpasses Marston
and reveals brilliant dramatic talent. Full of thrills and
unspeakable juxtapositions, it is governed by a sheer
delight in horror and unrelieved by any moral standard.
Webster, on the contrary, made his horrors impressive
in both poetry and moral. Dependent at every step on
the work of predecessors, he succeeded as did no other
poet except Shakespeare in transforming the revenge
play into a work of art and truth. Chapman was, perhaps, his chief model, but the processes of his transforming art, though not its results, bear resemblances to
Shakespeare's. He was possessed by an interest in the
effects of crime upon character, and had the power to
realize these momentarily with amazing truth. Hence
his great portraits of Vittoria, the Cardinal, and the
Duchess, and the ingeniously and vividly though not
very consistently drawn figure of Bosola. As Shakespeare
in "Macbeth" and "Lear," fascinated by the wickedness of the world, reveled in images of blackness, corruption, and despair, so Webster, more laboriously and
inquisitively, was ever seeking fantastic expression for
the old truth that all is vanity. In his masterpiece, "The
Duchess of Malfi," and in a lesser degree in "The White
Devil," his recognition of moral values again recalls
Shakespeare. We are moved by the pitifulness of the
suffering as well as by the horror of the evil. There is
no confusion of good and bad; and if the prevailing view

of life is cynical, it is not unrelieved by respect for forti-
tude and conscience. The tragedy of revenge reached
a new altitude in this play, which, though poorly constructed, tells a story of criminal and horrible revenge
with a vivid delineation of character, a pervading moral
sense, and with flashes of speech that attain both poetic
and dramatic sublimity.[1]

The collaboration of Beaumont and Fletcher was
finished by the time that Webster published his acknowledgment of their mastership. Gentlemen by birth and
breeding, they began writing for the stage apparently
as pupils of Jonson, entered into collaboration by 1607,
and in the next five years, by the time that Beaumont
was twenty-seven and Fletcher thirty-three, produced
some ten plays that gained them a popularity surpassing that of Shakespeare's later years, and extending well
through the Restoration. So far as tragedy is concerned,
the main result of their collaboration was the formation
of a new species of heroic romances, some tragedies and
some tragicomedies. Six plays serve to define the type,
though other plays of the collaboration have resemblances
to it and, after Beaumont's retirement, the type was continued in the work of Fletcher and others. These six
plays, "Four Plays in One," "Thierry and Theodoret,"
"Cupid's Revenge," "Philaster," "A King and No
King," and "The Maid's Tragedy," probably owe more

[1] For a somewhat different view of the play, emphasizing its crudity
as a drama, see Mr. William Archer's "Webster, Lamb, and Swinburne,"
New Review, January, 1893.

to Beaumont than to Fletcher. "The Maid's Tragedy"
and the two tragicomedies, "Philaster" and "A King
and No King," are the masterpieces, but the six plays
resemble one another so closely that one analysis will
answer for all.

Beaumont and Fletcher did not, like most of their predecessors, turn to English or Roman history for their
plots, and they preserved but few traces of the Marlowean
tragedy with its central protagonist and dominating
passion, or of the revenge type in any of its amplifica-
tions. Their plots, largely of their own invention, are
highly ingenious and complicated. They deal with heroic
actions in imaginary foreign realms. The conquests,
usurpations, and passions that ruin kingdoms are their
themes, but there are no battles or armies, and the action
is usually confined to the rooms of the palace or a neigh-
boring forest. Usually contrasting a story of gross sen-
sual passion with one of idyllic love, they introduce a
great variety of incidents, and aim at a constant but
varied excitement. Love of one sort or another, honor
also of many kinds, and friendship, which is somewhat
more steadfast, are ever in conflict. We are given seats
in an anteroom of the palace, and at once the flow of
events engrosses us, — conspiracies, imprisonments, in-
surrections, wars, adultery, seduction, murder, the talk
of courtiers, gossip of women, banquets of the monarch,
and the laments of the love-lorn. Or, after a tumultuous
hour, we may retire to the adjoining forest, where the
lovers wander to forget their misfortunes, and by its

fountains weave their laments into lyrical garlands. A
few hours, and kingdoms have trembled in the balance;
the heroine has been proved guilty and innocent again;
and the lover has been ecstatic, frantic, jealous, cowardly,
implacable, and forgiving, and finally wins or dies with
his honor secure.

The tragedies differ from those preceding in structure
as well as in material. Their main purpose is theatrical
effectiveness; their means of securing it the constant
use of surprise. Beaumont and Fletcher did not follow
their narrative sources closely; they invented their own
stories or used old ones as the frame for their favorite
situations and characters. The tragic, idyllic, and sensational matter is skillfully constructed into a number
of theatrically telling situations which lead by a series
of suspenses and surprises to very effective climaxes or
catastrophes. All signs of the epic methods of construction found in the early drama have disappeared, and
the interest in the action is maintained at fever heat. In
"The Maid's Tragedy," the climax of the play comes
at the end of the fourth act with the murder of the king
by his mistress, Evadne, the wife of Amintor. But in the
fifth act the main action absorbs the sub-plot and continues its course of thrills and surprises until the very
end. In "A King and No King," the love of Arbaces
for his supposed sister furnishes many entanglements,
and it is not until the end of Act V that we know that
the princess is not his sister, and the tragedy of incest
is resolved into romance. There is no inevitableness in

the action of these plays. Usually, until the last moment there is a chance for either a happy or an unhappy ending, and in every case the *dénouement* or catastrophe is elaborately planned and complicated.

From the nature of their material and treatment there is little difference between the tragedies and tragicomedies. Tragicomedy as a species had up to this time hardly been recognized in the English drama, although there are sporadic instances of the use of the term and although romantic comedy usually offered tragic elements. Fletcher's definition (borrowed from Guarini) in the preface to "The Faithful Shepherdess," may be taken as sufficiently distinguishing the form from other species, — "A tragicomedy is not so called in respect to mirth and killing, but in respect it wants deaths, which is enough to make it no tragedy, yet brings some near it, which is enough to make it no comedy, which must be a representation of familiar people, with such kind of trouble as no life be questioned; so that a god is as lawful in this as in a tragedy, and mean people as in a comedy." The example of Beaumont and Fletcher, moreover, gave popularity and importance to this class of plays. Borrowing motives familiar in romantic narrative and the preceding drama, they yet created a departure from preceding romantic comedy, both in the constant emphasis which they place upon the contrast between the tragic and idyllic elements of their plots and in the especial attention they pay to surprising and complicated *dénouements*. They aim not merely at a mixture of the sentimental and tragic but at involving every one in a tangle of disastrous complications, resolved only by a series of final surprises. Although only two of the six romances are tragicomedies, the imitators of Beaumont and Fletcher most frequently adopted the form, realizing apparently the theatrical value of keeping the spectators thrilled and excited until the end and then relieving their sympathetic suspense by a happy solution.

The *dramatis personae* of the six plays belong to the impossible and romantic situations rather than to life, and are usually of certain types, — the sentimental or violent hero; his faithful friend, a blunt outspoken soldier; the sentimental heroine, often a love-lorn maiden disguised as a page in order that she may serve the hero; an evil woman defiant in her crimes; and the poltroon, usually a comic personage. With the addition of a king, some gentlemen and ladies of the court, and a few persons from the lower ranks, the cast is complete. The various persons introduce one another in long descriptions; and, after the introductory speech, the character remains fixed, except as the shifting situations demand some unexpected revolution. There is no shading or subtlety in the characterization, little discrimination or individuality in the different representatives of the favorite types, who, however, are by no means wanting in originality. They do not reveal the depths or complexities of human nature, but they exhibit fresh and ingenious variations of the old types, audacious humor

and abundant spirit, and the power of their creators
to rise to a situation and to express dramatic emotion.
Thus, their type of evil woman acquires tremendous
force in the scenes where Evadne plays her part; and
their heroines suffer, serve, weep, love, forgive, and die,
in lines that somehow preserve the grace of simplicity,
though they wear all the jewels of allusion and imagery
that the authors possess. Moreover, their men and
women talk like real persons. Dryden declared that
they understood and imitated the conversation of gentlemen much better than Shakespeare, a distinction that
in some respects is clear to-day. The men of preceding
tragedies had spoken a language elevated and removed
from ordinary discourse, but in Beaumont and Fletcher
the romantic scenes and impossible changes of character
are made plausible by an absence of archaism and a
directness and lucidity of speech.

In the main, what reality the characters retain in our
memories is due to the power of the verse to reflect
clearly the emotions of the moment. There is a notable
absence of the merely sonorous, the turgid declamation,
the mouthing ,of strange words, and an absence of over-
crowding thought or fancy. Beaumont and Fletcher
had no desire to make their style sententious, weighty,
and philosophical. They knew what they wanted to say,
and they said it clearly and rapidly. They had room for
ornament and rhetorical device, but none for eccentricity
or obscurity. Another remark of Dryden's, that they perfected the English language, deserves consideration as

the view of a century later, and can be appreciated even
now. The characteristics of their style, so far as it can
be considered as a common property, seem due to an
effort to make dialogue correspond as nearly as possible
to natural speech. This is particularly true of Fletcher,
who is the more revolutionary of the two and the more
persistent in his mannerisms. His structure is loose and
conversational, and his blank verse overruns the borders
of the rigid pentameter and approaches the irregularity
of prose. Numerous added syllables and a large percent-
age of feminine endings further mark his departures from
past models, and, combined with his end-stopped lines,
give his verse a peculiar monotony. Both writers rise
now and then to an intensely imaginative phrase or a
beautifully wrought description. The verse of neither
is suggestive of the intricacies of human feeling or the
splendor of human intellect, but the verse of both, of
Fletcher preëminently, reveals a fertility of imagination
and an extraordinary mobility of words.

These merits of style gave Beaumont and Fletcher
their seventeenth century reputation and have continued
to attract readers in the generations since. Ethical ob-
jections to their plays drove them from the stage in spite
of their theatrical effectiveness. They wrote with little
ethical intention. Unlike some of their contemporaries,
they did not seek to discover the abodes of sin and to
chastise the monster, nor did they study human nature
in the light of moral law. They dealt with themes that
would please their audience and would offer a sufficient

range of emotions for the exhibition of their poetic powers. Without imaginations that touched spiritual heights or penetrated to the real significance of moral conflict, they entered unhesitatingly upon the task of holding up a mirror to a society loose in manners and unprincipled in morals. They were not so much guilty of intentional immorality as impotent to produce moral effect. If their imaginations kept too frequent company with the gross and the unhealthy, they also sought at times the sweeter and nobler aspects of life. What won for their ethics high laudation from their contemporaries was their rhetorical and dramatic exaltation of ideals of magnanimity and dreams of idyllic love and devoted friendship.

Their masterpieces, despite their limitations, must be given high rank in the English drama. Outside of Shakespeare it would be difficult to find in our language another tragedy that as an artistic achievement can be counted the superior of "The Maid's Tragedy." But the main contribution of their collaboration took the form of a type, limited in themes and characterization, brilliant often both in dramatic discovery and in execution, but tending toward artificiality and convention. Their most important innovations, the products of serious artistic effort as well as of cleverness and ingenuity, mark the acquirement by the drama of new habits of doubtful value. Their sacrifice of character to situation, their devotion to theatrical effectiveness, their lack of moral purpose, their dalliance with the artificial and abnormal aspects of passion, and their disregard for the limits of blank verse, all these characteristics furnished examples eagerly followed by the dramatists of the next generation, examples that did not promote in tragedy a true or comprehensive or noble reflection of life.

Immediately after Beaumont's retirement Fletcher probably collaborated with Shakespeare on "Henry VIII" and "The Two Noble Kinsmen," and possibly on a lost play, "Cardenio." The partnership resulted in no distinct departures from the methods of either dramatist, but it seems to have been full of incentive for the younger man, whose poetic gift nowhere displays itself more splendidly. From this time on he wrote constantly for the theatre, composing three or four plays a year, collaborating on many of these with Massinger, and maintaining his position as the most popular dramatist of the time until his death in 1625.

Perhaps if Beaumont had lived, the two might have advanced to maturer and worthier achievement, but Fletcher's work alone rather displays the superficialities and artificialities of the collaboration. His amazing cleverness appears in every scene, but he evidently wrote more and more for immediate success, and relied more and more on his readinesss of wit and invention to take the place of earnest and serious purpose. The long series of plays in which he had at least a considerable share, range in kind from comedies of manners to tragedies of blood and revenge, but practically all may be described

as romantic drama, having, that is, strange improbable
events, foreign and remote scenes, variety and surprise
in action, and love as the central motive. His sense of
dramatic value in theme or incident was constantly alert,
and in Spanish stories, especially the "Novellas Exem-
plares" of Cervantes, he found mazes of complicated
action which exactly suited his fancy, and which he
managed with adroit dramaturgy. The Spanish influence
is more noticeable in the comedies than in the more
serious plays; but, whatever the theme or the source,
Fletcher added bustle and excitement. The distinctions
between tragedy, comedy, tragicomedy, and romantic
comedy often become barely discernible. The material
and treatment are similar. Tragic situations occur in
comedies as well as tragedies, and in either case, though
finely conceived and admirably expressed, are yet
always directed by the desire for surprise and thrills.
The tragicomedies conform most closely to the conventionalities and repetitions of the heroic romances, though
they exhibit abundant originality of invention. Through
their example, romantic and melodramatic tragicomedy
became perhaps the most popular and characteristic
dramatic species of the reign of Charles I, and a direct
progenitor of the heroic plays of the Restoration.

In his tragedies Fletcher's prostitution to theatrical
effectiveness admits a recognition of the literary tradition. At least, the two which are the result of his unaided
efforts are composed with more care and with more evidence of artistic responsibility than his other dramas.

In "Valentinian" [1] he turned from his usual sources and themes to those long approved in pure tragedy, and found in Roman history a story of revenge and lust. Though treating the material with great freedom, he unfortunately followed his source in continuing the action beyond the murder of Valentinian through the counter revenge on Maximus. The first two acts, that tell of the attempted seduction of Lucina and her final ruin, are among the best sustained tragic developments in Fletcher, and, in comparison with many similar scenes in contemporary drama, testify to his remarkable poetic gifts. But the later scheming and the overthrow of her husband involve a conversion of character and a descent into absurd improbability. In "Bonduca," Fletcher's invention moved unhampered. Historical sources are used merely as hints and incentives. The stories of Bonduca and Caratach are combined; and the interest in their tragic fates diversified by the stories of Bonduca's daughters and their Roman lovers, by the episode of the noble Poenius, by the pathos of the child Hengo, and also by some gross and brutal comedy. All these interests are skillfully interwoven and focused upon the great central scene of the battle. There is stirring presentation of camp life, and throughout the action moves with abounding spirit. The play is not tragedy at all if one judges it strictly by Aristotle's precepts or by Shakespeare's example, or even in comparison with the emotional ten-

[1] See Coleridge, *Notes on Beaumont and Fletcher*, for a characteristic and valuable criticism of the play.

sion of "The Maid's Tragedy." But it is an admirable example of the blending of the romantic, historical, heroic, pathetic, comic, and tragic, full of human nature as well as incident, conspicuous for poetic expression as well as theatrical ingenuity, one of the masterpieces of the romantic drama.

The tragedies in which Fletcher collaborated with Massinger or others offer few amendments of his usual dramatic habits. "The Queen of Corinth," "The False One," "The Double Marriage," and the spectacular "Prophetess" are all melodramas in which Massinger's moral earnestness and rhetorical seriousness contrast with Fletcher's vivacity, and in which clever stage-craft, noble poetry, and slipshod and hasty workmanship are indiscriminately manifest. "The Tragedy of Sir John van Olden Barnavelt" carries on the practice of treating contemporary foreign history, already exemplified by Marlowe and Chapman. Hurriedly written within a few months of Barnavelt's death, it can lay no claim to be a thorough or impartial study of historical events, but it affords a remarkable illustration of the readiness with which both authors could summon their talents to an occasion. Given a theme that had a current theatrical interest, and Massinger's declamation and Fletcher's pathos came nimbly to the task, and almost at their very best.

The most striking illustration, however, both of Fletcher's genius and its prostitution to theatrical effectiveness is to be found in "The Bloody Brother; or Rollo,

Duke of Normandy." Here in collaboration with Massinger and possibly Jonson and Middleton, he returned to one of the stock themes of tragedy, the story of family feud and a bloody tyrant. In comparison, however, with any preceding dramas of this class, whether in early imitations of Seneca or later treatments of lust and revenge, the play shows the alteration that had come over dramatic ideals and methods. Its purpose is neither to follow literary tradition nor to expose the evil of tyranny, but to make some startling theatrical effects out of the familiar material. Fletcher accomplishes this purpose with his usual recklessness of talent. When the height of tragic passion is required he rises to it, or very nearly, in the scene where Edith pleads with the tyrant to spare her father's life, a scene which Dyce pronounced the most real in its passionate earnestness of anything in Beaumont and Fletcher's writings. But the most astounding display of his power comes where there is no genuine passion but only make-believe. It is the final scene of the play.

Edith, whose father has been killed by the bloody and lustful Rollo, is planning to murder him. She has pretended to yield to his solicitations, and has arranged a secret meeting with him at her house. Enter Edith, splendidly dressed — a banquet prepared. She kneels and prays to her father's soul that she may forget all pity and kill the tyrant —

"His heaven forgot, and all his lusts upon him."

Then, as her boy sings the lovely song, perhaps Shakespeare's,

" Take, oh take those lips away
    That so sweetly were forsworn — "

Enter Rollo. By one of Fletcher's sudden conversions, he has changed to a subtle hypocrite and appears humble, repentant, begging for pity and love,

> "in whiteness of my wash'd repentance,
> In my heart's tears and love of truth to Edith,
> In my fair life hereafter."

Edith, surprised and unnerved, gradually forgets her purpose, and as she informs the audience in several asides, is yielding; when — Enter Hamond and the guard. Hamond, a brave blunt soldier, is seeking revenge on Rollo because the tyrant has killed his brother and outraged him by commanding him to murder the noble Audrey. Hamond announces that he has come to kill Rollo, who seizes Edith and interposes her as a defense. She, aroused now to Rollo's real nature, draws her dagger, but he snatches it from her. In the struggle that follows Rollo and Hamond are both killed.

All this occupies only one hundred and fifty lines of verse and must be accounted a most skillful bit of playmaking, a scene such as only Fletcher among the Elizabethans could contrive. But there is neither truth to life nor dramatic logic; on the contrary, there are two improbable conversions of character. It is not tragedy, it is hardly serious drama, it is theatrical claptrap; yet Fletcher's poetry is as fine, and, for all that one can see, as sincere as in the scene of genuine passion. Such dramatic impossibilities as this Fletcher faced with eager recklessness, and gayly spurred his Pegasus for the leap.

"The Bloody Brother" further illustrates the union of the material and methods of the Beaumont-Fletcher romances with the conventions of the tragedy of revenge and lust. That union, manifest also in Fletcher's "Valentinian," is henceforth characteristic of the tragedy of the age. The dramatists belonged to a late period of an artistic development and had many examples both native and foreign to draw upon. They were men of talent or even genius whose creations were independent and original but rarely without large indebtedness to their predecessors. While Shakespeare and Jonson were often borrowed from, the majority of the tragedies clung to the examples of Webster and Tourneur or mingled revenge and horrors with the romantic plots and novel technic of Beaumont and Fletcher. A marked similarity consequently exists in the plays of men of different temperaments and purposes. Lustful tyrants and their intriguing favorites, love crossed by honor and often allied with revenge, illicit and abnormal passion, romantic princes and princesses, an action confined to the rooms of a palace, situations involving seduction or temptation, stage-effects whether by horrors or by masques and pageants, and a style more equable, less fantastic than in the early drama, — these are the ingredients which characterize tragedy for the quarter century after Shakespeare's death.

Middleton's tragedies and tragicomedies came late in his career, following a period of realistic comedies, in which his observant and satirical imagination found free play. Though affected by Beaumont and Fletcher's romanticism, he preserved most of the traits of the tragedy of revenge in its late development, including such penetrating analysis of character swayed by evil as we have

found in Marston and Webster. In some of his romantic
dramas, as the tragicomedy "The Witch," there is little
of this serious purpose. The various revenge motives —
of the duchess on the duke who has compelled her to
drink from the skull of her murdered father, of the
lover upon the husband who has married his betrothed,
and of the jealous husband upon his wife — are all treated
with melodramatic insincerity though with an ingenious
accompaniment of spectacular and supernatural interference on the part of the witches. Attempted murder
results in wounds that easily heal; the deadly potion
proves harmless; the duke discovered dead comes to
life. In the single tragedy written by Middleton alone,
"Women Beware Women," the revenge species appears
unadulterated. Isabella's illicit relation with her uncle,
the use of a masque to bring about the final slaughter, the
scenes of seduction, and the abominable wickedness of
all the persons, are elements that recall the Tourneurian
group. The fluency and eloquence of Middleton's style
and his admirable delineation of character by rapid dialogue are best shown in the early scenes; after the old
mother, so beautifully and truly drawn, has disappeared
from the action, the rest is unrelieved murder and lust.

The two famous plays that were the results of Middleton's collaboration with Rowley have somewhat different
characteristics. Rowley, a playwright used to rude and
fantastic comedy, and the author of "All's Lost by Lust,"
a clumsy tragedy of revenge, wrote most of the comic
scenes and had some share in the serious plots. In "The

Fair Quarrel," the hesitation of Captain Ager to defend
the honor of his mother unless convinced of her purity;
and in " The Changeling," the entanglement of Beatrice
with the loathed follower whom she has persuaded to
murder her accepted suitor, offer situations novel and
ingenious. In both plays, the opportunity for mere melodrama with sudden conversions of character is refused,
and the series of startling situations made the basis for
a study of human motive. It is this which gives "The
Fair Quarrel," in spite of its absurdities, superiority over
most of the tragicomedies of the time. In "The Changeling," one may easily imagine what havoc Fletcher would
have made of the characterization in order to over-
emphasize situations, sensational enough in themselves;
but Middleton and Rowley followed the best tradition of
Webster. The rash and pampered Beatrice retains our
sympathies even in her degradation, and remains con-
vincingly alive, whether in her incipient love for De
Flores or her final cry for forgiveness. De Flores, clear-
headed and well-motived, is the most powerful and
individual of the post-Shakespearean villains. The comic
relief supplied by the mad scenes spoils the tragic unity
of the play. But, except in Shakespeare and Webster,
the old combination of murder, revenge, sinful love,
villany, madness, and ghosts had never been made so
consistently the result of human motive and so effective
in its appeal to our sympathies.

Massinger's dramatic career, ranking in productive-
ness with Shakespeare's or Fletcher's, extended from

the time of Shakespeare's withdrawal from the theatre
to within a few years of the Civil War. For ten years he
was mainly occupied in collaborating with Fletcher for
the king's men; and of the nineteen plays usually classed
as his own, none were acted before 1622. His work,
therefore, falls roughly into two periods, the first when
he was the assistant of Fletcher, the second when he had
succeeded Fletcher as the main reliance of the leading
London company.

Of his work with Fletcher the tragedies have already
been considered. In most of the plays of the collaboration, Fletcher's share is the more important, especially
in the treatment of the dramatic crises. In plays, as
"The Queen of Corinth" and "The Laws of Candy,"
where Fletcher's hand is least apparent, there is an excess of melodramatic ingenuity without the Fletcherian
vivacity. Massinger's temperament reveals itself, however, from the first in the gravity of his style and the
seriousness of his morality. From Fletcher he acquired
his stage-craft and his attachment to the romantic drama
of thrills and surprises, but his art was meanwhile developing a responsibility and purposes all its own.

Of the plays written without the aid of Fletcher, two,
"A New Way to Pay Old Debts" and "The City Madam,"
are domestic comedies of manners. The others are romantic dramas which can be classified only with some
difficulty as comedies, tragicomedies, and tragedies.
A number of the tragicomedies are to be distinguished
from the tragedies only by the happy endings and the

absence of bloodshed. Nor are these always decisive. Of the tragedies, "Believe as You List" and "The Virgin Martyr" result in victory as well as death, and in the tragicomedy, "The Maid of Honor," suitors worthy and unworthy are rejected and the vindicated heroine enters a nunnery. The tragedies in the main deal with more serious and important actions and rely less on intrigue than the tragicomedies; but it may be said of Massinger, with even more truth than of Fletcher, that he dealt with romantic stories abounding in tragic possibilities, usually resulting in happy endings, but occasionally taking a loftier tone and a fatal conclusion.

The plays as a whole reveal a remarkable variety of stories and a treatment of sources fully as free and ingenious as Fletcher's and often contriving a political as well as a moral lesson. Honor and religion play conspicuous parts as in contemporary Spanish drama, to which Massinger apparently owed a considerable debt; although in only one instance, "The Renegado," has direct indebtedness to a Spanish play been traced. The earlier drama is also freely drawn upon. At this date it was in fact almost impossible to compose a play without traversing motives and incidents that were familiar on the stage; and Massinger borrowed from many, from Shakespeare as freely as from Fletcher, and from minor dramatists as well. The story of the usurper Sebastian, told in "The Battle of Alcazar," is retold in "Believe as You List"; and the poisoning by kissing the painted corpse, related in "The Second Maiden's Tragedy," reappears in his

"Duke of Milan." In spite of their variety and ingenuity, his plays are very like others of the period. There are the same court and courtiers, general, favorite, rival lovers, rival mistresses, and the same trials of chastity or intrigues of lust and malice.

Yet the independence of Massinger's invention and the truth of his conceptions of human motive are by no means small. In "The Bashful Lover" there is a presentation of idealizing and self-sacrificing love, far surpassing the courtly compliments of Fletcher and rivaling the magnanimity of Browning's conceptions. In such themes, just removed from the exaltation and the horror thought necessary for tragedy, yet serious and exalted above the average of comedy, Massinger is at his best. An outline of his "Maid of Honor" may serve to illustrate both the independence of his imaginative conceptions and the careful integration of his structure.

Act i opens at the court of Roberto, King of Sicily, who, after much eloquent solicitation, permits his natural brother Bertoldo to lead an expedition against Gonzaga, a knight of Malta, who is relieving Sienna, captured by Ferdinand, Duke of Urbin, in his effort to win the duchess by force. Camiola, the maid of honor, after some buffoonery on the part of Sylli, a Malvolio-like wooer, has a parting interview with Bertoldo and confesses that his vow as a knight of Malta is the only bar to her acceptance of his offers of marriage. In act ii, after some further buffoonery by Sylli, who serves throughout as a comic contrast to Camiola's other suitors, Fulgentio, the King's minion, solicits Camiola, but is tartly repulsed, and threatens to slander her. The scene changes to Sienna, the camp of Gonzaga, and then to the citadel held by Ferdinand. Bertoldo and his followers are defeated and made prisoners, Gonzaga tearing the cross from Bertoldo's breast. In act iii all the prisoners are released by ransom, except Bertoldo, who thereupon bewails the falseness of his brother the King. The scene changing to Sicily, Adorni, a faithful follower of Camiola's father, soliloquizes on his love for her and his intention to take vengeance on Fulgentio. Later he appears wounded before Camiola and presents the minion's recantation, but is blamed by her for his presumption in assuming a task proper only for her lover. Upon the arrival of news of Bertoldo's plight, Camiola, who is as energetic as loyal, decides to sacrifice her fortune to pay her lover's ransom, and summons Adorni to act as her agent in freeing Bertoldo. Adorni dutifully undertakes the mission that promises to ruin his hopes. In act iv the Duchess Aurelia arrives at Sienna and Ferdinand surrenders. Bertoldo in prison reads Seneca, soliloquizes on suicide, falls on the ground, and threatens to rend the bowels of the earth, quite in Kydian fashion. Adorni enters, and Bertoldo, upon hearing of Camiola's sacrifice, blesses her name and promises marriage. It is now Adorni's turn to soliloquize on suicide. Bertoldo is brought before Aurelia, who, suddenly enamored, offers him herself and duchy. After some resistance he yields. Adorni now begins to hope. In Sicily Camiola has convinced the King of Fulgentio's worthlessness. In act v Camiola receives from Adorni the news of Bertoldo's fickleness, but she still scorns Adorni and resolves to seek redress from the King. Accordingly, at the marriage of Bertoldo and Aurelia, she breaks in, states her case with eloquence and temper, and appeals to the King. Aurelia suddenly feels all her love quenched, and Bertoldo pleads for pity. All await the fulfillment of Camiola's promise that she will declare whom she will marry, and are astonished when Father Paula announces that she has decided to become the bride of the church. Before taking the veil, she obtains Fulgentio's pardon, gives one half of her wealth to the faithful Adorni, and commands Bertoldo to resume the cross of Malta.

In his six tragedies there is less of romantic love and more of the blacker passions. "The Unnatural Combat," "The Duke of Milan," "The Fatal Dowry" (in collaboration with Field), and "The Roman Actor" deal with lust and revenge in the quantity and quality long prescribed. In the last named, however, Massinger broke away from the conventional treatment and made his protagonist neither the cruel tyrant nor the lustful queen, but a dignified and noble representative of the actor's profession, and took the opportunity of effectively expanding the old device of a play within a play. The other two tragedies present still more originality of conception and treatment: "Believe As You List," dealing with the fortune of a rightful claimant to the crown, and "The Virgin Martyr," perhaps a revision of an early play by Dekker, returning to the old material of the Miracles, the story of a martyrdom that converts the persecutors. In each of these tragedies, as in "The Maid of Honor," a number of stories are organized into a single action, introduced by admirable exposition, and usually carried through with direct and logical progress. In the treatment of catastrophe, always heightened, prolonged, and sometimes full of surprise after Fletcher's fashion, Massinger is less competent. Massinger could not keep to the inevitable development of character as did Shakespeare, nor could he sacrifice character to situation as light-heartedly as did Fletcher. In consequence he falls between two stools; and his fifth act is usually clumsy and unconvincing.

Massinger's art was not only less reckless than Fletcher's; it was linked to a serious moral view of human affairs. He always worked under a sense of responsibility both as a dramatic artist and as a preacher of political and personal morality. Neither the heedlessness of Fletcher nor the perversion of Ford is discoverable in his plays. Bad and good are clearly differentiated, despite the improbabilities of the romantic vicissitudes; and poetic justice is administered with decision. Following his venturesome and nimble master, he pursues his pathway gravely, judicially, somewhat heavily. His careful art and sincere morality lack the leaven of dramatic genius. The orator and the rhetorician are always elbowing the dramatist off the scene. His style, never splendid, never excessively figurative, is always contained and clear. At its best in sustained declamation, it often descends to a tone approaching prose and rarely rises to the more stirring or impelling emotions. His abundant inventiveness also fails him in the great crises of passion. Again and again when the heroine is at bay, or the hero within the jaws of ruin, Massinger resorts to oratory. As in "The Maid of Honor," eloquence is the *deus ex machina* which solves the difficulties of the plot. In consequence, the characterization, though involving subtle and penetrating conceptions of human nature, and often logical and consistent, rarely results in living beings. An exception must be made of some of his men, whose virility and dignity are akin to his own temper and can be made real through his favorite rhetorical means. The women, with few exceptions, of whom Camiola is chief, are, for reverse reasons, bad failures. Chastity cannot be revealed by an oratorical appeal, and the evil women only grow impossible when they add rhetoric to lust.

The passing of the greatness of the Elizabethan drama is manifest in Massinger as in his contemporaries. He retains, to be sure, most of the external characteristics of his predecessors; he writes constantly in the light of their achievements; he would restrain Fletcher's theatricality by a more cautious and responsible art. Like Shakespeare he maintains a moral standard despite the exigencies of a romantic plot. But the old fervor as well as the old extravagance of diction have gone; and a careful dramaturgy now finds itself incompetent to meet the requirements of great tragic crises. His tragedies recapitulate what has been done before, without important advance or departure, and without attaining one unforgettable phrase or one moment that electrifies the reader with an undeniable conviction of its dramatic truth.

In Ford the results of servile imitation and original genius were curiously combined. The first dramatist to feel the overshadowing effect of Shakespeare's tragedies, he borrowed freely from "Lear," "Othello," and "Romeo and Juliet," and he was hardly less indebted to Beaumont and Fletcher and the school of Webster. As a playwright he was, in fact, usually imitative and often unskillful. As a poet his consciousness of the greatness of earlier dramatists now chilled him to bald copying and now incited him to a unique development of some of the old tragic motives. With Dekker and Rowley he collaborated on "The Witch of Edmonton," a tragicomedy dealing with a contemporary crime and linking itself with the domestic tragedies. "Perkin Warbeck," a revival of the chronicle history, is without battles or pageants, and is less concerned with the scenic presentation of history than with the delineation of the character of the claimant. His other tragedies, "Love's Sacrifice," "The Broken Heart," and "'T is Pity She's a Whore," are at once both more in accord with prevailing modes in the drama and more characteristic of Ford's imaginative temperament. In spite of their worthless comic scenes, their conventional material, and their melodramatic situations, they present tragic passion with an intensity and truth possible only to dramatic genius.

Love is the theme, and an excess of sentiment and passion in conflict with friendship, right, or natural law, is the particular province that Ford makes his own. A favorite in love with the wife of his lord, a brother in love with a sister, are the situations over which his genius casts an oppressive melancholy that lasts until the final heartbreaks. The monarch, his favorite, a buffoon or two, and lords and ladies, love-sick or passion-inflamed, play with the casuistry of love and mingle dances and revels with bloodshed and horror. Villany and revenge appear but are not very essential. The seeds of fatal passions have been already sown when the play begins; it is the stifling hothouse in which they luxuriate. The end is inevitable, though it may be long held in suspense and attained through some surprise in the final act.

"The Broken Heart" is the most healthy of his plays. Orgilus, whose life has been blighted because Penthea has married Bassanio through the intervention of her brother, the great General Ithocles, pursues his revenge upon Ithocles in spite of much delay and apparent reconciliation. Finally he stabs Ithocles to death just as Ithocles is to be married to the princess Calantha, and just as Penthea dies of madness and starvation. The familiar round of revenge, madness, and torture here reappears, but it is told in a story full of romantic sentiment and human passion, and not without sunshine as well as shadow. It is the final scenes, however, which every reader remembers. Calantha is dancing when the tidings of the deaths of her father and her lover are brought to her, and she dances on, hiding her grief and playing her part nobly, until, duty accomplished, her heart is free to yield to its bursting sorrow.

It is in scenes like these, showing passion restrained or overborne for the moment, or the strain and suspense preceding the crash, that Ford is at his best. The marvelous parting scene between brother and sister in "'T is Pity" is perfection itself. His imagination dissolves the horrible story into the very language of the breaking heart. His verse, lacking both the old rhetorical artificiality and the vivacity and adaptability of Fletcher's, possesses a restraint and moderation of language and a complex and beautiful melody all its own. At times it is the thinnest of translucent veils "through which passion is burning as the radiant lines of morning."

One may find in him somewhat of the perverse inquisitiveness of Donne. A wayward and solitary searcher in the realms of poetry, he voyaged only to regions unexplored or forbidding. But, as we have seen, his imagination, wayward though it was, took direction from his contemporaries, and he was representative of much in current tragedy. Though Ford's ethical attitude is perhaps more non-committal than that of any of his contemporaries, yet his casuistical interest in moral problems, and the emphasis which he places on such problems at the expense of his stories, are traits common in the drama of the time, and especially in the collaborative work of Middleton and Rowley. His absorption with questions of sex, his searching for new sensation, his attempt to bestow on moral perversion the enticements of poetry correspond with what is most decadent in Fletcher and Shirley. Like his fine-spoken and well-mannered courtiers and impulsive ladies, Ford imagined in an atmosphere of unhealthy emotion. His plays are immoral because their passion is so often morbid and their sentiment mawkish. His power to reveal character and passion, which rank him with the greatest of the Elizabethans, was discovered in his searching the by-paths of the abnormal and pathological. Pathos for him was a flower plucked from a poisonous exotic.

Beginning about 1625 and extending to the Civil War, Shirley's dramatic career overlapped and continued

Massinger's as Massinger's did Fletcher's. After leaving the university he took orders, but shortly became converted to Catholicism, and then, after a volume of poems, turned to the public theatres for employment. The last of the brilliant series of poets who made the London stage the home of poesy and contributed to the great period of the English drama, at the closing of the theatres he was the dean of his profession. His thirty odd plays, while naturally continuing the methods and types of Massinger and of Fletcher, his avowed master, and while reminiscent of much in earlier writers, especially Webster and Shakespeare, also reflect about all the characteristics manifest in the drama during the reign of Charles I.

Shirley's remarkable talents challenge comparison with his predecessors. He had a share of Massinger's seriousness of purpose and painstaking art, and of Fletcher's freshness of fancy and sprightliness of style. In invention he is hardly less ingenious than either, and in careful construction and theatrical craftsmanship he approaches Massinger's undoubted mastership. His verse seems modeled on Fletcher's, but it often has a spontaneity of movement and a richness of decoration that recall Elizabethan style in its early flights. Little of early aphorism, however, or of the later obscurity and confusion remains; these are replaced, sometimes indeed by a hackneyed declamation, but often by natural and fluent dialogue.

Yet, in spite of his talents, Shirley's own position and his contribution to the drama are difficult of definition, because he is so constantly reminiscent of his predecessors and so constantly approaching, though never quite equaling, their preëminent models. His plays, like Massinger's, seem to the reader of to-day repetitions of one another. Each coalesces in the mind with other comedies of manners, or other tragedies of blood, or with the tragicomedies of Massinger and Fletcher. Whatever the species, love is the theme, lust is pursuing, chastity is tried by intrigue and by declamation; but the real interest is in the plot, the tricks, disguises, subterfuges, villains, and surprises that end — as the case may be — in the discomfiture of the fools, or the marriage of the lovers, or the downfall of a dynasty.

The drama had become conventionalized. The dramatists were no longer searching for new themes and characters in a wide range of stories; they were inventing their plots but were restricted in their materials. The ingredients of early plays served Shirley's purpose, and by a few new devices or changes in motive he gave his fashionable ladies, his lustful monarchs, scheming favorites, and exiled heroes new names and adventures, and so produced a play. The cleverness of the plot occupies your attention, or occasionally a beautiful passage or a fine conception of character arrests the mind, but at the close you are at a loss to separate the play from a dozen similar ones.

In Shirley, as in Massinger, the most representative plays, and certainly those most satisfactory to our taste, are the tragicomedies. Bloodshed and horror and

grossness of language and situation may all be absent,
and the story of love and intrigue, even if it does not
exalt the mind or purify the passions, may be altogether
delightful. In "The Royal Master," one of the best,
the rôle of the lustful monarch is assumed for a single
scene, only to cure a really charming heroine of her infatuation for royalty; and the intriguing favorite is foiled,
the banished noble vindicated, and two love matches
completed with gracefulness of language and dexterity of
plot. Unfortunately Shirley's land of romance is rarely
so wholesome as here or the inhabitants so agreeable.

His tragedies mainly conform to the hackneyed models,
no matter what the sources may be or how large his own
invention may seem. The earliest, "The Maid's Revenge," relating a Spanish story of the rivalry in love
of two sisters that ends in a fatal duel between brother
and lover, is wholly in the tone of romantic melodrama.
"The Politician," a more ambitious effort, combines
the villain play with the Beaumont-Fletcher romance.
Gotharius, the politician, is the villain; Marpisa, the
evil woman, is his mistress and about to be married to
the king; Albina, the loyal and long-suffering heroine, is
the villain's wife; Turgesius is the prince and hero; and
Olaus, a blunt soldier, is his faithful friend. There is an
insurrection, as so often in Fletcher; and after a long
intrigue the villain and the evil woman perish, and the
prince marries the heroine. In "Love's Cruelty," a more
original conception is worked out with telling realism
and a good deal of dramatic truth. Clariana becomes

infatuated with her husband's friend Hippolito; and, even after the guilty lovers have been permitted to go unpunished by the husband, her passion continues until her jealousy at her lover's approaching marriage to Eubella drives her to his murder. Rarely elsewhere in the Elizabethan drama is the story of illicit love told with less of glamour and more veracity. These merits are perhaps counterbalanced by the extreme realism of the language and the stage action.

In this play the deceived husband dies of grief, but Eubella, who had earlier resisted the lustful duke, is solaced after the death of her betrothed by a promise of marriage from the duke himself. Both "The Politician" and "The Duke's Mistress," a tragedy along hackneyed lines, end with reward for the virtuous and punishment only for the vicious. Such application of poetic justice had been earlier expounded by Ben Jonson in defense of the punishments inflicted in his comedy, "Volpone." The applications of the doctrine in Shirley and Massinger were, however, probably due not so much to theoretical criticism as to the popular preference for the restriction of the catastrophe to the bad, a preference recorded by Aristotle and evidently shared by a generation in which romantic tragicomedy was the most popular dramatic form.

Shirley's tragic masterpieces, however, offered no alleviation of horror and bloodshed. "The Traitor" and "The Cardinal" are plays of revenge, lust, intrigue, and villany, in which all the accretions of this kind of

tragedy from Kyd and Marlowe down to Webster and
Massinger seem to be represented. The villains are as
black as Barabas and as crafty as those of Webster;
plots are as intricately entangled with counterplots as
in Tourneur; and surprises follow as rapidly as in
Fletcher. The corpse kissed by the repentant duke is
again presented; there is attempted rape and assumed
madness; in each play a bridegroom is murdered as he
takes his place in the wedding procession; and in each
revenge strews the final scene with the dead. But the old
motives still had power to convey poetic inspiration, and
the examples of all his predecessors summoned Shirley
to his best efforts. Perhaps in no other plays does he so
constantly recall their work; certainly in no others do
the poetic quality of his language, the vigorous delineation of character, and the dramatic depiction of passion
so worthily maintain what were even for men of his day
the great traditions of English tragedy.

Tragedies by minor writers during the years from
1620 to 1642 offer little that is distinctive. Occasionally,
as in the anonymous "Nero" of 1624, we have a play
spontaneous in phrase and lifelike in characterization,
worthy of the best days of the drama; but in the main
the plays only repeat what is to be found in Massinger,
Ford, and Shirley. In spite of the vogue of tragicomedy,
tragedy was by no means neglected, nearly fifty tragedies
being preserved from the twenty years, in addition to
those by the authors mentioned. These include several
by Suckling, Glapthorne's pastoral tragedy, "Argalus

and Parthenia," and his worthless "Wallenstein," May's plays on classical history, and others by Killigrew, Davenant, Carlell, Heming, Davenport, and less known men.

The large majority conform to the later type of revenge play as exemplified in Massinger and Shirley. Sometimes the romantic love element supersedes the intrigue and horrors, but oftener the horrors have full sway. A double plot, usually with an elaborate surprise in the fifth act, revolves about lust and revenge with some attention to untarnished honor and unconquered chastity. The lustful duke and his intriguing favorite, or the tyrannical usurper and the rightful prince alternate at the centre of the stage along with the evil woman, perhaps a Lady Potiphar, and a distressed maiden, likely to be disguised as a boy. Madness is frequently represented, eyes are plucked out, brains dashed upon the stage, and many of the old horrors reproduced, but ghosts rarely appear. The action consists largely of adultery, seduction, and rape; and these are represented with a horrid detail that rivals Marston. When chastity is preserved it is often by a device similar to that used in "Measure for Measure," although occasionally there is an exchange of men instead of women. Tragedy is for the most part confined to stories of crime. The monstrous politicians and libertines differ from their sixteenth century predecessors chiefly in the greater ingenuity and complexity of their intrigue, their subordination of ambition or other motives to those of love or lust, and in the prosaic flatness of their blank verse.

Often there are manifest borrowings, and occasionally a dramatist evidently strove to include everything that had ever been known on the tragic stage. "The Rebellion," by Thomas Rawlins, presents Machiavel, a villain, whose soliloquies might be burlesques on Barabas and Richard III, two mad scenes, a nurse from "Romeo and Juliet," a Moor, who is another villain, attempted rape, and frequent bursts of poetry:—

> "The lazy moon has scarcely trimm'd herself
> To entertain the sun; she still retains
> The slimy tincture of the banish'd night."

On the other hand, the usual type of tragedy, with reminiscences of Shakespeare and Fletcher, sometimes shows a genuine poetic gift, as notably in Lord Falkland's "The Marriage Night." The most marked trait, however, of these minor tragedies is their eagerness to out-Herod Herod and to make good their weakness in dramatic truth by means of stage horrors or rant. "The Valiant Scot," a tragedy dealing with the career of Wallace, represents the cutting out of the tongue of one English ambassador and the putting out of the eyes of another. In "Mirza" the protagonist kills his seven-year-old daughter, — "Takes Fatima by the neck, breaks it, and swings her about." The taste for atrocities seems to have been most highly developed at Oxford, where the students acted Goffe's outrageous plays and a Samuel Harding published "Sicily and Naples," a medley introducing revenge for a father, a maiden disguised as a boy, a villain-favorite, the Mariana device, and combining rape, murder, madness, and incest in a fashion not equaled since "Titus Andronicus."

Absurd plays of this sort were common enough from the days of "Cambyses," and cannot be fairly taken as evidences of the drama's decadence. Nor do the main differences that are apparent between tragedy after 1620 and that of the early or of the Shakespearean period point to decadence as unmistakably as critics are wont to assume. There is a waning of poetic power; blank verse descends to prose, and its flowers have a jaded air; but there is poetic imagination in Glapthorne as well as in Shirley, noble rhetoric in Massinger, and sheer poetry in Ford. The ethical tone has in general suffered deterioration. The moral insight of Shakespeare or even of Webster is not maintained; courtly and sophisticated ideals ring false; the language becomes gross; the vulgarities of the early plays are replaced by mawkish sentimentality or lewd suggestiveness. There seems to be increasing difficulty in presenting persons normally good. The reiteration of scenes of rape and seduction bespeak an unhealthy moral atmosphere. Yet tragedy, though at times perverse or forgetful, still clings to its moral standards. It still endeavors to expose and chastise sin and to incite to virtue.

Decadence is more manifest in the restriction and conventionalizing of the material of tragedy. The love for the impossible, the craving for stupendous emotions and supernormal passions had given place to theatrical court intrigues. The daring attempts of Marlowe and

Shakespeare to depict the great round of the emotions had given way to a continual harping on illicit love. Dramatists were no longer striving to give beautiful expression to the terrible, heroic, or pitiable in story, but seeking to construct acting plays out of stock situations and stock characters. There was a lack of fresh impulse. French romance and Spanish drama seem to have encouraged no marked innovations, and French classicism was only just making itself heard at the closing of the theatres. A man of original genius like Ford staggered under the recognition of the greatness of earlier achievement and turned to the abnormalities and excesses of passion for his themes. Shirley, more typical of the period, devoted talents of a high order to repeating familiar models.

Yet there was progress as well as stagnation. Dramatists had shaken off the medieval adherence to sources and learned to invent, though their invention unhappily followed current theatrical fashions rather than fresh creative impulses. The art of making plays had advanced, not as Shakespeare had pointed the way, by making construction dependent upon character, but as Beaumont and Fletcher had fashioned, by making character subordinate to a varied and rapid action. There is more complication, more coherence in plot, more ingenuity in situation, and a far greater use of surprise than in the early plays, but no great gain in consistent motivation. Yet many of the early absurdities have disappeared; and in discovering what is to be acted and what not, in

the quick excitement of the spectator's interest, and in
the careful integration of the various lines of action, the
dramaturgy is, in comparison with the period before
Shakespeare, noticeably modern.

The differences which distinguish the different periods
do not conceal the essential unity of the entire development from 1562 to 1642. The changes that take place
in the prevailing types are of degree and not of kind.
Nearly all the tragedies might be called tragedies of
blood, for nearly all deal with crime and bloodshed. A
narrower division like that of the tragedy of revenge
keeps its integrity from Kyd onward, the hesitation motive finding transformation in "Hamlet," the union of
revenge, intrigue, and madness finding a different development in Webster and others, and remaining until the
end the most prevalent type of tragedy. A majority of
Elizabethan plays are romantic rather than classical or
realistic, though the romance is of many kinds and drawn
from many widely different sources, as Boccaccio, D'Urfé,
or Lope de Vega. For a time it is mainly confined to
romantic comedy, but it soon enters into tragedy and
tragicomedy. In tragedy it plays a fitful part, but in tragicomedy it conquers the theatres. The course of tragedy
from its inception in an amalgamation of medieval and
classical elements, through its establishment by Marlowe,
its development of types and methods, the transformation of these by Shakespeare into a dramatic form that
changed and enlarged the meaning of tragedy for the
centuries since then, the further development of types and

methods under the innovations of Beaumont and Fletcher, and the splendid contribution that tragedy still received from Webster, Middleton, Ford, and Massinger, — all this was comprised within a single century; all that was most significant, within a single lifetime.

Tragedy throughout this development remained popular. Less than the ballad but more than any other form of literature prior to the pamphlet, novel, and newspaper, the drama was the result of popular taste, thought, and desire. Tragedy early shook off the bonds of classical tradition, and it never ceased to aim first at pleasing the audiences. Shakespeare as well as Dekker or Shirley was their servant. Even in the later days when increasing Puritanism alienated a large portion of the public from the theatres, literary standards failed to overthrow the sovereignty of the people, though, as the dramatists paid allegiance to a restricted and less representative audience, the drama waned. Without a guiding criticism, without any reliance on authority or tradition, appealing first to the public theatre and only secondly to court or culture or posterity, tragedy at its best was not distinguished by impeccability of literary art. It lacked simplicity of theme and precision of treatment; it was fantastic in design and language. It lacked refinement; it was vulgar in diction and scene; it was revolting in its horrors and bloodshed. It lacked reserve and definiteness of literary purpose; it was sensational, incongruous, or naïve in its address to the intelligence. But from the same conditions that gave rise to its faults and excesses came its excellences. A delight in verbal felicity, a welcome for diverse excitement, and a craving for story on the part of the public made possible the wealth of incident and character, the varied emotional appeal, and the fervid poetry of Elizabethan tragedy. It was free to avail itself of every resource of poet or playwright in order to present human passion of all kinds, human individuals of many varieties. Its virtues as well as its faults are summed up in Shakespeare. After his death it developed in dramatic dexterity rather than in the comprehensiveness of its mirror of life. Yet, without Shakespeare, the fabrics of its vision comprise

> "The cloud-capp'd towers, the gorgeous palaces,
> The solemn temples, the great globe itself."

Even without him, the legacy of Elizabethan tragedy is an unfaded pageant of the greatness and the pain, the passion and the poetry of our little life.

NOTE ON BIBLIOGRAPHY

Ward, Fleay, Schelling, and the bibliographies in the Shakespeare *Jahrbuch* continue to be the best guides. Dyce's admirable edition of Beaumont and Fletcher (11 vols., 1843–46) has long been the standard, but two new complete editions of their works are now in progress, one under the general editorship of A. H. Bullen (London, 1904–), the other edited by A. Glover and A. R. Waller (Cambridge, 1905–). The discussion in this chapter is in part based on my *Influence of Beaumont and Fletcher on Shakespeare* (1901) and my edition of *The Maid's Tragedy* and *Philaster* in the *Belles-Lettres Series* (Boston, 1906). I must refer to the latter for a full bibliography of both texts and critical works. Miss Hatcher's *John Fletcher* (Chicago, 1905) should be added. Webster has been well edited by Dyce and Hazlitt; and his two principal tragedies by M. W. Sampson in the

Belles-Lettres Series, with full bibliography. E. E. Stoll's monograph, *John Webster*, referred to in chapter v, has been drawn upon in the discussion in this chapter. Tourneur has been edited by J. Churton Collins (1878); Middleton by A. H. Bullen; Massinger very poorly by Gifford (2d ed., 1813); Ford by Gifford (1827, revised by Dyce, 1869); and Shirley by Dyce (1833). Editions of selections from all these dramatists will also be found in the *Mermaid Series of Old Dramatists*, with introductions of varying value. Bibliographical references to all dramatists of this period will be found in Ward and Schelling, and in general more comprehensive discussion of their plays than are to be found elsewhere. Of especial value in the study of sources are E. Koeppel's two volumes, *Quellen Studien zu den Dramen Ben Jonson's, John Marston's und Beaumont und Fletcher's* (1895) and *Quellen Studien zu den Dramen George Chapman's, Philip Massinger's und John Ford's* (1897).

Among the critical appreciations of the dramatists of this and the preceding chapters are: Lamb's *Specimens of English Dramatic Poets*, Hazlitt's *Dramatic Literature of the Age of Elizabeth*, Jeffrey's *Essay on Ford*, Lowell's *Old English Dramatists*, G. C. Macaulay's *Francis Beaumont* (1883), Swinburne's *Ben Jonson* (1889), and his essays on other dramatists.

CHAPTER VIII

THE RESTORATION

HE drama of the Restoration was separated from the earlier periods by sixteen years of closed theatres and a virtual cessation of all dramatic composition. To the drama, as to other forms of literature, the Restoration brought not only a revival but also a revolution— new fashions, new models, new foreign influence, a new age, and a changed society. No such break in theatrical conditions has occurred since then, and nothing so nearly revolutionary in the history of the drama. Since then the theatres have been always open, the dramatists always writing. Changes have been gradual, the history continuous. Due recognition must, therefore, be given to the last years before the closing of the theatres and the first years after their reopening as marking an end and a beginning. Really, however, the new was a continuation of the old; the pause was by no means a severing of traditions; and the Restoration drama inherited far more from the Elizabethan than it imported from France or originated under the inspiration of that illustrious patron of poetry, Charles II.

Signs of continued interest in the theatre had not been wanting during the Commonwealth. The theatres were

reopened in 1648 but promptly suppressed and dis-
mantled. Drolls or short farces derived from popular
plays were performed here and there in London or in
the country, and the continued publication of old plays
revealed a considerable demand from the reading public.
In 1656 Davenant obtained permission for the performance of his "Siege of Rhodes" "made a Representation
by the Art of Perspective Scenes, and the story sung in
Recitative Music." Thus, even before the revival of
the regular drama, came its rival the opera, and the important innovation of movable scenes. Two years later
Davenant produced another entertainment, and was
performing regular plays before Monk had entered London. Two companies, the King's and the Duke of
York's, were presently licensed; these, united from 1682
to 1695, sufficed for sixty years to supply the needs of the
London public, and maintained their monopoly until
well into the nineteenth century. Before 1642 the open
public theatres had largely given place to the "private"
theatres in inclosed rooms. These and the contemporary French theatres served as models for the Restoration buildings. The stage still protruded into the
auditorium and was frequently crowded with gallants as
in the Elizabethan days, but the use of scenery, a drop
curtain shutting off all the stage but the proscenium,
the performances by artificial light, together with the
women actors, who now for the first time interpreted
Shakespeare's heroines, brought the Restoration stage
closer to that of our own day than to that of the preceding

generation. This transformation from a half-medieval to a nearly modern stage resulted in far-reaching changes in the drama; among others, in a new importance to female parts and in alterations in structure due to the use of scenery and curtain. Few of the old actors were still alive, though enough had been gathered to make up the nucleus of the companies and to transmit the traditions of the Globe and the Blackfriars. The acting of the Restoration probably soon surpassed that of the earlier period, and the great triumphs of Betterton and Mrs. Barry set new and long influential traditions in English tragedy. The changes which most fundamentally affected the drama were those in the stage and the actors.

The influence exerted upon the drama by the new opera may also be described as largely theatrical. The opera of the Restoration is to be distinguished from the form as it has prevailed since the introduction of Italian opera into England at the beginning of the eighteenth century. The term was loosely used to describe a variety of entertainments, in which the dialogue might be altogether sung, or in part spoken, and in which the dancing and decoration were regarded as not less essential than the music. Derived from France, where the opera gained great favor and attracted the services of Corneille and Quinault, the English species was closely related to two national forms of drama, the masque and the tragedy. In music, dancing, and machinery it resembled the former; in theme, plot, and persons, often the latter. A resemblance between the opera and the heroic tragedy is also observable in the prominence given by each to heroic love. Tragedies were readily transformed into operas as in the case of Lee's "Theodosius" and Tate's "Brutus of Alba," and of Fletcher's "Island Princess" and "Prophetess." Throughout the period the relations between the two remain close. They were presented in the same theatre; the same actors often played in one and sang in the other; an orchestral band was provided to play between the acts in tragedy; and tragedy availed itself of songs, scenery, and machines. Entirely apart from its place in the history of English music, English opera is of some importance in the development of tragedy, partly as a rival and partly because it promoted operatic elements in tragedy itself. Tragedy came in the Restoration period to rely more than ever before upon the externals of its stage presentation, and on elements then considered distinctively operatic, — scenery, spectacle, and music.

From changes in theatrical conditions, friends of the drama doubtless found hope for its higher development; but the main source of promise seemed to lie in the patronage of the court. The court of Charles II indeed exerted a greater influence on the drama than any court since or, perhaps, before, but the influence was mainly toward social and political immorality. Patronage rather than public support was relied upon by both dramatists and actors. In consequence, the theatres became servile purveyors to the amusement and taste of the king and his favorites, and blindly partisan adherents of the royal politics. The failure to represent the nation and the consequent loss both in range of artistic impulse and in soundness of moral standards that had characterized the drama in the reigns of the two earlier Stuarts were now greatly intensified. In tragedy, grossness of language and manners had less opportunity than in comedy, but political subserviency had freer play. Political allegory combined with tragedy in plays contemptible as specimens of either species. This unworthy partisanship and this catering to a society mean and corrupt necessarily maimed that branch of the drama supposed to devote itself to heroic and lofty themes.

The influences making most for innovation in the poetry and art of the drama came from France, partly owing to the instigation of the court. The character of this French influence, like its sources, differed from time to time, but from 1660 until after the death of Voltaire it was continuous and powerful. In tragedy, shortly after the Restoration, the heroic romances of Calprenède, Scudéry, and others, and the French plays which they had fostered, were the sources and models of much in the English heroic plays. There was constant borrowing and adapting from French romances and tragedies, as from French comedies. The "Cid" had been translated and acted in the reign of Charles I; several other of Corneille's plays were translated before 1670, his subjects and style were often imitated, and toward the end of the century the influence of Racine was marked upon English drama. The French influence on tragedy, however, was less a matter of models than of rules and theory. The English dramatists never in this period got very close to Corneille or Racine, but they were greatly impressed by French criticism and precept. In an age of reason and modernity, English tragedy, like other forms of literature, found its reaction from the crudities of an earlier age and its reform of the excesses of an untrained art in the pseudo-classicism of France.

An effort was made, which proved far more portentous than preceding ones, to wrest tragedy back into conformity with the supposed rules of Aristotle. The conflict between English and French models, between Shakespeare and Corneille, between romantic license and classical proprieties had begun, a conflict to be continued in criticism as well as practice for over a century. Dryden's "Essay on Dramatic Poetry" introduces us at once to the questions at issue and the state of the debate. The main questions were: first, the unities, recognized in French drama as necessities and supposedly derived from Aristotle; second, the mixture of tragedy and comedy, or, more especially, the introduction of low comedy into tragedy; and third, the use of rhyme as in French tragedy or of blank verse as in English, prose by general consent being restricted to comedy. In these the English tradition was directly opposed by French practice and theory, and in many minor matters as well: in the *liaison* of scenes, favored, as was the unity of place, by the use of scenery; in certain proprieties in the conduct of kings and of subjects to kings; in the restriction of tragedy to historical, classical, or at least heroical persons and themes; and, notably, in the avoidance of violence and bloodshed in the action. Dryden's discussion reveals French practice and classical practice, not clearly differentiated, set up against the English tradition, and recognizes much in the former that seems reasonable and authoritative. But, on the other hand, it insists on the excellence and impressiveness of the English achievement. Such was the state of opinion shortly after the Restoration, and such, with varying emphasis and refinement, remained the consensus of opinion of dramatists and critics for a century. The laws of the pseudo-classicists were held to be measurably good, but Shakespeare without those laws had been undeniably great.

Throughout the Restoration the main influence on the theatre was that of the earlier English drama. When the theatres were opened the old plays were acted. Literally hundreds were revived, many of which long held the stage. After a time changes in taste and theatrical conditions led to revisions and alterations; but the alterations of Shakespeare and others not only illustrate this perversion of taste, but also testify to the continuance of the English tradition. Not merely revisions and adaptations, but the whole drama bears witness to its descent. The characteristics of the tragedy of 1630 are those of the tragedy of 1670. The influence of the Beaumont-Fletcher romances and of the tragedy of revenge are hardly less marked after 1660 than before. The comic scenes, blank verse, complicated plots, physical horrors, and supernatural agents, the mixture of idealization and realism that characterize Elizabethan tragedy, persist throughout the Restoration period.

The conflict between the contending theories of tragedy may be studied in criticism. Dryden's various essays recur again and again to the main issues of the war, and define with changing emphasis his attempted reconciliation of the two opposites. Rymer came forward as a thoroughgoing exponent of classicism, and at the beginning of the next century Dennis, Gildon, and Addison carried on the discussion. The conflict is also represented in the work of nearly every dramatist. There are tragedies in blank verse and tragedies in rhyme, tragicomedies, tragedies with comic scenes, tragedies without deaths and with happy endings, tragedies translated from the French, others based on Greek originals, and still others in their medleys of farce, horror, and rant as Elizabethan as "The Jew of Malta" itself. Many of these varieties are represented in the work of a single writer, as Crowne, or Lee, or Otway. The career of Dryden sums up and reflects nearly all the changes in opinion or practice. His plays, and with them the whole course of tragedy from 1660 to 1700, fall roughly into certain divisions. For a few years after the Restoration, ending at about the time of the "Essay," is the period of the dominance of the earlier drama, a period of which Davenant is the leading figure. About 1664 began the heroic tragedies in rhyme which for a time carried all before them. In a dozen years, however, the fashion wore out, and Dryden's "All for Love" in 1678 marked the abandonment of rhyme and led the return to Shakespeare. From 1678 on, the course of tragedy again takes to varied streams. To this period belong the most notable alterations of Shakespeare, the most permanent of Restoration tragedies in the plays of Dryden, Lee, and Otway, and also the growth of French methods and of the influence of Racine, culminating in the pseudo-classical triumph at the beginning of the eighteenth century.

At the opening of the theatres, tragedy and tragi-comedy took up their courses about where they had left off. The plays of Davenant, the main connecting link between the two periods, might be treated in connection with either, without seeming in the least out of place. Tragicomedy of the type current in the thirties continued in the sixties; tragedy oscillated between honor and horror, fine writing and perverted lust, as in Massinger, Shirley, and Glapthorne. Spanish stories, long influential in the drama, promised for a time to prove still more important. Dryden's first two plays, "The Wild Gallant" (1663)[1] and "The Rival Ladies" (1664), were based, like many other contemporary plays, on Spanish originals; but the second introduced rhyme and some of the elements of the plots of the heroic plays.

---

[1] In this and subsequent chapters the dates in brackets give the year of the first presentation in the case of acted plays. The date of publication usually coincides with the year of acting.

It was, however, the Elizabethan plays that the audiences went to see, and that the dramatists had constantly before them. The plays of the Marlowean period were regarded as out of date, and very few were revived, practically none of the tragedies except the early ones of Shakespeare. Of the later Elizabethans, Beaumont and Fletcher were the most popular, for a time surpassing Shakespeare. Over thirty of their plays were revived, and many of these were constantly acted. Of tragedies and tragicomedies, "The Maid's Tragedy," "Philaster," "Bonduca," "A King and No King," "Valentinian," and "Rollo" held the stage till the end of the century, the first three much longer. Jonson's tragedies, as well as his comedies, were revived; and Massinger's "Virgin Martyr," Webster's "White Devil," Chapman's "Bussy D'Ambois," Shirley's "Cardinal" and "Traitor" were among the plays that carried on the traditions of the tragedy of blood. Shakespeare's comedies fell into disfavor, but his tragedies were popular from the start. This was due in part to the genius of Betterton, who found his best opportunities in depicting their protagonists, in part to their merits as stage plays for both actors and audiences; but, whatever the causes of their success, they soon exercised a large and increasing influence upon the theory and practice of tragedy.

The Elizabethan plays, however, had almost from the first to encounter a rivalry with a new fashion. Davenant, their reviver, was also the first with the new. His "Siege of Rhodes" (1656), with its scenery, machines, music, rhyme, and heroics, may be said to inaugurate both the opera and the heroic play. Howard's "Indian Queen" (1664), in which Dryden had a hand, was followed by Dryden's "Indian Emperor" (1665), in rhyme and displaying the full-fledged heroic formula. The love-complications of its plot are of a kind constantly reappearing not only in the heroic plays but in later tragedy as well.

Montezuma and Cortez are the historical heroes; Almeria, daughter of the Indian Queen, is the vengeful passionate heroine; Cydaria, daughter of Montezuma, is the angelic heroine. Montezuma's sons, Odmar and Guyomar, Almeria's sister, Alibech, and her brother, Orbellan, all in love with some one, add to the criss-crossing of affections. Almeria is loved by Montezuma, but loves Cortez, who does not love her. Cydaria is loved by Cortez and also by Orbellan. The two heroines, as well as the two heroes, are thus rivals, and the vengeful one directs the intrigue. The brothers Odmar and Guyomar, to say nothing of a Spanish captain, both love Alibech, and provide the usual story of fraternal rivalry. After duels, captures, imprisonments, conflicts of honor, renunciations, and jealousies, finally the vengeful heroine succumbs. One of the brothers is preserved for Alibech; Cortez weds the angelic heroine; the rest, including six of the leading actors and several supernumeraries, are killed or commit suicide.

Dryden's dedication of "The Rival Ladies" to the Earl of Orrery gives some support to the latter's claim to have been the introducer of the rhymed heroic species, though his first play acted was probably "Henry V," in 1664. Whoever the originators, their example was soon followed by Crowne, Lee, Settle, Otway, and most of the dramatists of the day; and for fifteen years or so English efforts in tragedy were confined to the heroic model.

The use of the heroic couplet was its distinguishing mark; of course, an imitation of French practice. The plots, too, were direct borrowings, or close imitations, of contemporary French romances or dramas. Moreover, the themes and their treatment, the conception of honor, the importance given to love, and the pseudo-history, all followed French ideas. The unities were attended to, if not strictly observed; incidents, persons, and scenes greatly reduced in number in comparison with Elizabethan practice; and fixed rules of propriety in characterization and language observed, all in French fashion.

The English plays, however, formed a type unknown in France or anywhere else on sea or land. The plots of all the "Sieges," "Rivals," and "Conquests" are mainly concerned with love, which inspires heroic sentiment and valor, encounters much jealousy and intrigue, runs counter to friendship and honor, and works its sorrows and joys among persons illustrious in history. In the end, the hero, a man of prodigious valor and most exemplary honor, weds the heroine, who is equally skilled in the artificial code of honor, while the deaths of the ambitious villain and the evil princess, in love with the hero and seeking revenge on the heroine, provide a tragic catastrophe. The persons are usually historical, English, Classical, or Eastern, and a little

historical fact was intended to give a kind of grandeur
to the story. The Alexanders and Montezumas, however,
have manners and sentiments drawn partly from the
courts of Louis and Charles and partly from the world
of romance. The curious conception of honor as superhuman valor and magnanimity combined with formal
propriety leads to impossibilities like those in a child's
book of wonders. Duels and rescues take the place of
pitched fields; the valorous champion puts to rout an
army, exchanges compliments and courtesies with the
grace of a fashion-plate, boasts and rants in Cambyses'
vein, and is near to expire in an ecstasy of declamation
when the heroine extends her hand for him to kiss. The
two rival lovers and the two rival ladies generally play
their game of jealousy, ambition, and wounded honor
during a conquest or a siege; but world and empire count
for naught. *Amor vincit omnia.*

A mere summary of their leading traits may suggest,
what a careful examination of the various representatives
of the class will confirm, that the heroic plays were by
no means a fresh importation from France, but rather
a result of tendencies distinctly manifest in the English
drama, at least since the Beaumont-Fletcher romances.[1]
The *genre* of heroic romances begun by Beaumont and
Fletcher, continued in tragedy and especially in tragicomedy by Fletcher, Massinger, and Shirley, here takes
a further but not very diverse development under the

---

[1] *Cf.* James W. Tupper, *Relation of the Heroic Play to the Romances
of Beaumont and Fletcher.* Publ. Mod. Lang. Assn. 1905.

spell of French romance and drama. The conflicts of honor, the rivalries in love, the few types of character constantly recurring, the extraordinary surprises and discoveries, the women, sentimental and sensational, offered nothing new in English drama. The avoidance of bloodshed, the observance of poetic justice, the exaltation of love as the whole theme, the preference for the sensational and astounding rather than the natural or inevitable, have all been found distinguishing drama since Fletcher. On the other hand, the hateful intrigue and abnormal lust, the horrors and gloom of Webster and Ford found little place in the heroic plays. One survival from the revenge plays, however, took on new life. Ghosts became as numerous and voluble as in the days of Kyd. But in the main the heroic plays represent the continuance of the heroic romance and tragicomedy corrected in accord with French standards of dramatic art and French conceptions of gallantry and heroism.

It is in this aspect that they are of the most interest in the history of English tragedy. They are not a freak variation but a species lineally related to those which precede and follow. They carry the restriction and conventionalization of the material of tragedy much farther than did the plays of Shirley and his contemporaries; and, somewhat before Racine, they confine the main course of tragedy to sentimental love. Though their main innovation, the employment of rhyme, did not prevail, and though their changes in technic were rejected by many later Restoration dramatists, yet they

were a powerful force in habituating the theatre to the
structure and methods of French tragedy and in promoting the triumph of these methods in the next century.
They also mark a further change in the conception of
the field and functions of tragedy. The result of developments from tragicomedy rather than from tragedy,
they exhibit a blending of the two forms and a redivision
along new lines. Before the Restoration, nearly all tragedies had presented a mixture of comedy or of farce.
Tragicomedy had been distinguished from tragedy not
by the presence of comedy but by the fact that its leading
persons were brought near to death yet saved for a happy
ending. Moreover, tragicomedies as a class developed
along the lines of the Beaumont-Fletcher romances.
The heroic plays inherited the traits of this class and also
to some extent the happy endings. In some, as Orrery's
"Henry V," there is no suffering and everything turns
out well; in others, as Orrery's later plays, there is bloodshed enough; but in nearly all death is visited only on the
evil; the heroic are married. All plays with heroic themes,
however, were called tragedies. There was no hint of
heroic comedy as in France. The distinction between
tragedy and comedy, which the Restoration drama
drew much more closely than the Elizabethan, came to
depend less on the presence of deaths or of an unhappy
ending, and more on the nature of the material and form.
After the decline of the heroic plays, tragedy returned,
as we shall see, to bloodshed, deaths, and horrors, but
meantime the heroic plays had emphasized as essential

certain elements that long continued their ascendency in both critical and popular views of tragedy. Henceforth every one associated with tragedy heroic actions, illustrious persons, verse, whether rhymed or blank, a love story, and an inflated diction. The curious heroic rant, indeed, supplied a vocabulary and a manner that lasted long after the jingle of the rhyming couplets had been abandoned. Its "furies," "vows," "chains," "transports," "ecstasies," and "Etnas burning within the breast" remained the language of despairing innocence and palpitating passion. Tragic became almost synonymous with artificial and inflated.

A worthier achievement must also be credited to the heroic plays. The spacious realms of romance which the Elizabethans had loved were closing their gates to the imagination of the later seventeenth century. Even Shakespeare's isles of the blest that so delighted Elizabeth and James were strangely inaccessible to Restoration fancy, which took pleasure in only the "Merry Wives of Windsor" among his comedies. The narrowing of romance had been manifest in the drama since 1600, and it was a theatrical and artificial domain of thrills, sentiments, and honor that the Restoration received for its heritage. Poor enough as is this kingdom, absurd its inhabitants, it is still the land of the wonderful and impossible, and its monarchs now and then remind us of Tamburlaine and Hotspur. At the time of Wycherley's comedies and Rochester's patronage of literature, men and women sighed and thrilled with Albumazor, dreamed of love, and fancied themselves kings and queens in China and Peru. When Romance was banished from other forms of literature, — unless in pastoral or opera, — tragedy still remained dedicated to the banished goddess, and in its precincts scanty flames still burned on the altars of heroism, enthusiasm, romantic aspiration, and extravagant love.

The rise and wane of the heroic plays is sufficiently illustrated in the career of their chief exponent. After his "Indian Emperor" (1665), Dryden turned in "Secret Love" (1667) to tragicomedy with a mixture of verse, rhyme, and prose and a mixture of heroic and lively comedy. After various comedies and the adaptation of "The Tempest," "Tyrannic Love" (1669) and "The Conquest of Granada" (1669) accomplished the full triumph of rhymed verse and "the grand scale." At times Dryden's rapidity and vigor almost justify the rhymed couplets and redeem the absurdities of the conventions. It was in the Epilogue to "The Conquest" that he attacked the Elizabethans, vaunting the superiority of an age when

> "Our ladies and our men now speak more wit
> In conversation, than those poets writ."

In 1671 came the burlesque "Rehearsal," which, if its attack did not centre on heroic plays, made Dryden and the popular "Conquest of Granada" the butts of its most telling fun. Then followed Dryden's "Essay of Heroic Plays," two comedies, his inexcusable tragedy of "Amboyna" (written in a month to support the war with the Dutch, yet, in conformity to the fashion, tracing the Dutch atrocities to a heroic love), and the opera based on Milton's "Paradise Lost." In 1675 came "Aureng Zebe," the last of his heroic plays, without supernatural machinery, and somewhat tamed in style.

The vogue of the heroic play was about over. In 1678 came Rymer's attempt at a model heroic tragedy and his "Tragedies of the Last Age," a severe attack upon the Elizabethan drama from the point of view of extreme pseudo-classicism. But in the same year was acted Dryden's "All for Love," in blank verse, with a preface extolling Shakespeare, rejecting the models of the ancients as "too little for English tragedy," discarding "the nicety of manners of the French," yet claiming credit for an observance of the unities. This was the one play in which, as he declared, Dryden followed his own bent unheedful of stage fashions, and it seems to have set the fashion and led the way back to blank verse and to Shakespeare. Rhymed plays continued to appear occasionally, but blank verse was henceforth recognized as the proper medium for tragedy.

Even Dryden's praise of Shakespeare is modified by his respect for French rules, and by the prevailing opinion that Shakespeare's genius lacked the improvements readily secured by an application of the accepted formulas of art. That a certain improvement is accomplished cannot be denied. The incoherent profusion of scenes, the host of distracting incidents are reduced to order, the unities of time and place give a directness and rapidity to the action that "Antony and Cleopatra" greatly lacks. In characterization and poetry Dryden's play is, to be sure, not comparable with Shakespeare's, but in both respects it far surpasses the numerous other English dramas on the subject. This is faint praise. By following Shakespeare without imitating him, and by adapting a play to the stage requirements of the day without bowing to the absurdities of the heroic models, Dryden succeeded in producing a great and original poetical drama. Not in response to mere theatrical fashion or to French taste or theory, but in response to the inspiration of Shakespeare came the finest product of Restoration tragedy.

In this same year as "All for Love" appeared "Œdipus," written in collaboration with Lee, in which the authors brought to their classical model the methods of the Elizabethans. Eurydice and Adrastus furnish the necessary love story, and Creon becomes the hateful rival and intriguing villain. The declamation sometimes shows Dryden at his best, the bombast and horrors are in Lee's worst vein. In the next year appeared Dryden's improvement of "Troilus and Cressida" with his careful essay on "The Grounds of Criticism in Tragedy," in which he criticises after the fashion set by Rymer the errors of Shakespeare and Fletcher, insists on the necessity of unity, order, and greatness in action, and praises the excellence of Fletcher and especially of Shakespeare in character and passion. Nowhere else, perhaps, has Dryden expressed so discriminatingly and so finally his own views and, on the whole, the views of his age, on tragedy. Shakespeare's greatness is recognized as preëminent in the presentation of character and passion; his faults in coherence and unity of structure and his archaism in manners and proprieties are admitted.

From this time on Dryden's contributions to the drama were less frequent. In "The Spanish Fryar" (1681), he added the best Restoration example of tragicomedy, availing himself of Fletcher's example, a double plot, and a happy ending. "The Duke of Guise" (1682), a political allegory, written in collaboration with Lee, deserves little consideration as satire or drama. After two operas and an absence of several years from the stage, came "Don Sebastian" (1690), which Sir Walter Scott thought the best of his tragedies. It is heroic in its pairs of lovers and tangle of love and jealousy, and in the exploits, boasts, and love-making of the hero; French in its general structure; Elizabethan in its mixture of comedy, its use of horror and incest, and its imitation of Shakespeare. It recalls the tragedies before 1642, with their heroic love after the style of Beaumont and Fletcher, their horrors and incest following the Websterian school, and their emulation of famous passages in Shakespeare. "Cleomenes" (1692), which repeats the Potiphar's wife story, is still more Elizabethan, and "Love Triumphant," a tragicomedy (1693), deals with an incestuous passion proved innocent at last, a motive very popular since "A King and No King."

Dryden never gave the theatre a whole-hearted service. Responding readily to its conditions, he wrote with facility and vigor comedies, tragedies, operas, and political allegories of the kind that changing fashion or patrons demanded. When, after a long slavery, he had acquired mastery of his art and confidence to lead rather than to follow, circumstances arose to call him away from the theatre. We may wish that he had earlier and oftener tried to do his best, as in " All for Love," " The Spanish Friar," and " Don Sebastian"; but his genius was not essentially dramatic, and we may not regret the time taken from the theatre for the Satires and Fables. His greatness can be best seen by comparison with the work of his contemporaries. Whatever he tried, he did on the whole better than they, and in comprehensiveness and adaptability as well as in sheer poetic faculty he was their master.

Up to " Aureng Zebe " Dryden's tragedies reflected the prevailing fashion; his " All for Love " marked a turning-point in the course of tragedy; and his criticism reviewed, summed up, and discriminated the current views of Shakespeare and the French. His later work was less representative of the general course of the drama, yet the various species exhibited in his work recur in that of his contemporaries, and the partial return to Elizabethan methods that marks his latest plays is perhaps the leading characteristic of the last twenty years of the century.

Crowne's " Thyestes " is the only attempt besides Dryden's " Orestes " to adapt a classical play to the popular stage, and neither returns much nearer to the Greek than Seneca. The only play closely modeled on the Greek is Milton's "Samson Agonistes." The preface renounces the stage with a scorn that includes not only the Restoration tragedies but apparently those of Shakespeare as well. Though the play stands by itself, it may be said to represent a tendency to turn to Greek rather than to French models, a tendency boasted of by Dryden and Crowne, and fully manifest in the next century. And it takes its place at the head of the numerous, if sporadic, tragedies on Greek models that extend from the Restoration to the present day.

In the return to Shakespeare, Dryden's influence was more potent, though here, as in the case of the Greeks, an increased appreciation was shown partly through alterations and adaptations. Before "All for Love," only "Measure for Measure," "Macbeth," and "The Tempest" of Shakespeare's plays had suffered alterations, and in two of these Dryden had a share. In the four years after 1678, no less than ten alterations were produced, the majority of which long usurped the stage. The restorers, sincere enough in their admiration for Shakespeare, were following Dryden's precept and example, correcting Shakespeare's faults in diction or structure, and preserving his poetry and characters. While their entire readiness to cut or to add resulted in part from ignorant vanity, it depended far more on their confidence in the panacea afforded by Art for all diseases of genius. Art, according to their prescription, was compounded of closeness of structure in the French style and a declamatory vocabulary in accord with the latest pseudo-classic conventions. The alterations are so various in their audacities that a brief general description is hardly possible. The main purpose in each case was the remaking of Shakespeare's disordered beauties into "a play," and, beyond the formulas of Art, the most usual improvement was the addition of a love story. Thus, Alcibiades marries the daughter of Timon, and Cordelia's loyalty is rewarded by the hand of Edgar. Perhaps the most that can be said for the restorers is, first, that they rescued for the stage some of the less dramatic plays, as "Troilus and Cressida," "Timon," "Henry IV," "Coriolanus," and "Cymbeline," and thereby greatly extended the knowledge and appreciation of Shakespeare; and, second, that they left "Hamlet" and "Othello" untouched. Adaptations were made of practically all Elizabethan authors, and Shakespeare fared as his fellows. A more elaborate history of the drama than the present one might trace the changes in the conception of tragedy and in the taste of the theatres as indicated by these alterations. The main consideration here is that, however mutilated or embellished, a half dozen of his tragedies were among the favorite plays of the Restoration. Before the end of the century they had outclassed the other Elizabethan plays, even those of Beaumont and Fletcher, in popular regard. The Restoration did what his own age had not done; it recognized Shakespeare's supremacy in English tragedy.

It would be tedious to trace the infatuation for the

heroic plays and the partial return to the Elizabethans in the work of the various dramatists whose careers paralleled Dryden's. His rival, Settle, wrote heroic plays, a sensational political play on the Whig side, "Pope Joan, or the Female Prelate," and a long series of tragedies and comedies extending well into the next century. John Crowne, another contemporary, began with tragic comedies and heroic rhymed plays, proceeded to Shakespearean alterations, "Thyestes," and blank verse plays in the Elizabethan tradition, and ended his career with a rhymed "Caligula." Among those who in tragedy confined themselves mainly to adaptations or borrowings from the Elizabethans were Tate, Ravenscroft, and D'Urfey; and a group of women should be mentioned, — Mrs. Behn, Mrs. Manley, Mrs. Pix, and Mrs. Centlivre, — who in the later half of the period devoted considerable attention to tragedy without creating any marked departure from the commonplace. We must confine ourselves to the authors whose tragedies had a more extended interest.

Nathaniel Lee wrote his first play in 1675, when he was eighteen years old, and produced ten tragedies, in addition to the two in which he collaborated with Dryden, before the close of 1684, when he became insane. The first three, "Nero," "Sophonisba," and "Gloriana," were rhymed, but the fourth, "The Rival Queens" (1677), preceded Dryden in its return to blank verse and won an enormous success, maintaining itself on the stage long after the death of Betterton. His remaining tragedies were in blank verse, "Mithridates," "Œdipus," "Theodosius," "Cæsar Borgia," "Lucius Junius Brutus," "Duke of Guise," "Constantine," and "The Massacre of Paris," which with the tragicomedy "The Princess of Cleve" was acted after his release from the madhouse.

All his plays are pretty much of a kind. The juvenile and worthless "Nero" unites the conventions of heroic love with the ghosts, lust, bloodshed, and madness of the later Elizabethan revenge plays. The later blank verse plays, though to a large extent based on French romances, envelop the love interest in a Tourneurian medley of depravity and horror. They revive the late Elizabethan type of tragedy that united the sentimental and the terrible and delighted to present loving and devoted womanhood in an environment of undiluted villany, abnormal lust, and physical torture. They add somewhat of the closeness of structure of French models, the spectacle of an improved stage that displays ballets and temples along with bloody heavens, human sacrifice, and crucifixions, and a style that out-Herods the Elizabethans in the extravagance and vehemence of its rant. "Theodosius" tells of the fatal result of the rival love of brothers for the same woman; "Brutus" of the judicial murder of a son by a father; "Cæsar Borgia" introduces Machiavelli again as a machinating villain in a story of fraternal rivalry in love; "Constantine" and "Gloriana" deal with the rival loves of son and father. This theme, a favorite with Lee, reappears in

"Mithridates," the contents of which are fairly typical of the revolting intrigues to which Lee mainly confined himself.

The leading persons are Mithridates, the lustful dotard; his two sons, Ziphares and Pharnaces; Monima, the gentle heroine, contracted to Mithridates; Semandra, the chief heroine, in love with and loved by Ziphares; her father, a noble soldier; and two conspiring villains. The Romans are at the gates of Synope, where the scene is placed. Pharnaces, at feud with his brother and desirous of Monima for himself, conspires with the villains to thwart the marriage of Mithridates to Monima and direct the passion of the king to Semandra. Mithridates condemns Ziphares to death and pursues Semandra, but is persuaded to relent in order that Ziphares may lead the army against the Romans. Semandra and Ziphares exchange parting vows of fidelity as he leaves for battle. The conspirators again incite Mithridates; and Semandra, in order to save the life of her lover, repulses him upon his return in triumph. In consequence he believes her false and leaves her in the power of his father. The fourth act opens with Mithridates, who has ravished Semandra, "encompassed with the ghosts of his sons, who set daggers to his breast and vanish." He is attacked by remorse; Pharnaces betrays the city to the Romans; Semandra and Ziphares have a last interview and commit suicide; Mithridates dies after condemning the captured conspirators and Pharnaces to execution.

It is interesting to compare this with Racine's play of the same title and dealing with the same historical incidents, acted four years earlier. Though neither play represents its author at his best, and Lee's was apparently written without any knowledge of Racine's, the two illustrate the differences between the two theatres,

and may remind us how far Lee was from forsaking
the English tradition for the French. In Racine, all the
stage spectacles, temples, portents, and ghosts, all the
horrors and frenzy are lacking; so, too, are the characters of Archilaus the noble soldier and Semandra the
all-important person in Lee. In addition to Mithridates,
Monima, and the two sons, the only persons are two
confidants and a servant. The intrigue is of the simplest.
Monima, contracted to Mithridates, is loved by both of
his sons and returns the love of Xipharés. In the end
Pharnaces forsakes his father, who dies, leaving Monima
and Xipharés to face impending ruin. Mithridates is
not the lustful tyrant traditional on the English stage,
but a monarch who cherishes great projects and counts
magnanimity a royal duty. Nor is Pharnaces the traditional English villain with accomplices, as in Lee,
though he has a villain's part to play. The interest is
psychological, centring on emotional crises in the lives
of all, and without resort to sensationalism, horrors, or
complication of incident.

Otway, like Lee, began with rhymed plays, "Alcibiades" (1675) and "Don Carlos" (1676), the second
winning an extraordinary and long-continued success
on the stage. The next year appeared his "Titus and
Berenice," a free and sympathetic translation of Racine's "Berenice" that was surpassed in the favor of
the theatre by Crowne's treatment of the same subject.
After several comedies he followed the fashion for Shakespearean adaptations in his "History and Fall of Caius

Marius " (1680).[1] This monstrous play, about half of
which, as Otway acknowledged in his prologue, is from
" Romeo and Juliet," provides a large mixture of comedy,
and presents Juliet (Lavinia) dressed as a page, the
servant of her lover, after the style of Beaumont and
Fletcher's Bellario. For sixty years this play superseded "Romeo and Juliet" upon the stage. Otway's two
other tragedies, "The Orphan " (1680) and "Venice
Preserved" (1682), are his masterpieces. They continued to be stage favorites for a century and a half, and
procured for Otway the place next to Shakespeare in
the admiration of the eighteenth century.

"Venice Preserved" may be classed with the many
tragedies of the day that maintain the Elizabethan traditions. These are manifest in the general structure,
the large number of actors, the changing scenes, the
gross comedy, the abundance of incidents, the terrors,
ghosts, and madness. Not only the frequent reminiscences of Shakespeare and Fletcher, but the whole conception and treatment testify to an inspiration from the
earlier and better days of the drama.

The story, not long ago too well known to need retelling,
relates how Jaffier, in poverty and desperation, is induced to
join a conspiracy against the state, and is then persuaded by
his wife, Belvidera, to save the state and her father by turning
informer. He seeks to sacrifice himself for the friend whom he
has betrayed, and in the end stabs both himself and his friend

---

[1] Ward (iii, 415) is in error in crediting public taste with condemnation of this play. Lavinia seems to have been one of Mrs. Barry's most
successful parts.

upon the scaffold. A curiously Elizabethan prolongation of the catastrophe follows in the apparition of the ghosts of the friends, and the madness and death of Belvidera.

The essentials of great tragedy, of Shakespearean tragedy, are here. The opposition of character, the struggle of the generous but pliable Jaffier under the conflicting influences of his wife and the steadfast 'Roman' Pierre, the joy and tenderness and ruin that come with his love for Belvidera, are all drawn with a truth of passion in conception and language that reaches the heart. "Nature is there," wrote Dryden, "which is the greatest beauty." Marred as a whole by buffoonery and excess, the play is still among the two or three best tragedies of the Restoration. If it were all equal to the tremendous fourth act, Otway would be sure of a place among the immortals.

Marked by the same power of swaying the emotions of tenderness and pity, "The Orphan" attains these effects by means of the situations rather than through the study of motives. The plot deals with the rivalry of two brothers in love with their father's ward. She is secretly married to one; the other substitutes himself by trick on the marriage night. The situation, which has parallels in preceding tragedy, is abhorrent enough to kill all interest in the persons concerned; but Otway's power to depict love and distress triumphs over one's repugnance. The play is remarkable in many ways. Its few characters, its observance of the unities, its confinement of the action, give it the simplicity and directness of French tragedy. Its theme and its poetry recall Elizabethan rather than Restoration examples. But it departs from the canons of either theatre in presenting neither historical persons, nobles, kings, nor illustrious actions. Based on a story, supposedly of fact, related in a contemporary pamphlet, it merely transfers the scene to Bohemia, without adding the usual accessories of tragedy. Though it keeps something of a court setting and does not venture into middle-class society, it is like the Elizabethan plays of crime in its presentation of contemporaneous fact, and like Heywood's "A Woman Killed with Kindness" in telling a story of domestic distress. It might by a little extension of the term be called a domestic tragedy, and it still further departs from the canons in relating the misery of an innocent sufferer who is the victim of a cruel mistake. Otway should, therefore, be remembered as a dramatist who, in a time when tragedy was largely artificial, imitative, and conventional, painted suffering and tenderness with truth to nature, and who violated the accepted rules of his art in order to reach the hearts of his audience. That he could not also escape the moral perversion of taste that marked his time has brought its punishment in the final neglect of his masterpieces; but it is a sign of genius to turn away from heroic plays, Racine, and Shakespeare, to write plays different from any written before, and to stir all men's hearts for over a century.

Of the many dramatists who wrote tragedies in the last decade of the seventeenth century and bridged the

way from the age of Dryden to the age of Pope, only
Banks, Southerne, and Congreve produced plays of continuing popularity and influence through the eighteenth
century. Banks ended a prolific career with "Cyrus the
Great, or the Tragedy of Love" in 1696, but his popularity was mainly due to his three English historical
tragedies, "Virtue Betrayed, or Anne Bullen," "The
Island Queens" (Elizabeth and Mary Stuart), and "The
Unhappy Favorite" (the Earl of Essex). These plays
are interesting as an illustration of the survival on the
stage of a dramatic species in a debased form. Though
in blank verse, their material is that of the heroic play;
their formula, much love-making and a pretense of portentous events; their persons, rivals in love, — two men with
the same woman or two women with the same man, —
a wicked minister, a revengeful woman, and the queen
at the centre of the stage. There is no comedy, no
physical horrors, and even the portents are reduced to a
peculiar decorum:—

> "Last night no sooner was I laid to rest
> But just three drops of blood fell from my nose."

The construction is on French models with few actors,
continuity of scenes, and observance of the unities.
Puerile in conception and more ridiculous in their bombast than Fielding's burlesque, they have enough rapidity of action, vivacity of claptrap, and extravagance
of changing emotions to account for their stage success.

Thomas Southerne finished "Cleomenes" for Dryden,
with whom he was closely associated, and his tragedies

follow Dryden's later work in maintaining the Elizabethan traditions of blank verse, comedy, double plots, shifting scenes, horrors, and persons of varied ranks. His "Loyal Brother" (1682) is wholly commonplace, and "The Spartan Dame" (1719) and "The Fate of Capua" (1700) do not depart from usual themes and methods, though the latter is in some respects Southerne's best play; but his two most successful plays, "The Fatal Marriage" (1694) and "Oroonoko" (1696), both based on novels by Mrs. Behn, present decided innovations in theme. "Oroonoko, or the Royal Slave" contains much comedy, and has little merit besides the novelty of the story, presenting the virtues of a negro slave. "The Fatal Marriage, or the Innocent Adultery" introduces the Enoch Arden story, attached to an outrageous comic underplot derived in part from Fletcher's "Nightwalker."

In the main plot, Biron, oldest son of Baldwin, has been captured by pirates and is supposed to be dead, his letters being kept secret and answered by his villanous brother, Carlos, who urges his wife Isabella to marry. After Baldwin, instigated by Carlos, has thrust her out from his house, she accepts the devoted Villeroy. Biron returns; she goes mad in a scene of great imaginative power; Carlos and his assistants endeavor to kill Biron, who is rescued by the returning Villeroy. Biron, however, dies; and an accomplice of Carlos, tortured upon the rack (on the stage), confesses and exposes Carlos. Then "enter Isabella distracted, her little son running in before, being afraid of her." She stabs herself.

Like Otway's "Orphan," this is virtually a domestic

tragedy, for there are no interests of state or court, and our sympathy is centred solely on the innocent distress of the heroine. Like Otway, again, Southerne gains his greatest effects by an appeal to pity. The sentimentality that we attribute to the days of Richardson's "Clarissa" earlier triumphed on the stage in the heroines of Lee, Otway, and Southerne.

Not less successful on the stage than the plays of Banks and Southerne was the single tragedy of Congreve. First acted in 1697, "The Mourning Bride" continued without alteration through the next century, and furnished Mrs. Siddons with one of her greatest parts. Congreve's remarkable dramatic ingenuity was skillfully exercised in combining all the elements that the average audience delighted in, and yet presenting these draped sufficiently to avoid offending the judicious. Classical form and technic permit a sensational and gruesome fifth act; dignified and facile verse gives way at times to outrageous rant; the usual plot of the rival ladies and rival lovers is ingeniously complicated to supply suspense, surprise, and a happy ending.

It is the day after the death of King Anselmo, prisoner of Manuel, King of Granada, whose daughter Almeira has been secretly married to Alphonso, son of Anselmo, and then separated from him by shipwreck. She confesses this marriage to her confidant, mourns Anselmo, and declares that she will never yield to her father and marry Garcia, son of the premier Gonzales. King Manuel returns from battle, having slain the Moorish king, and brings the queen Zara and other prisoners, among them a valiant warrior, Osmyn — Alphonso in disguise. At the tomb of Anselmo, Osmyn-Alphonso and Almeira meet and dissolve in grief.

The king is in love with Zara and Zara with Osmyn. She offers to procure Osmyn's escape and to fly with him; but later on, discovering him with Almeira, she betrays them to the king. The king and Zara are now torn by love and jealousy. She obtains permission to have Osmyn strangled by one of her mutes, and the suspicious Gonzales assumes the costume of the mute in order to make sure of the execution. Meanwhile the king, learning of Zara's passion for Osmyn, determines to have him killed and then assume his clothing in order to confront Zara. Osmyn makes his escape; Gonzales kills the king, taking him for Osmyn; Zara, taking the body to be Osmyn's, drinks poison; Almeira is about to make the same mistake, when the soldiers enter with Osmyn at their head.

Perhaps no other single play is so representative of the various features of Restoration tragedy. It is not a tragedy at all if one insists that tragedy should be logical and psychological; but it was praised by Voltaire and Dr. Johnson and approved by the London public for over a century.

Although the years from 1660 to 1700 offer little in tragedy that has proved of permanent value, they mark the continuance of the *genre* in a full tide of popularity. Probably in no forty years since then have so many original tragedies appeared in the London theatres; certainly in no forty years since have so many Elizabethan tragedies been revived. Tragedies and tragicomedies together are in numbers almost equal to the comedies which we think of as especially distinguishing the Restoration stage. There was hardly a writer for the theatre who did not try his hand at tragedy. In spite of the rivalry of opera and comedy, it continued from Davenant to Southerne to delight the age. Its literary as well as its theatrical importance was maintained. Noble authors as well as the greatest wits, the Earl of Orrery, Granville, Dryden, and Congreve, courted the tragic muse. Tragedy written for the popular stage had, indeed, a literary eminence hardly recognized before, even in the generation preceding the Civil War. In comparison with their Elizabethan predecessors the tragedies of this time are, in fact, literary rather than popular. They draw their themes from French or English plays; they display little innovation and still less study of life; they adopt rules and regulations; they are conventional and artificial. They respond to literary traditions ; they hardly express the sentiments or ideas of their age. Some exceptions there are; but even plays like those of Banks, which gained theatrical success without literary distinction, resembled their more worthy brethren in their adherence to convention rather than nature.

In the main Restoration tragedy must be regarded as a continuation and development of Elizabethan. The influence of Beaumont and Fletcher continued in the heroic plays and their after-effects. The wane of the heroic plays brought a return to the Elizabethans, and, notably in Lee, to some of the most characteristic features of the later revenge plays. The increasing influence of Shakespeare was felt not only in the worthy emulation of " All for Love " and in the various adaptations, but

also in the debates of the critics and through the whole
warp and woof of tragedy. But what were preëminent
in many of Shakespeare's contemporaries as in Shakespeare himself, poetry, passion, and characterization,
were beyond the reach of any of the playwrights except
Dryden, Lee, and Otway at their best. The worst excesses, the most undesirable conventions of the Elizabethans, excited imitation as much as their excellences.
The Elizabethan bloom had gone to seed in unfavorable
soil. It is not strange that after the horrors, bloodshed,
and supernaturalism of Lee and Otway, and after the
gross buffoonery that spoils tragedies otherwise so noble
as "Don Sebastian," "Venice Preserved," and "The
Fatal Marriage," there should have followed in the opening years of the next century a marked reaction to the
decencies of French tragedy. In the Restoration period,
however, the French influence, though manifest in the
great vogue of the heroic plays and in a wide adoption
of French ideas of structure and propriety, won only
a partial triumph in checking and modifying the Elizabethan tradition. Its effect in supplying fresh incentives
for worthy endeavor was slight, indeed, hardly discernible
unless in the influence of Racine upon Otway. Tragedy,
then, as handed down to the eighteenth century, was
not a fixed and definite form, though measurably more
so than a century before. It was still a conglomerate of
various forms and tendencies, mingling relics of the
medieval stage with reminiscences of Shakespeare and
the manners of the court of Louis XIV. The sentimental

tragedies of Southerne and Otway, telling stories of distressed womanhood and exciting pity without any accessories of grandeur, were perhaps the most independent achievements of Restoration tragedy; the preservation of Shakespearean influence was its most important. But, in comparison with a century before, the changes in tragedy that were most noticeable and permanent were the restriction of themes, the narrowing of structure, and the conventionality and artificiality that extended to character and language as well as to themes and plots.

NOTE ON BIBLIOGRAPHY

Ward continues to supply the best history of the drama. Henceforth the standard authority for the history of the stage is Genest's *Some Account of the English Stage from the Restoration in 1660 to 1830*, 10 vols., Bath, 1832. This is an invaluable collection of facts in regard to plays and actors, superseding preceding books on the subject and supplying material for subsequent ones. Other histories of the theatre are: Chetwood's *General History of the Stage* (1749); *The Dramatic Mirror* (1808); D. E. Baker's *Biographica Dramatica* (1764, continued by Isaac Reed and Stephen Jones, 3d ed. 1812); Dibdin's *Complete History of the English Stage* (1800). Lowe's *Bibliographical Account of English Dramatic Literature* (1888) will guide in their use. More recent histories of the theatre are: P. Fitzgerald's *New History of the Stage* (1882); Lowe's new edition of Doran's *Their Majesties' Servants* (1888); and H. B. Baker's *The London Stage, 1576–1903* (1904).

Works of the Restoration period on the drama or theatre include a number of Dryden's essays, notably, *The Essay of Dramatic Poesy, The Defence of the Essay, The Defence of the Epilogue, Of Heroic Plays,* and *The Grounds of Criticism in Tragedy;* Wright's *Historia Histrionica* (1699, reprinted in Dodsley and in Cibber's *Life*); Edward Phillips's *Theatrum Poetarum* (1675); Langbaine's *Account of the English Dramatic Poets* (1691); Rymer's *Tragedies of the Last Age* (1678) and *A Short View of Tragedy* (1693); Dennis's *The Impartial Critic* (1693); and Jeremy Collier's *Short View of the Immorality and*

Profaneness of the English Stage (1698). Downes's *Roscius Anglicanus* (1708, facsimile reprint, 1886) also contains interesting information on the period. Corneille, Boileau, Saint Evremond, the Abbé D'Aubignac, and Rapin are the French critics of most influence on the drama of this period, especially Rapin, whose *Reflexions sur la poëtique* was translated by Rymer (1674). J. E. Spingarn's *Seventeenth Century Critical Essays* (now in press) will contain all the critical work of the period of importance, with a valuable discussion of its relation to French criticism.

There are collected editions of the works of most of the Restoration dramatists, but none of Settle or Banks. The Scott-Saintsbury edition is the standard for Dryden. Individual plays are to be found in many collections: *The Modern British Drama*, 5 vols. (1811); Oxberry's *New English Drama* (1812-25); Mrs. Inchbald's *Modern Theatre* (1811); Bell's *British Theatre* (1797) and supplement. *Dramatists of the Restoration*, edited by Maidment and Logan, 14 vols., Edinburgh, 1872-79, includes the plays of Crowne, Davenant, Tatham, and John Wilson. Ward and the *English Drama* (by K. L. Bates and L. B. Godfrey, *op. cit.*) direct to editions and monographs of the individual authors of this period.

J. J. Jusserand's *Shakespeare en France* (1898), Professor Lounsbury's *Shakespeare as a Dramatic Artist*, and Miss Canfield's *Corneille and Racine in England* (1905) are important for certain phases of the drama. Concerning the heroic plays there is a considerable literature; see, especially, P. Holzhausen on Dryden's heroic plays, *Englische Studien*, vols. xiii, xv, and xvi (1890-92); L. N. Chase, *The English Heroic Play* (1903); J. W. Tupper, *The Relation of the Heroic Play to Beaumont and Fletcher*, Mod. Lang. Assn. Publ. 1905. C. G. Child, *The Rise of the Heroic Play*, Mod. Lang. Notes, 1904. Alex. Beljame's *Le Public et les Hommes de Lettres en Angleterre au xviiie siècle* (1881) deals fully with Dryden and has an elaborate bibliography.

CHAPTER IX

THE EIGHTEENTH CENTURY

N tragedy the division between the seventeenth and eighteenth centuries is less marked than that which distinguishes in general the literatures of the Restoration and the Augustan eras. Yet by 1700 most of the leading dramatists of the preceding generation had ceased to write for the stage; and the death of Dryden marked the end of the old, as the beginning of the reign of Anne, with its important changes in politics, society, and literature, marked the beginning of a new development in tragedy. The attack of Jeremy Collier (1698) was also an important landmark in the history of the drama, assisting in a notable change from the preceding licentiousness and toward a moralized and sentimentalized comedy. A similar change in tragedy was its most apparent departure from Restoration models. Chastened language and a stricter moral censorship of both subjects and sentiments reflected that refinement of which the age of Addison and Pope was wont to boast.

The theatrical conditions governing the reign of Queen Anne were not very different from those of the Restoration. There was a general complaint, as there has been ever since, that operas and spectacles were crowding the serious drama out of favor, but there was still abundant opportunity to see many of the best plays of the Elizabethan and Restoration periods. Of tragedies, we find in a single season, 1703–04, "Hamlet," "Othello," "Julius Cæsar," and alterations of "Macbeth," "Lear," "Richard III," "Timon," and "Titus Andronicus," Shirley's "Traitor," and Beaumont and Fletcher's "Maid's Tragedy," "Valentinian," and "A King and No King," "The Loyal Subject," and other of their tragicomedies. "Henry VIII," "Rollo," "Bonduca," and "Philaster" were performed within the next few years. Of Restoration tragedies, Banks's "Unhappy Favorite" and Lee's "Rival Queens" were perhaps the most popular, and other plays of Banks, Lee, Otway, Dryden, Congreve, and Southerne were acted yearly. A number of the heroic plays also still kept the stage, including Howard's "Indian Queen," Dryden's "Conquest of Granada," "Indian Emperor," and "Aureng Zebe." Throughout the century both the London and the provincial theatres presented each year a large number of old plays, including many of these already mentioned. The Elizabethan tragedies, except Shakespeare's, and the heroic plays gradually disappeared from the regular repertoire, but Shakespeare's tragedies steadily gained in popularity, and "The Unhappy Favorite" (rewritten as "The Earl of Essex"), "The Orphan," "Venice Preserved," "Oronooko," "The Fatal Marriage" (altered as "Isabella"), "All for Love," and "The Mourning Bride" maintained their places into the nineteenth century. Tragedy thus had its permanent representatives in this group of stock plays, to which newcomers gained admission only by marked success on the stage.

To these stock plays no writer of the eighteenth century made more notable additions than Nicholas Rowe, the first editor of Shakespeare, whose work began the century, borrowed much from his predecessors, and yet introduced most of the changes which distinguish the eighteenth century type of tragedy from that of the Restoration or Elizabethan period. His first play was followed by four other tragedies by 1707, and, after an interval of seven years, by " Jane Shore " (1714) and "Lady Jane Grey" (1715). Of the first five, three are of little interest except as representing common variations of the prevailing type. They all relate love stories of rivalry and intrigue among heroic personages, and all observe the French proprieties in structure. " The Ambitious Stepmother," like so many predecessors and successors, places the scene in an oriental court; " Ulysses " more daringly invades Homeric territory; and " The Royal Convert" turns to early English history, a field which literary patriotism was appropriating for tragedy.

In "Tamerlane" (1702), love and intrigue play subordinate parts to the political and moral interest which the author endeavored to centre upon his protagonist. Tamerlane, who, we are told, was patterned on William III, is an extremely pious pagan, who overtops conquest with mercy and adorns every occasion with a moralizing discourse. Had he ever encountered his Marlowean namesake, he would have shed the pitying tear. In general, the structure is on the French plan, but the large number of characters and the considerable amount of action recall Elizabethan models. The verse, too, with its feminine endings, occasionally reminds one of Fletcher, and the figures of speech are feebly patterned on Shakespeare, while the ravings of Bajazet are worthy of Nat Lee. The play, long acted every November fifth, seems to have owed its great success to its high moral tone and its patriotic eloquence. It set the key for many similarly patriotic tunes.

"The Fair Penitent" (1703) links itself with the two later " She-tragedies," to borrow a term from one of their epilogues. Its prologue proclaims an innovation from the usual tragic themes of monarchs' cares and lost royalty, because —

> " We ne'er can pity what we ne'er can share
> .   .   .   .
> Therefore an humbler Theme our Author chose,
> A melancholy Tale of Private Woes."

This was the play of which Dr. Johnson said that " scarcely any work of any poet is at once so interesting by the fable and so delightful by the language." The domestic theme, the female protagonist, and the insistent appeal to pity were all already familiar in the plays of Otway and Southerne. Rowe gave these a larger popularity; and from his Lothario and Calista Richardson received suggestions for Lovelace and Clarissa.

"The Fair Penitent" is also interesting as an adaptation of an Elizabethan play. Rowe borrowed the plot and some hints in the characterization from "The Fatal Dowry" of Massinger and Field, but he refashioned the scenes and rewrote the verse in accord with current modes. While "The Fatal Dowry" is by no means one of the best of Elizabethan tragedies, a comparison of it with Rowe's version of the story emphasizes the losses which tragedy was suffering as it moved farther and farther from its old traditions.[1] "The Fair Penitent" reduces the host of *dramatis personae* to eight, the fair penitent, her husband, his rival, his sister, and three friends or confidants, and confines the action to one place and something over twenty-four hours. Much of the action of the early play is omitted or reduced to narrative, including all the opening scenes of the funeral of the husband's father and the origin of his friendship with the father of the heroine. The various attempts of the faithful friend to mend matters are also restricted, and Massinger's usual trial scene omitted. The result of these structural changes is a loss of verisimilitude. The old play had something of the illusion of a true history; in "The Fair Penitent" the action, though narrowed, is still far too much for the time supposed, and improbabilities are solved by well-worn theatrical devices. The guilt is discovered by means of a lost letter and an over-

---

[1] For comparisons of the two plays, see Sir Walter Scott's "Essay on the Drama," Cumberland's *Observer*, Nos. 77, 78, 79; and Gifford's introduction to his edition of Massinger.

heard conversation, and throughout literary and moral
proprieties lead to a reduction of action and an increase
of talk. This is well illustrated in the scenes in which
the husband confronts the guilty wife. In "The Fair
Penitent," the wife and Lothario are having a final meeting, or declamation contest, on the day after the wedding.
She upbraids him and incidentally relates the story of
her seduction; the husband overhears. In "The Fatal
Dowry," the husband comes unexpectedly to the house
of Aymer where the lovers have an assignation. Aymer
is attempting to divert him with music, when a laugh
is heard within, — more music, and the lady's laugh
again. The husband rushes from the stage and returns
driving in the lovers. Further, the restricted action of
Rowe's play causes a conventionalizing of the characters.
The wife and her lover are shallow persons in Massinger's play, but they have some plausibility. In Rowe,
he becomes the avenging rival; she, an impossible de-
claimer, now the evil woman of the heroic plays, now the
lachrymose moralizer. The moralizing, emphatic in all
of Rowe's plays, also adds to the general artificiality.
Calista dies after most voluble repentance, and her husband matches her "groan for groan and tear for tear."

If the Elizabethan play is confused, long spun out,
and not especially edifying, it is yet occasionally intense
in its emotional effect and maintains some verisimilitude
of life and character. Rowe's artificially ingenious and
morally mellifluous play, if edifying, is never thrilling.
Its conventional persons and scenes do not depict life

by action; they declaim sentimentally a story that ends in a sermon. In its conventionalization and moralization Rowe illustrates the main tendencies of the drama, tendencies derived largely from the French, but it must not be thought that either his play or the majority in the century altogether forsake English models for French. Rowe's declamations and laments, immeasurably inferior in all respects, differ essentially from Racine's in that they fail to disclose psychological moments and emotional crises. They also differ from Racine in their retention of spectacle, incident, and business in accord with English tradition. Like other of his contemporaries and successors, Rowe was prone to copy the Elizabethans at their worst. The most Elizabethan thing in his play, though not found in "The Fatal Dowry," is the setting for the long famous fifth act. "The Scene is a Room hung with Black; on one side, Lothario's body on a Bier; on the other, a Table with a Scull and other Bones, a Book, and a Lamp on it. Calista is discovered on a Couch in Black, her Hair hanging loose and disordered: After Musick and a Song, she rises and comes forward" — and begins her midnight soliloquy. Perhaps, as Dr. Ward surmises, this business went far to give the act its great effectiveness.

Of the two later "She-tragedies," "Lady Jane Grey" presents the usual love intrigue (fomented here by the discarded rival), the female protagonist, and much Protestant and Whig patriotism, but nothing not paralleled in Rowe's other plays. "Jane Shore" (1714), one of the most popular plays of the century, represents another treatment of "the fair penitent," this time not only in a story used in the Elizabethan drama, but in a style avowedly in imitation of Shakespeare's.

Gloster, who is closely modeled on Shakespeare's Richard III, plays an important part, usually in consultation with his two confidants, Catesby and Radcliffe. Hastings, suspected by Gloster of loyalty to the child prince, becomes enamored of Jane Shore, the former mistress of Edward IV. She, now dedicated to penitence, resists his persuasions, in which she is encouraged by Dumont (her husband in disguise) and his confidant Bellmour. When Hastings resorts to force, Dumont comes to the rescue and disarms him. Alicia, deserted by Hastings, is the jealous and vengeful woman, well known in tragedy; and she denounces Hastings and Jane Shore in a letter which she substitutes for the petition for the release of Dumont, imprisoned through Hastings, that Jane Shore presents to Gloster. Gloster, upon testing Hastings and Jane Shore, is met by frank protestations from both of their loyalty to the prince. Hastings is condemned to death, but has time for a final interview with Alicia, and the exchange of mutual upbraidings, confessions, and forgiveness. Jane Shore is condemned to public penance. She has a parting interview with Alicia, who has gone mad, and then encounters Dumont, who, after a long discussion with his confidant, has decided to reveal himself and forgive his wife. She dies and he is led away to prison.

> "Let those who view this sad Example, know
> What Fate attends the broken Marriage Vow;
> And teach their Children in succeeding Times,
> No common Vengeance waits upon their Crimes,
> When such severe Repentance could not save
> From Want, from Shame, and an untimely Grave."

The play is undoubtedly Rowe's masterpiece, the closing scenes having a natural pathos that he rarely attains elsewhere. The only Shakespearean imitation now discernible is in the character of Gloster, though Rowe may have endeavored in his female characters to supply the naturalness and greatness of emotions which he recognized as characteristic of Shakespeare's men, but curiously thought lacking in his women. Here and elsewhere in language and metaphors Rowe reverts at times to the Elizabethans, as also in the admission of much action and spectacle, in pale horrors, and in the plots of his two best known plays. In the general conception and structure of his plays he follows Otway. Taken as a whole, however, his plays, without comedy, with much heroic love, with few persons, and a restricted action, come nearer to French models than those of any preceding writer of large reputation. Sentimentalized, moralized, conventionalized as the plays are, Rowe may be said to have made a novel departure in tragedy, though one accomplished a century before by Heywood's "A Woman Killed with Kindness." Penitence is the sole theme of his two famous plays, and the moral lesson is constantly enforced. The protagonist is a repentant sinner for whom we feel pity because of her punishment, which we nevertheless regard as just.

Rowe's plays, tame as they are, seem to have been too exciting and too rude for the coterie of wits who set the standards of criticism; and before the appearance of "Jane Shore" an effort was made under the direction of Addison toward still greater refinement and closer accord with French rules. Smith's "Phædra and Hippolitus" (1706), an adaptation of Racine, failed on the stage in spite of Addison's approval, but it was later often revived, and it prepared the way for the great success of Ambrose Philips's "Distrest Mother" (1712), a translation of the "Andromaque." This success, promoted by the zealous support of Mr. Spectator and Sir Roger de Coverley, was due in large measure to the story, sentimental and moral in accord with the taste of the day.[1] In these respects "The Distrest Mother" had the advantage of "Phædra," though both illustrate the tendency, growing since Lee and Otway, of making the heroine the protagonist. At all events, the success of Philips's translation was not only great for the moment, but long continued. It remained a popular stock play through the century, gave a favorite part to Mrs. Siddons, and introduced Macready to a London audience.

In the flush of Philips's first success, Addison was emboldened to present his long withheld "Cato" upon the stage. The political circumstances made the first night one of the most memorable in the history of the theatre, and gave the play what was then the enormous initial run of a month. Voltaire praised; and, with the exception of the doughty Dennis, English critics seemed agreed that here at last was an English tragedy in full accord with classical precedents and the rules of reason. The play continued a favorite on the stage into the nine-

[1] See *Corneille and Racine in England.* Dorothea Canfield. New York, 1904.

teenth century, and even after the retirement of Kemble, who found in Cato one of his great parts. It would be vain to search for dramatic merits to account for this great success. The play combines love intrigues, as absurd as those usual in contemporary plays, with lucid declamation and aphoristic moralizing. Aphorism and declamation have, indeed, rarely been absent from the tragedy of any period or nation, but they were especially delightful to the taste of the Augustan era. Addison was only continuing the success of Rowe's "Tamerlane," reducing its rant to a more reasonable pattern. The reforming classicists, like the theatre-pleasing Rowe, hit on the two themes which pleased the public, the distressed female and the patriotic moralizer.

The success of "The Distrest Mother" and "Cato" was the beginning of the long triumph of French influence over English tragedy, yet the victory was never more than half won. There was no capitulation, and the battle continued through the century both among the critics and on the stage. Rowe's plays maintained at least a feeble English tradition, and Shakespeare's won increasing admiration. If critical opinion was for a time warm in support of French classicism, the theatre still clung to Elizabethan practices. Later, when imitations of the French models had established themselves in some degree upon the stage, criticism turned to condemnation of the unities and renewed its laudations of Shakespeare. The lines of battle were often obscured. Between Rowe's refinements of Elizabethan plays and

Addison's imitation of the French there is little difference; and later, in spite of the din of critical essays and prefaces, the representatives of " Shakespeare's school" and of " correct taste " have a great similarity.

The Elizabethan tradition was directly represented by Elizabethan imitations and revivals, by many new plays that reverted in one way or another to the early methods, by the conservatism of actors and playgoers, and by the tragedies of Shakespeare. As Shakespeare grew in the appreciation of readers and critics, there was a tendency toward the restoration of a real Shakespearean text to the stage. There were, to be sure, innumerable new alterations and adaptations, but these were mostly of little importance on the stage. They dealt with the minor plays, as " Cymbeline," " Coriolanus," or " Timon;" or they were the essays of admiring amateurs with a bent for restringing the rough diamonds of the original, or of playwrights trying to meet the theatrical demands of the moment. Cibber's " Richard III " and Tate's " Lear " held the stage well into the next century, but " Julius Cæsar," " Hamlet " (except for Garrick's alteration, 1772–80), and " Othello " admitted no alterations. After 1744 Shakespeare's " Macbeth " took the place of Davenant's, and " Romeo and Juliet " of Otway's " Caius Marius." " Coriolanus," variously revised, altered, and finally combined with Thomson's play of the same name, was toward the end of the century given a great vogue by Kemble; and, indeed, the only one of the tragedies neglected during

the century was "Antony and Cleopatra." [1] Dryden's
"All for Love" had usurped its place. As the critical
tone toward Shakespeare grew more admiring and less
tainted by condescension, so the attitude of actors and
audiences grew in heartiness of appreciation. The revival of the romantic comedies marked an important
change of taste, though not calling for more than mention here. Year after year his comedies, histories, and
tragedies were acted oftener and to larger audiences,
and gave opportunity for the best efforts of a long series
of great actors and actresses. Garrick's revivals and triumphs were followed by those of Mrs. Siddons and
Kemble. Now one play became a favorite, now another,
under the influence of a great impersonation; but few
were neglected, and over the theatre Shakespeare's
domination was unquestioned.

Except for Shakespeare the direct influence of the
Elizabethans was small. A few of the tragedies were
acted intermittently in the first half of the century, and
a few comedies kept their places in the stock list much
longer. Revivals, though not infrequent, were rarely
permanent. Revampings sometimes resulted in an
almost unconditional surrender to the French. Theo-
bald in the first half of the century attempted a reversion
to the Elizabethans without much success, and later a
revival of interest in Massinger succeeded in restoring
only his two comedies to the theatre. As sources of

---

[1] Its only appearance on the stage recorded by Genest was in Capell's
adaptation, acted six times by Garrick in 1759.

incentive for those writers who shunned French modes,
Otway, Southerne, and Rowe took the places of the
Elizabethans other than Shakespeare. The English
tradition which these names represent had, as we have
seen, already been much subject to French influence,
though protected by the adherence of the theatre to old
custom. Consequently, while the majority of eighteenth
century tragedies retain some Elizabethan practices,
there is not one of importance that is a thoroughgoing
representative of the old methods and technic.

French influence, on the contrary, had many representatives among the new plays. The success of "The
Distrest Mother" led to a number of translations. In the
first quarter of the century there were ten of Racine's
plays and four of Corneille's; and of these fourteen,
eight were acted, and several with success. Later on,
Whitehead's "Roman Father" (1750), an adaptation
of Corneille's "Horace," won a place in the stock list.
But the leading factor in the French influence on English
tragedy during the century was Voltaire. The long
critical debate which he waged in behalf of the rules
and against the barbarities of Shakespeare has its importance in English as well as French literary history. But
while the English critics grew more and more eager as the
century advanced to uphold the glory of Shakespeare and
to denounce an atheist who denied this, or to proclaim
their freedom from the narrowing rules which were
French, yet the triumphs of Voltaire's plays upon the
English stage continued unabated. Adaptations of no less

than nine of his tragedies had appeared on the London
stage before the English translation of his full works
in 1779–80, and there were manifold borrowings from
him in many other plays.[1] A number of the translations,
Hill's "Zara" and "Merope," Miller's "Mahomet,"
and Murphy's "Orphan of China," made notable successes. From the production of "Brutus" to that of
"Semiramis" in 1776 Voltaire may be said to have been
the most popular and influential of the writers of tragedy
for the English theatre.[2]

The translations of these tragedies, however, indicate
the influence of English traditions. The long speeches
are shortened, the dialogue is broken and enlivened,
the minor proprieties disregarded, the sentiments and
morals Anglicized, and some business and bloodshed introduced on the stage. In Hill's "Merope," for example,
the great scene where Merope strives to kill the murderer
of her long-lost son and discovers the supposed murderer to be her son himself, loses all its simplicity as well
as its poetry. It is ornamented by Hill with processions,
virgins in white, music, a sacrificial song, and many
starts and strains. Where on the French stage Egisthe

[1] *Brutus* (1734), *Zara* (1736), *Alzira* (1736), *Mahomet* (1744), *Merope*
(1749), *Orphan of China* (1759), *Orestes* (1769), *Almida* (1771) (from
Tancrède), *Semiramis* (1776). See, also, Hoole's *Cyrus* (1768), Crad-
ock's *Zobeide* (1771), Murphy's *Alzuma* (1773), and Brooke's *Imposter*
(1778), not acted.

[2] Professor Lounsbury seems mistaken in finding a "sudden cessation of interest in Voltaire" after 1750. *Shakespere and Voltaire*, pp.
304, 305. He neglects the later popularity of *The Orphan of China* and
the continued popularity of plays earlier translated.

decorously withdraws behind the scenes as' his mother approaches with the dagger, on the English stage everything was in full sight. If some of the other translations are less altered, the imitations and unavowed adaptations are much more so. Hoole's "Cyrus" (1768), a popular play, is obviously based on "Merope," but adds a much complicated plot, a mad woman, a love intrigue between the long-lost son and the daughter of the old tutor, and a returning husband for Mandane (Merope). The great success of Voltaire in England did not, in fact, produce any very marked change in the course of tragedy. He represents the continuance of French influence but established no departures of note from the general type established in the English theatres by 1725. Virtually no English tragedies in the eighteenth century introduced comedy; few reveled in horrors and bloodshed, the majority observed the unities, nearly all had few persons, a restricted action, and themes and situations confined to slight variations of a stereotyped love story; and nearly all had regard for poetic justice. The differences between French and English tragedy were largely those which adapters of Voltaire eliminated when they made over his plays for the London theatres and gave them a more broken dialogue and more stage action, and perhaps a mad woman or a villain. Moreover, the amelioration of the differences between the two theatres was not all on one side, as is shown by Voltaire's own imitations of Shakespeare and his introduction of ghosts and horrors, and by the growing interest

in France in Shakespeare and other English dramatists.[1]
Voltaire, with his ingenious plots and telling crises, was
nearer than Racine to the English tradition, and he
wrote at a time when the differences between the two
national theatres were minimized to a degree that made
intercommunication easy. His talents gave him an easy
superiority over any English writer of tragedies after
the classical formulas.

In the course of the century there were also a considerable number of plays that turned from French to
Greek models. While these cannot be regarded as wholly
representative of a reaction from a pseudo to a truer
classicism, they certainly offered hardly more resemblance to Voltaire than to Shakespeare. The Greek
influence was, however, variously manifested. Adaptations of Euripides were numerous, half a dozen of which
were presented at the theatres. In addition, a number
of original plays were written, following the Greek form.
Most famous of these were two by Gray's friend Mason,
"Elfrida" and "Caractacus." The latter, while stilted
and academic, compares favorably in point of literary

---

[1] *Le théâtre anglais* (1746–49) of Pierre de La Place contained in
its 8 vols. synopses and partial translations of the following plays:
*Othello, 3 Henry VI, Richard III, Hamlet, Macbeth, Cymbeline, Julius
Cæsar, Antony and Cleopatra, Timon of Athens, Merry Wives of Windsor, The Maid's Tragedy, Catiline, The Fair Penitent, Venice Preserved, Aureng Zebe, The Mourning Bride, Tamerlane, Siege of Damascus* (by Hughes, 1720), *Busiris, Love for Love, The Innocent
Adultery, Cato, The Funeral* (Steele, 1702). This list, in which it will
be noticed tragedy greatly predominates, represents fairly the English
taste of the time.

excellence with most tragedies of the century, and not altogether unworthily takes its place in a series that includes "Samson Agonistes" and "Prometheus Unbound." "Read Shakespeare," wrote Lyttleton to Aaron Hill, "but study Racine and Sophocles." But the classicists were occupied in the main with neither poet, but in discussing various minor questions of dramatic propriety: Should any violence or bloodshed be permitted? Should rhyme tags end the scenes? Should the epilogue be comic or serious? Should figures of speech be allowed? Should long speeches be shortened for presentation? Classicism in both England and France was not greatly imitative of either Sophocles or Racine, but mainly insistent on immaterialities.

If we attempt to follow the diminishing differences between English and French standards in the work of individual authors, Young's "Busiris" (1719) and "Revenge" (1721) are the most important of those tragedies in the first quarter of the century which cling to some of the characteristics of the early English drama, while his "Brothers," written at about the same time but not acted until 1753, is based upon Thomas Corneille's "Persée et Demetrius." In "Busiris" there is no villain, but tyranny, conspiracy, and a passionate revenging queen play their usual parts. There is an attempt, both in incidents and expression, at Elizabethan force and horror; the main action deals with a rape, and five of the principal persons are killed upon the stage. "The Revenge" is still more Elizabethan, being a palpable imitation of "Othello." The prologue declares that the proper field for tragedy is not villany but "the tumults of a Godlike mind," yet the villain, the Moor Zanga, is the chief character and was acted by Garrick, Kemble, and Kean. The villain's part, it is interesting to note, affords the most striking difference between this popular play and the even more popular "Zara." In both, the heroine, pure and innocent, is killed by the husband, Othello-like in both magnanimity and jealousy; but in Voltaire the jealousy is occasioned by the heroine's meetings with her brother, a captive Christian, in Young by the busy and ponderous intrigues of a Moorish Iago.

In opposition to Young, Thomson represents the vogue of classicism both in literary circles and in the theatres. His early tragedies, "Sophonisba" (1730), "Agammemnon" (1738), and "Edward and Eleonora," prohibited by the censor because of its attacks upon Walpole, won little favor except in the circle of wits who attempted to dictate the national taste in letters and among the opponents of Walpole. The first was dedicated to the Queen and the two later to the Princess of Wales, and "Tancred and Sigismunda" (1743) to Frederick, Prince of Wales, the patron of the drama and the hope of the Tories. This play, the presentation of which was fathered and superintended by Lyttleton and Pitt, achieved a large popular success; and portions of "Coriolanus," acted after the author's death in 1749, were combined with Shakespeare's tragedy in versions by Thomas Sheridan and Kemble, and supplied the latter with his greatest part. All Thomson's plays endeavor to retell stories often used in tragedy, in strict accord with the rules, with absolute propriety of diction, some reference to political events, and a due inculcation of moral sentiments. In the language of one of their admirers, they were intended to be "reasonable entertainments becoming virtue itself to behold with tears of approbation."[1] "Sophonisba" is sternly heroic in its subordination of love to patriotic hate of Rome in the character of its heroine, and sternly classic in the simplicity of its plot and the heaviness of its inflated rhetoric. "Agammemnon," also a "She-tragedy," is designed after the school of Racine rather than of Corneille; and its wavering, inconsistent Clytemnestra, who closes the play with a torrent of remorse and a faint, its Melisander saved from a desert island, and its courtly love-sick Egisthus are queer denizens of the house of Atreus. "Edward and Eleanor," telling of the queen who sucked poison from her husband's wound, and of the sultan who, suspected of the attempted murder, bore a truly miraculous antidote to the Christian camp, owes allegiance to Voltaire. Its emotional changes and elaborate intrigue bring it also more closely in accord with the prevailing English type. "Tancred and Sigismunda," based on the story as told in "Gil Blas,"[2] makes the lover a claimant to the throne and the intervention of the father due to reasons of state. The plot is developed with more skill

---

[1] Dr. Rundle, Letters, quoted by Morel, *James Thomson*, p. 82.
[2] *Gil Blas*, Book 4, "Le Mariage de vengeance."

than is usual in Thomson, and the rival lovers, the marriage in revenge, the midnight interview, the duel, and the murder of the heroine are quite in conformity to the prevailing model. "Coriolanus," the subject of many French tragedies and of Shakespearean alterations by Tate and Dennis, illustrates the inferiority of the classic scheme to the Elizabethan in the presentation of history. The action, beginning with the arrival of Coriolanus as a suppliant for Tullus's hospitality, crowds the remaining events and the changes in the two rivals within the impossible confines of the unities of time and place. Coriolanus himself exemplifies the effort toward "Nature," that is, typicality and reasonableness, in pseudo-classical characterization. He expresses the sentiments and manners approved by the eighteenth century, and, even when pride and revenge most fire his passion, is a very tame lion. The moral lessons, somewhat clouded in Shakespeare, are distinctly enunciated and finally summed up by Galesus:—

> "This man was once the glory of his age,
>   Disinterested, just, with every virtue
>   Of civil life adorn'd, in arms unequall'd.
>   His only blot was this; that, much provok'd,
>   He rais'd his vengeful arm against his country," etc. (v. 4).

In Thomson's other plays the inflated declamation occasionally gives way to a bit of description that recalls "The Seasons," but in "Coriolanus" he follows the promise of the Prologue to "Tancred" with unerring fidelity:—

"Your taste rejects the glittering false sublime,
To sigh in metaphor, and die in rhyme.
High *rant* is tumbled from his gallery throne;
Description, dreams, — nay, similes are gone."

He was obviously seeking what he called Shakespeare's "simple, plain sublime," and his declamations occasionally reach a sententious lucidity worthy of Addison, but the pseudo-classic diction freezes every emotion with its "transports," "charms," and "nuptial loves." This is Volumnia's appeal to Coriolanus, her husband in Thomson's play:—

"Ah Coriolanus!
Is then this hand, this hand to be devoted,
The pledge of nuptial love, that has so long
Protected, bless'd, and shelter'd us with kindness,
Now lifted up against us? Yet I love it,
And, with submissive veneration, bow
Beneath th' affliction which it heaps upon us.
But O! what nobler transports would it give thee!
What joy beyond expression! couldst thou once
Surmount the furious storm of fierce revenge,
And yield ye to the charms of love and mercy.
Oh make the glorious trial!" (v. 1).

Thomson's plays were not esteemed even by his master Voltaire as contributing greatly to that perfection of art possibly attainable by a "due mixture of the French taste and English energy." For, though "wisely intricated and elegantly writ," Voltaire found him, like Addison, lacking in warmth, an "iced genius." [1] Frigid to his contemporaries, the tragedies were long since

---

[1] For various references to Thomson in Voltaire's Letters, see Morel, *op. cit.* pp. 192–194; and a letter on the French translation of *Tancred and Sigismunda*, p. 153.

decently interred. They constitute, nevertheless, the most considerable attempt made by any author of the eighteenth century to conserve the classic theory of tragedy, and they recall nearly every variety of pseudo-classic endeavor. Of classicism it might be said, as of Thomson, that it attempted classic and early English history, that it found in partisan patriotism its favorite theme for rhetoric, that its French rules and taste usually pleased readers better than spectators, but that when it took one of Shakespeare's tragedies as the basis for an infusion of classical theory, or when it was tempered with a love story and a lively action, it triumphed in the theatre.

Thomson's friends, Mallet and the versatile and indefatigable Aaron Hill, joined him in his efforts to redeem the tragic muse. Hill's efforts, if no more successful than Thomson's and much less consistent, are at least more amusing. His general theory seems to have been not unlike that which actually controlled theatrical practice; he purposed a combination of French rules with romantic incident, theatrical bustle, and his own inimitable style. His "Fatal Vision, or Fall of Siam" (1716), he boasted, had "a deeper and more surprising plot than any play which has been published, that I know of, in the English tongue; and yet is written in strict observance of the dramatic rules" and affords "room for topical reflections, large description, love, war, show, and passion," and also "a very high regard to decoration." The play is noticeable for its tangle of trite dramatic motives.

The emperor's vision is of a son who shall kill him and usurp the throne. The two elder sons are in love with the Princess of Siam. Sworn by her to kill their father, and condemned by him for a murder they did not commit, they die fighting in his behalf. The third son kills the emperor, marries the princess, and ascends the throne. In his rapid advance he is aided by the banished empress, who has returned to court and attained high power, disguised as the favorite eunuch.

Hill adapted three of Voltaire's plays, " Zara," " Alzira," and " Merope." To the first he wrote some comic choruses intended to be sung between the acts, and to the third he prefixed his revised and final opinion of Voltaire and French tragedy : —

" Our unpolished English stage (as he assumes the liberty of calling it) has entertained a nobler taste of dignify'd simplicity, than to deprive dramatic poetry of all that animates its passions; in pursuit of a *cold, starv'd, tame abstinence*, which, from an affectation to shun *figure*, sinks to *flatness :* an *elaborate escape* from *energy* into a groveling, wearisome, bald, barren, unalarming *chilness* of expression, that *emasculates* the mind, instead of *moving it.*"

"Athelwold" (1731), a revision of his early "Elfrid," is colorlessly conventional; "The Roman Revenge" (1753) is an alteration of "Julius Cæsar"; "The Insolvent" (1758) is a rewriting of "The Fatal Dowry," making the heroine an innocent object of jealousy. Most Aaronic of all is "Henry V" (1723). Here he gives up French unities and technic, and introduces many characters, shifting scenes, a bit of comedy, and the "genius of England," who sings a song. His greatest addition to Shakespeare is his Harriet, who starts out

like one of the evil queens in the heroic tragedies. When
abandoned by Henry, she is still jealous and revengeful;
next she appears disguised as a page in the French camp,
and, Viola-like, relates a story of a love-lorn sister;
then recaptured by Henry, she storms and melts; but
the Jane Shore mood is transient, and, like a tragedy
queen again, she stabs herself. A man who could write
a comic duet for Voltaire's "Zaïre" and could supply
Prince Hal with a paramour whose grandmothers were
Viola and the Indian Queen, ought not to be wholly
forgotten.

Hill's career may remind us both of the din of the
critics over Voltaire and Shakespeare, and also of the
virtual compromise and amalgamation that had taken
place on the stage between French and English traditions. English tragedy, after a long national development,
had become materially modified by French influence
and had assumed a fixed and restricted form. This
type, recognizable early in the century, continues to
prevail nearly to the end. The century had little power
of innovation, little that can be called a development
in the history of tragedy. The pendulum swings now
toward French, now toward Elizabethan models, but
its oscillations are slight and regulated. The plays thus
far considered offer unimportant variations from the
type, and plays after the middle of the century vary still
less. Home's famous "Douglas" (1757), that thrilled
every heart and in the opinion of the judicious redeemed
the stage anew from barbarism, fails now to distinguish

itself from its fellows, unless by its touches of melancholy, medievalism, and nature, that hint of romanticism. Here, as so often, a much suffering woman is beset by villany and jealousy. Home's other tragedies and those of Glover, Hoole, Brown, Murphy, and Cumberland offer even less of novelty, except that toward the end of the century refinement in sentiments and morals becomes increasingly attenuated. Miss Hannah More best represents this feminization of the type. Her "Percy" (1777), a very successful play, is devoted to the sentiment: —

> "Will it content me that her person's pure?
> No, if her alien heart doats on another,
> She is unchaste."

"The Fatal Falsehood" (1779) presents in a domestic guise the usual plot of rivals in love and an intriguing villain, with the addition of a love-sick lady who runs mad. "The curtain falls to soft music." The century has one marked innovation in the realistic plays of Lillo and Moore, and after 1780 there are signs of the romanticism stirring elsewhere in literature; but in the main the new tragedies are hopelessly commonplace representatives of an extremely conventionalized form.

Yet tragedy was by no means neglected in literature or on the stage. Several hundred tragedies were published during the century and many of them went through several editions. Three or four were brought out every year in the theatres, and many of these maintained themselves for a time as stock plays. Most men of letters essayed tragedy, — Addison, Johnson, Young, Thomson, Gay, the laureates Cibber, Rowe, Whitehead, Pye, and a host of minor celebrities. Besides the tragedies acted, there were almost as many not acted but printed. Closet dramas, common in the Elizabethan period, grew more numerous after the Restoration. Whether the writer scorned or was scorned by the manager, an appeal to the reading public was always easy and apparently sometimes profitable. Tragedies were bought and read; a popular play might start with an edition of five thousand and run through a number of editions. Even after the novel had supplanted the drama among readers, there was no diminution of printed plays. The non-acted plays, however, offer nothing of importance for the history of the drama. The majority are unactable; others follow the usual formulas; a few Greek plays, alterations of Shakespeare, and sacred dramas have some interest as curiosities. The increase in the number of these plays does indicate a growing separation between the drama and the theatre. Plays were no longer written by a set of dramatists who made a profession; they were written by any one who had literary pretensions. Only a few new plays were required; the supply greatly exceeded the demand. The theatrical monopoly maintained by the two patented theatres offered no great encouragement to dramatists, and the number who wrote without any acquaintance or knowledge of the stage increased. Literary fame rather than success in the theatre was perhaps the greater incentive in the case of tragedy. Whatever the incentive, individual ambition resulted in no individuality of expression. The popular ballad of tradition is scarcely less expressive of personality than the average eighteenth century tragedy. Even the plays of temporary importance have no flavor of their own.[1]

The features of this type have often been mentioned in connection with particular plays, but it may be convenient to collect them in a composite picture. In structure and technic French models are mainly followed. Very long speeches, indeed, are rare, bloodshed and violence are permitted on the stage, and there is a good deal of incident; but bloodshed and horrors after the Elizabethan style no longer appear. Comedy also has disappeared, and is tabooed even in adaptations of Shakespeare or of Restoration plays. Comedy is reserved for the farce which is always performed after a tragedy. Each tragedy concerns itself with a single plot, involving only from six to ten persons, and observing the unities, even after Johnson's salutary condemnation of them. There are few changes of scene, ordinarily none within an act. With the disappearance of other medieval characteristics there has also departed the

[1] The following list includes all eighteenth century tragedies, not mentioned in the text, that achieved any considerable popularity. These all became stock plays, and most were acted in the nineteenth century. Hughes, *Siege of Damascus* (1720); Fenton, *Mariamne* (1723); Jones, *Earl of Essex* (1753), which superseded Banks's play as a stage favorite; Brown, *Barbarossa* (1754); Francklin, *Earl of Warwick* (1766); Hartson, *Countess of Salisbury* (1767); Murphy, *Zenobia* (1768), and *The Grecian Daughter* (1772), which gave a famous part, Euphrasia, to Mrs. Siddons and later to Miss Fannie Kemble.

medieval freedom in respect to the suitability of an action
for the stage. The range of incidents possible for presentation is very limited; exposition is largely by narrative; supernatural elements, common in Lee, are
unusual; the ghost at last rests in peace. Madness,
however, is still retained, especially in the case of the
long-suffering heroine. Battles, armies, stage spectacles
of all kinds, are restricted, though the scenes may be
elaborate, and processions, sacrifices, even music and
songs are permissible. The first essential for the action
is a love story, the second some kind of historical setting.
The fatal or hazardous loves of princes and queens are
the themes; Eastern, classic, or early English courts are
the scenes.

The love story itself often keeps to the form customary
in the heroic plays. Two rivals in love, two heroines,
major and minor, a tyrant, an intriguing minister, and
the accompanying confidants appear again and again to
assist in similar stories of jealousy, ambition, and villany.
The old Elizabethan motives continue, as "Rape" and
"The Fate of Villany," the titles of two plays acted in
1729–30, may witness, but usually they are refined and
tamed. Incest and rape are averted; the tyrant in love
with the heroine only threatens; the villain who pursues
casts suspicion on her virtue but abstains from violence;
the two brothers, or the son and the father, in love with
the same lady sometimes find renunciation possible.
Unjustified jealousy is perhaps the leading motive, and
there are many feeble imitations of "Othello." A secret

marriage, a long-lost son, and marriages, either for revenge or in order to save a lover, are common elements in the plot. Hero and heroine are examples of virtue. Their difficulties or ruin are sometimes due to one fatal error duly emphasized, or they may be due wholly to the machinations of the villain. In the latter case, poetic justice is usually regarded and the good are saved.

The villain is the most constant reminder of Elizabethan tragedy. He has all the traits of the stage Machiavellis of Marlowe and Kyd, and sometimes imitates Iago. He is wholly black at heart, but he is apparently frank and honest; his revenge or ambition works by most devious intrigue; he confides his schemes to the audience in long soliloquies, yet his accomplished hypocrisy long baffles the rest of the *dramatis personae*. As in late Elizabethan and Restoration plays, he is often a prime minister. A collection of these villains' speeches would illustrate the conventionalized character of eighteenth century tragedy and the tendency of stage types to perpetuate themselves in theatrical tradition. A few lines from two may be sufficient. The first is the opening soliloquy of Seyfert in "The Heroine of the Cave," a play of some popularity acted in 1774.

> " Revenge, thou art the deity I adore! —
> From thy auspicious shrine I hope a cure
> For the corroding pain that rends my heart.
> The vain Alberti being thus preferr'd
> By fair Constantia, passeth all enduring!
> Colredo I have rouz'd — another wooer —
> And in his name are such reflections dropp'd,
> As 'twixt the two a duel must provoke —

My purpose is, whoe'er the conqu'ror be,
To reap advantage for my private views," etc.

The second is the opening soliloquy of Bertrand in Miss Hannah More's "Fatal Falsehood" (1779).

"What fools are serious melancholy villains!
I play a surer game, and screen my heart
With easy looks and undesigning smiles;
And while my actions spring from sober thought,
They still appear th' effect of wild caprice,
And I, the thoughtless slave of giddy chance.
What but this frankness has engag'd the promise
Of young Orlando, to confide in me
That secret grief which preys upon his heart?
'T is dangerous, indiscreet hypocrisy
To seem too good: I am the *careless* Bertrand,
The honest, undesigning, plain, blunt man:" etc.

The continuance of the stage villain is worthy of some note beyond its ·evidence of conventionalization. It calls attention to the fact that English tragedy has always been largely concerned with evil persons. Though the utterly bad were condemned as tragic figures by Aristotle, and the overthrow of the wicked as a tragic theme has ever since been held in some contempt by theorizers; yet from the time of Marlowe, or even earlier, English tragedy has told the stories of evil-doers with careers of cruelty or lust, or of machinators who have turned to bitterness and disaster the lives of the pure and the good. Of the first class are the tyrants, usurpers, lustful monarchs, and bloody avengers; of the second, the Machiavellian prime ministers, the hypocritical counselors, and the traitorous friends; and the two are often united as in Barabas or Richard III. English authors, actors,

and audiences have delighted in a visible representative
of the devil upon the stage, in an impersonation of the
source of evil. Given grandeur of ambition, the evil one
becomes the protagonist; given mere revenge and hatred
as motives, he is still the main opponent of the hero.
Perhaps the highest kind of tragic feeling is not aroused
either by the fall of the depraved or by the ruin of the
noble through trickery and cunning, yet "Richard III"
and "Macbeth" deal with the one theme, and "Othello"
and "Lear" with the other. Shakespeare's tragedies,
indeed, represent other conflicts than this between good
and evil, and in the representation of that conflict they
are not confined by theological or dramatic formulas.
Such formulas were just what eighteenth century writers
enjoyed, and in attacking the problem of evil they clung
to one of the most artificial if also one of the most typical
persons in literature, the Elizabethan stage machinator.
The conflict of bad and good, a natural if not inevitable
motive of a drama descending from medieval times,
found its expression in the excessively amiable hero and
heroine and the utterly black villain, stage types that
have maintained themselves in fiction as well as the
drama through Scott and Dickens down to the present
day. The stage villain, a theory of poetic justice that
refused to punish the good except for some distinctly
emphasized fault, and a faith in the potency of moral
precepts, these are the devil, providence, and salvation of
a theatrical theology, which, along with conventional
technic, narrowed plots, and some refinement in moral

taste, distinguish the eighteenth century type of tragedy.

The bird, caged and clipped, no longer sang. There was no poetry left in tragedy, and no human nature. Was there anything, then, in this type that showed advance over the preceding centuries, or anything that offered promise for future development? Not one of the literary forms in which the eighteenth century excelled, and not one fully representing the pseudo-classical theories, tragedy cannot be fairly judged as representing classicism *versus* romanticism. It merely presents a deteriorated English tradition modified and narrowed by pseudo-classical rules and theory. Yet it corrected and modified English tradition where it needed corrections and modifications, without quite denationalizing it. The admixture of comedy, prone to become gross farce, the horrors and bloodshed, and the brutal and revolting themes were rightly abandoned. In structure there was a more positive reformation. Stage illusion and precision of effect may be aided by an observance of the unities, and the limitation of the action to a single plot, a few persons, and a few scenes, — Shakespeare and encomiasts of his art to the contrary notwithstanding. It must be added that in practice the unities are likely to result in a counterbalancing defect, in a concentration of incident improbable and artificial, as often in eighteenth century tragedies, and even in Ibsen. The pseudo-classicists erred mainly in taking their rules as masters instead of as guides. Yet eighteenth century tragedy deserves this meed of

praise that it sought for literary form, which preceding
tragedy had largely lacked; and its attempts to secure
this offered useful lessons for the future. But here the
usefulness of its dramatic art ends. In the limitation of
what could be acted and of what belonged to the species,
it was suicidal. French tragedy in its effort to imitate
Greek failed to take advantage of the resources of modern
theatres; and English tragedy, halting between English
and French precedents, simply confined itself to well-
worn theatrical customs. There are not only no new subjects or characters, there are no new situations, surprises,
or catastrophes, no new methods of exposition or dialogue.
Some of the worst of the old conventions survived, as the
soliloquies, which continue long, frequent, and undis-
guised, but it would be hard to find even a bit of stage
business that was new. Eighteenth century tragedy made
no adequate demands of its splendid theatres and great
actors.[1]

The only daring departure from the prevailing type,
and the most important contribution to the general development of European tragedy in the eighteenth century,
came in the success of " George Barnwell, or the London
Merchant" (1731). This was the first tragedy of George
Lillo, a London jeweler, who had hitherto had no known
theatrical or literary connections, save for one unsuccess-

---

[1] The eighteenth century was not blind to the absurdities of its
tragedies, but made fun of them without stint. The number of burlesque tragedies is large and includes: Gay's *What d'ye Call It* (1715);
Carey's *Chrononhotonthologos* (1734); Fielding's *Tom Thumb* (1730);
Foote's *Tragedy a la Mode* (1764); and Sheridan's *Critic* (1779).

ful play. It was followed within a few years by another
domestic tragedy, "Fatal Curiosity," two tragedies of
the regular type, "The Christian Hero" and the post-
humous "Elmerick," and by adaptations of "Pericles"
and "Arden of Feversham." The two domestic tragedies
differ somewhat in both form and purpose. "The London Merchant," in prose, tells the story of Barnwell's
downfall through the courtesan Millwood, his murder
of his uncle at her instigation, and the final execution
of both criminals. Barnwell's repentance is much dwelt
upon, and the moral lesson is enforced in every line.
"The Fatal Curiosity," in blank verse, tells of a fright-
ful murder of a son by a father at the instigation of the
mother. From the innocent "curiosity" of the long-
lost son in concealing his identity from his parents, there
is traced the chain of circumstances which finally drive
the poverty-stricken and wretched couple to the murder
of the stranger. The play is thus nearer to Greek than
modern ideas of tragedy, in that it represents destiny
as something separate from character, and it links itself
with the German species of *Schicksalstragödie*, which
indeed it directly influenced. "The London Merchant,"
on the contrary, seeks the causes and effects of crime in
a crude and popular presentation of character that always
makes the most of human will and sentiment.

Daring and important as was Lillo's innovation, it
was by no means without progenitors and near kinsmen. The relations of his plays to Elizabethan domestic
tragedies are evident. Like "Arden of Feversham,"

which Lillo may have been copying, "The London Merchant" presents a murder, portrays a monstrous woman, and ends with an execution. Like the Elizabethan plays, Lillo's are bald, detailed, and moralizing. The very pleas that he advances in his dedication for realism and liberty had been advanced in "Arden" and the "Warning for Fair Women." Moreover, while since 1660 no tragedies had dealt solely with middle-class society, there had been much chafing against the restrictions that limited tragedy to princes; and from English writers as well as Corneille had come forecasts of the sweeping democracy of Lillo's creed: —

"What I would infer is this, I think, evident truth; that tragedy is so far from losing its dignity, by being accommodated to the circumstances of the generality of mankind, that it is more truly august in proportion to the extent of its influence, and the numbers that are properly affected by it. As it is more truly great to be the instrument of good to many, who stand in need of our assistance, than to a very small part of that number." [1]

Southerne, Otway, and Rowe had won great success for domestic themes, and their examples were naturally cited in the prologue which introduced "The Merchant." Comedy might also have been summoned to support. After the scourging from Collier it had joined in the general movement at the beginning of the century toward sentiment and moralizing. Sentimental comedy, seeking both pathos and a moral, may be said to begin in Eng-

[1] Dedication to *The London Merchant*.

land at least as early as Colley Cibber's "Careless Husband" (1704) and Steele's "Tender Husband" (1705). Steele's "Conscious Lovers" (1722) shows the species in full development. More general but not less important encouragements for realism in tragedy came from the realistic tendencies manifest in the literature of the preceding generation, notably in the novels of Defoe, and from the moralistic tendencies everywhere manifest in both fiction and drama. Lillo was one with his time, though out with truth and art, in thinking "the more extensively useful the moral of any tragedy is, the more excellent that piece must be of its kind."[1] The ascendancy of the middle class in letters, their expanding social life, their attachment to a conventional morality and a utilitarian art, and their delight in sentimentality, all help to explain the appearance of "George Barnwell." Lillo was writing for a generation that had "The Fair Penitent" and was waiting for "Pamela."

Lillo's work, however, was none the less that of a pioneer. "The Fatal Curiosity" had a special influence, beginning forty years after its appearance, in the German tragedies of destiny; and "The London Merchant," soon after its publication, became of importance in both France and Germany. In France its welcome was prepared by the growth of a species of sentimental comedy paralleling the English, and it was translated in time (1748) to serve as an example and stimulant to Diderot's plays and theories. Even before the publication of his "Le Fils

---

[1] Dedication to *The London Merchant*.

Naturel "[1] (1757), and "Le Père de Famille "[2] (1758), Lessing's "Miss Sara Sampson" (1755) had appeared directly modeled on "The London Merchant." Through Diderot and Lessing and, a little later, through German translations of Lillo's plays, domestic tragedy continued its leavening work in the German drama. By that time, sentimental comedy and domestic tragedy were returning from France and Germany to influence the English drama.

In England the direct stream of domestic tragedy never flowed high. A one-act play, " Fatal Extravagance," in prose, had appeared in 1721 under the patronage of Aaron Hill, and was revived the year before the success of " Barnwell," and later enlarged into five acts. There were a few successors — " Caelia, or the Perjured Lover" (1732), by Charles Johnson, presenting a Lovelace-like protagonist; "Love the Cause and Cure of Grief" (1743), a three-act play in prose; and Victor's adaptation of "A Woman Killed with Kindness" (1776). Far more important than any of these was Moore's "Gamester" (1753), long a stock play, and almost as influential on the continent as "Barnwell." Like "The Yorkshire Tragedy," it pictures the horrors of gaming. The gamester, his long-suffering wife, a faithful servant, a spirited girl, her lover, the intriguing villain, and his accomplices

---

[1] Translated into English as *Dorval, or the Test of Virtue* (1767).

[2] Translated 1770, and as *A Family Picture* (1781). Also, cf. General Burgoyne's *Heiress* (1786), which borrows from *Le Père de Famille*, and Holcroft's *Love's Frailties* (1794), based on a German adaptation.

play a story of far more insistent dramatic power than Lillo's and of no less sentimental and moral conclusiveness. Cumberland's "Mysterious Husband" (1783) is a later and less crude representative of the same species.[1]

Lord Davenant has deceived his wife into marrying him by slandering her lover Dormer. Later he has entrapped Dormer's sister into a pretended marriage and then deserted her. She, supposing her husband dead, marries Lord Davenant's son. On their marriage day, Dormer returns; Lord Davenant is discovered and kills himself.

Though a man and not a woman is the central figure of this social entanglement, we are reminded of the Tanquerays and Ebbsmiths of a later day in its powerful and not unveracious presentation of domestic ruin.

One reason for the failure of Lillo's pioneering to arouse a larger following in tragedy was the possession which comedy had taken of both domestic sentiment and morality. The species of sentimental and tearful comedy, which had already by 1730 appeared in both England and France, soon flourished in both countries. Their vogue was diminished by the success of "She Stoops to Conquer" and "The Rivals," but there was a further development during the last thirty years of the century in the plays of Cumberland, Holcroft, Mrs. Inchbald, and others. A certain amount of low comedy was, after "The Rivals," admitted to be necessary, as Holcroft avows in the preface to "Duplicity," but in such plays as

---

[1] Criticised in *The Critical Review*, lv, 151, because of its introduction of a comic character.

his "Duplicity" and "Road to Ruin," or Cumberland's "The Jew" and "The Wheel of Fortune," suffering abounds, ruin is imminent, there is much weeping, and a salient moral lesson. The suffering usually is confined to loss of fortune or temptation of virtue, and the moral lesson is directed against gaming, or loose living, or marital infidelity upon the part of the husband. The intriguing villain in this kind of play sinks to insignificance, and the moving force is likely to be a humanitarian benefactor who rescues the lost fortune or saves the heroine from the hated marriage. Occasionally this type of serious comedy comes close to tragedy. In Holcroft's "Deserted Daughter" (1795), a revamping of Cumberland's "Fashionable Lover," the father has disowned his daughter by his first marriage, and, through his wicked agent, she has been sent to a house of ill-fame. Not knowing his own daughter, the father, ruined in fortune and conscience, plans to aid a friend to secure her, and himself visits her. The situation is ghastly enough, but all comes out happily. The happy ending was in fact the dram of eale that corrupted the whole substance of this sentimental comedy. The theatrical necessity of a happy ending forbade either tragedy or a serious study of life. It compelled the dramatist to devote a large part of a play to preparing for the reconciliation, to spend much time on youthful love, to maintain a lightness of tone throughout; and it destroyed the possibility of tracing out character and incident to anything like a logical conclusion. The domestic drama, devoted to a serious presentation of social life, had its opportunity in the eighteenth as well as in the twentieth century. It shrank from tragedy; it advanced as far as attacking fashionable excesses, or as dramatizing moral theses, but it never got beyond the lovers who must be united and the everything that must come out well. It resigned itself to sentimentality and false conclusions, and was naturally overwhelmed by the theatrically more captivating sentimentality and falsity of Kotzebue. When "The London Merchant" and "The Gamester" encouraged the vogue of sentimental comedy, they nourished an ingrate which destroyed the legitimate brood of domestic tragedy. In the theatres men took their realism sugared by a sentimentality that sent them home contented. But Lillo's work was not unheeded by the genius who in "Tom Jones" and "Amelia" gave literary greatness to a realistic study of manners and morals. The sentimentalizing and moralizing of the middle classes, which from the time of Southerne had threatened to have their say on the stage, found their spokesman in the author of "Clarissa Harlowe."

In the last third of the century the various social, intellectual, and imaginative changes that make up the beginnings of the Romantic movement had their effect upon tragedy, but only in a partial and secondary fashion. The drama was already losing place to the novel in popularity, and showing signs of becoming a sort of literary by-product. Successful novels were made over into plays, and the various romantic tendencies to medievalism, melancholy, supernaturalism, and naturalism found expression in novel or verse rather than in play. The reawakening interest in the Elizabethan dramatists was represented by a revival of a number of the plays of Massinger and of Beaumont and Fletcher,[1] and imitations of Elizabethan diction became frequent. A more important departure was furnished by the so-called Terrific School of fiction. Medieval stories and scenes, and the various accessories of horror, ghosts, graveyards, dungeons, vaults, and the midnight bell had never been lacking in eighteenth century tragedy, but the novels of Walpole and his successors offered some novelties. Walpole's own unacted "Mysterious Mother" (1768), perhaps the most powerful of the Gothic trage-dies, was the pioneer of the movement. Robert Jephson, whose "Braganza" (1775) was heralded as

"His; no French tragedy, — tame, polish'd, dull by rule! Vigorous he comes, and warm from Shakespeare's school,"

produced in 1781 an adapation of Walpole's "Castle of Otranto," called "The Count of Narbonne," which, as the epilogue boasts,

"Midst the placid murmurings of Love Rolls the rough tide of Gothick force along."

His "Julia" (1787), another popular play with his usual

[1] The elder Colman was a leader in this revival. Besides the few comedies which remained on the stock list and "Philaster," which was frequently acted at this time, the following Elizabethan plays were re-vived in the decade 1778–88: *Bonduca, Bondman, City Madam, Duke of Milan, Knight of Malta, A King and No King, Marcella* (based on *The Changeling*), *Maid of Honor, The Picture, The Pilgrim, Scorn-ful Lady* (altered as *The Capricious Lady*), *Triumph of Honor, Women Pleased*.

abundance of soliloquies, tells a story of Elizabethan villany; and there were a few other Gothic attempts, as Cumberland's "Carmelite" (1784), before Lewis's "Castle Spectre" (1797) carried the town by storm. The further history of the terrific tragedies belongs to the next chapter, as does that of the German importations which culminated in the craze for Kotzebue, but it may be noted here that "Werter," acted in 1785, and "Emilia Galotti," acted in 1794, were among the earlier indications of German influence on the stage.

By 1790 the decadence of English tragedy had apparently run its course and nearly come to a full stop. The freedom and independence of Elizabethan days had degenerated by the time of Charles I into a fairly definite type. That type, maintained in the Restoration period, though with modifications and innovations, had now become conventionalized, debased, sterile. French influence had proved unprocreative. In spite of the activities of the theatres, the inspiration of Shakespeare, and the assistance of great actors and actresses, tragedy had failed to produce literature comparable to that of its rival, the novel. The drama, to be sure, had played a large part, both in tragedy and comedy, in reflecting and promoting the sentimentality and moralizing common in the literature of the century; Otway, Southerne, and Rowe had in a way fathered the sentimental novels. But in tragedy their Isabellas and Calistas had no successors to rank with Clarissa and Amelia. If tragedy through its alliance with sentiment failed of permanent

advance, it was still more unsuccessful in representing
the reasonableness, typicality, and austerity which the
classical conception required. It was half-hearted, turning now to Shakespeare, now to Voltaire, but never producing anything not conventionalized and dull. The
escapes from its dullness remained until the very end
of the century only half-opened doors. Through the
door opened by "Barnwell" and "The Gamester," the
drama saw only the broad path that led back to sentimentality and overlooked the straight and narrow way
leading to realism and truth. Over the threshold that
opened to medieval castles and chambers of horrors it
was still hesitating. The divorce between literature and
the stage had widened, and tragedy failed to attract
genius to its rescue. Crabbe did not write a tragedy of
the village, and Burns did not summon poetry and passion to the stage.

NOTE ON BIBLIOGRAPHY

Ward's *History of Dramatic Literature* ends with the death of Queen
Anne; and there is no adequate history of the English drama for the
last two centuries, and no good bibliography. Genest continues to be
the main source of information. Lowe's *Bibliographical Account* and
the histories of the theatre noted in the last chapter are useful for the
matter of the present. In addition, *The History and Illustration of
the London Theatres*, by Chas. Dibdin, Jr. (1826); Victor's *History
of the Theatres of London and Dublin* (1761); W. C. Dalton's *History
of the Theatres*, 1771–95; and *The Dramatic Censor* (1770) become
available for this period. A large number of memoirs of actors also
supply information in regard to the drama. *An Apology for the Life
of Colley Cibber, Comedian, written by himself* (1750), reviews the Restoration period as well. Others of interest are: Davies's *Memoirs of*

Garrick (1780); Murphy's *Life of Garrick* (1801); Boaden's *Memoirs of Mrs. Siddons* (1827) and *Memoirs of Kemble* (1825); Cumberland's *Memoir* (1806); Mudford's *Critical Examination of the Writings of Richard Cumberland*, etc. (1812); Boaden's *Memoirs of Mrs. Inchbald* (1833); *Private Correspondence of David Garrick* (1831–32); Holcroft's *Memoirs*, ed. by Hazlitt (1816); Cooke's *Memoirs of Charles Macklin* (2d ed., 1808).

The plays by authors of note can be found in the collected editions of their works, the more popular plays in the various collections noted in the last chapter. The majority of the tragedies, however, have never been reprinted and can be obtained only in the original editions. Dramatic criticism of the period can be studied in various essays by Addison, Steele, Gildon, Dennis, and Dr. Johnson, especially his Preface to the edition of Shakespeare and his *Lives of the Poets*. Lord Kames's *Elements of Criticism* (1762) was highly approved in its own day; and several essays on tragedy are of historical interest: William Guthrie's *Essay on Tragedy* (1747); Mrs. Montagu's *Essay on the Genius and Writing of Shakespeare* (1769); Edwin Taylor's *Cursory Remarks on Tragedy* (1774): William Cook's *Elements of Dramatic Criticism* (1775); and Hodson's *Observations on Tragedy*, prefixed to his tragedy *Zoraida* (1780).

Beljame's *Le Public et les Hommes de Lettres en Angleterre* bears on this as on the preceding chapter. Voltaire's influence on English tragedy has never been fully studied, but the following recent books bear on his relations with England: A. Ballantyne's *Voltaire's Visit to England* (1893); J. Churton Collins's *Bolingbroke, a historical study, and Voltaire in England* (1886); Lounsbury's *Shakespeare and Voltaire* (1902), which gives much information on the drama and criticism of the period and sufficient directory to Voltaire's comment on the English drama; and Jusserand's *Shakespeare en France*, which is also very valuable for this period. Miss Canfield's study of *Corneille and Racine in England* is also of marked service; and L. Morel's *James Thomson* (Paris, 1895) gives a very full study of Thomson's plays and literary relations. The *Belles-Lettres Series* contains editions with introductions of plays of Rowe, ed. Miss Sophie Hart; and of Lillo, ed. A. W. Ward (1906). Dr. Ward's introduction is particularly valuable for its sketch of the course of domestic tragedy and sentimental comedy on the continent. From the notes in these various studies, and from *La Littérature comparée, essai bibliographique*, by Louis P. Betz, Strasbourg, 1904, direction can be had to a number of monographs dealing with special phases of the relations between the dramas of England and France, and, toward the end of the century, between England and Germany.

CHAPTER X

THE ROMANTIC MOVEMENT

HE last few years of the eighteenth century and the first few of the nineteenth made up a decade full of movement and change in the drama. The eighteenth century had been, as we have seen, a time of stagnation in tragedy and of little dramatic advance in any direction. The theatregoer of 1720 would in 1780 have found the same plays or others similar in kind; but, had he postponed his visit yet twenty years, he would have entered a new theatrical world of romance, musical plays, and German novelties. By that time nearly all the factors of importance in the history of the stage during the first half of the nineteenth century had made their appearance. New departures in both tragedy and comedy, and a theatrically important *tertium quid* were all instituted. And new ideas, new themes, and new stories witnessed the changing taste and gave promise of the enlargement of the imaginative horizon which the new romanticism was to produce.

We have seen that, while neither realistic tragedy nor sentimental comedy had experienced a notable development, they had been departures from long-standing conventions. Tragedies in three acts, tragedies in prose, tragedies on domestic themes, tragedies without princes, tragedies of the present, all gave some encouragement for further novelty and experiment, The several varieties of "soft tragedy and genteel comedy" departed far enough from the standards of both species to suggest a dramatic development that should discard the traditional limitations. This changing taste, however, was seized by German plays and dramatized "tales of terror." The large and varied influence of German poetry, criticism, and philosophy upon the romantic movement in England can be noticed here only so far as it affected the drama. The plays of Lessing and the early plays of Goethe and Schiller made little impression on the English stage, though they exercised an immediate influence on the reading public and on most of the young men "standing on the forehead of the age to come." The conquest of the English stage was made at its point of greatest vulnerability — its sentimentality — by one who seemed the very Napoleon of the drama, Kotzebue, the conqueror of the theatres of all western Europe. In 1798 "The Stranger" ("Menschenhass und Reue") took Drury Lane by storm, and the next year Sheridan's "Pizarro," an adaptation of "Die Spanier in Peru," plus some eloquence and some songs, gained a still more brilliant success and drew even George III to the theatre. For several years Kotzebue reigned supreme; twenty or more of his plays were translated; many were acted; "Pizarro" alone had passed through twenty-nine editions by 1811, besides other English and American versions of the play. Kotzebue's triumph was due in part to his great skill in stage-craft, and in part to his adroit appeal to the more superficial sentiments for social and political revolution that were everywhere stirring. When it is compared with preceding sentimental comedy, the success of "The Stranger" is easily understood. It has the theatrical merit of arousing curiosity at the beginning and keeping it on question until the last moment; and it deals, over-sentimentally of course, with a social question of dramatic value and of especial piquancy at a time when many conventions seemed tottering, — should an erring wife be taken back again by her husband? The theme of "A Woman Killed with Kindness," "Jane Shore," and "The Fair Penitent" was given a new interest and a new solution. "Pizarro," retaining much of the plot familiar in English tragedy since the time of Dryden's "Indian Emperor," has two lovers, opponents in war, and two heroines, one vengeful, the other angelic, but makes the real hero the renouncing lover, who sacrifices all for the happiness of the angel who loves not him but his friend. Under these new auspices the fair penitent and the renunciatory hero began long careers in English drama and fiction. But neither these nor any other of Kotzebue's plays offered any guidance toward a serious interpretation of life or any innovations of real consequence in the English tragic tradition.

If Kotzebue's plays offered little promise for the national drama, the native plays which rivaled them in popularity offered less. Castles, monks, dungeons, and so on had already become somewhat common in musical plays and operas[1] and occasionally in tragedies, when "The Castle Spectre" of Monk Lewis opened the floodgates to "tales of terror" and their medieval and supernatural paraphernalia. "The Castle Spectre," which in the season of 1797-98 surpassed "The Stranger" and for a while held its own with Kotzebue, represents a new reign of romance. The new queen did not come from "perilous seas, in faery lands forlorn." She belonged to the earlier days of the romantic movement, and made her conquest at the head of squadrons of medievalistic, terroristic, and Germanistic Goths. She is adequately described in the prologue to the play: —

> "Far from the haunts of men, of vice the foe,
> The moon-struck child of genius and of woe,
> Versed in each magic spell, and dear to fame,
> A fair enchantress dwells, Romance her name,
> She loathes the sun or blazing taper's light:
> The moon-beam'd landscape and tempestuous night
> Alone she loves; and oft, with glimmering lamp,
> Near graves new-opened, or midst dungeons damp,
> Drear forests, ruin'd aisles, and haunted towers,
> Forlorn she roves, and raves away the hours!
> Anon, when storms howl loud and lash the deep,
> Desperate she climbs the sea-rock's beetling steep;
> There wildly strikes her harp's fantastic strings,
> Tells to the moon how grief her bosom wrings,
> And while her strange song chaunts fictitious ills,
> In wounded hearts Oblivion's balm distils."

The "drama," as it was called, is in prose, and is a medley of the various terroristic novels, including the

[1] See *The Haunted Tower*, an opera (1789), acted eighty times in two seasons.

two most famous, "The Castle of Otranto" and "The Mysteries of Udolpho," and adding something from Schiller's "Robbers" and from Shakespeare. There is a haunted castle, a jocose monk, a fool, a marvelous dungeon, a fisherman's hut, a ghost, a midnight bell, and songs and elaborate scenery. The villain, a feudal baron attended by negroes, is finally killed by the heroine, who saves her imprisoned father and escapes with the hero.

The signs of life that succeeded the long petrifaction of the eighteenth century drama and the beginning of the revolutionary epoch thus resulted only in theatrical novelties and in no serious dramatic movement. All serious drama was, indeed, threatened by the ascendancy of the "illegitimate" drama of music and dumb show. The causes leading to the rise of this class and its ensuing history were in large measure connected with the theatres themselves. Even before the new romanticism had invaded the drama, changes in theatrical conditions of far-reaching importance were well under way. The monopoly exercised by the Drury Lane and Covent Garden theatres was first threatened about 1730 by the success of a few minor theatres which gave musical, acrobatic, or dramatic entertainments. The old theatres were successful in maintaining their monopoly in regular pláys, but the irregular houses gained permission to give performances under the loosely defined term "burletta." A "burletta" was supposed to have a musical accompaniment, but it proved difficult to say how little music and how much of a drama might be included under the term. Henceforth, the regular drama had, in addition to the rivalry of Italian and English operas, that of musical and dramatic medleys; and the patent houses had to face the rivalry of playhouses that infringed as far as they dared on the legitimate drama. The patent theatres, with their vested rights in the stock plays and their obligation to maintain Dryden, Otway, and Shakespeare, offered no great inducements to new authors. This was particularly true, after the rebuilding and enlargement of both theatres in 1791 and 1794, when the increased cost of bringing out a play and the increased difficulty in acting or hearing an unfamiliar play led Kemble practically to abandon any attempt to produce new tragedies. The minor theatres, which were growing in importance, legally limited to the field of musical performances, and excluded from the regular drama except by trick, could offer little support to the serious dramatist. As a result, musical plays, operettas, and finally a new type, the "melodrame," flourished in the minor houses and found their way soon into the two great theatres. When in 1808–09 these were burned, the rivalry with the minors had become acute. The old theatres were rebuilt of so great a size that they proved unsuitable for any spoken drama. Through their great actors, Kemble, Kean, and later Macready, they maintained Shakespearean drama and a few of the old stock plays; but they were forced for the rest of the time to resort to melodrama, spectacle, or pantomime. The

minors, though they now became more daring in their
invasions of legitimate drama, naturally continued the
kind of entertainments at which they had succeeded and
to which they had forced the great theatres to succumb.
The long struggle for a free stage was now nearing its
end; the patent theatres were maintained with increasing difficulty; the minors prospered. With the death of
Kean in 1833, a great prop of the patent theatres fell;
and though the agitation for parliamentary reform in
that year failed, and the final legislation against theatrical monopoly was not passed until 1847, the great
theatres ceased to determine the history of the drama.
Macready's two periods of management, 1837–39 and
1841–43, were the final efforts to restore the old régime
that had maintained tragedy since the Restoration.

The "illegitimate" drama that triumphed in the theatres comprised a wide range of entertainments, mostly
farcical in their dramatic elements. Toward the end of
the eighteenth century the rage for dumb show and musical additions invaded the regular drama. Even Kotzebue
had to be decked out with songs and choruses. Moreover, a peculiar species of the illegitimate drama developed in the plays of Andrews, Dibdin, Reynolds,
Boaden, and Colman the younger that served as a half
substitute for tragedy. This species seems to have been
mainly due to the ingenuity of George Colman. Those
of his plays verging on tragedy, of which "The Battle
of Hexham" (1789), "The Surrender of Calais" (1791),
"The Mountaineers" (1793), and "The Iron Chest"

(1796) are the chief, are lively medleys of tragedy, comedy, opera, and farce. In each a tragic story is told in blank verse, audaciously Shakespearean, and this is mixed with broad comedy or farce in prose. There is a bustling action with shifting scenes, much spectacle, many songs, solos, duets, or choruses, for which a crowd of soldiers, monks, beggars, foresters, or the like, is always within call. "The Surrender of Calais" tells the story of Queen Philippa's mercy; "The Iron Chest" is a dramatization of "Caleb Williams"; "The Battle of Hexham" is a sort of musicalized chronicle history, presenting the adventures of Adeline in search of her husband, who turns out to be a captain of a band of robbers and the rescuer of Queen Margaret and the prince after the battle of Hexham. "The Mountaineers," suggested by a story in "Don Quixote," finds its land of romance in Spain, where a Christian prisoner elopes with the daughter of his Moorish jailer, accompanied by a stage Irishman as *gracioso;* and this group, when recaptured, are rescued by Octavian, a half-mad tragic soliloquizer, who also recovers his long-lost love, and was thought to be extremely impressive when impersonated by Kemble. In his use of all the well-worn motives of serious drama and his constant imitation of Shakespearean and Elizabethan diction, Colman displays remarkable cleverness as well as the most cheerful effrontery. He represents, too, a curious stage in the history of tragedy. He was born and bred in the theatre and had an exceptional opportunity to become familiar with the Elizabethan drama through his father's revivals and editorial labors. His method was to start with some incident, like that of Queen Philippa, and to connect with it any scenes that suggested themselves as interesting and varied, so that the motives, types of character, situations, and the very phrases of the Elizabethan and the later stock plays reappear to play their parts in his variety shows. He did not burlesque; in fact, he imitated so well that, while the judicious might grieve, the vulgar subscribed to pity and terror when his plays were performed by the great actors of the day. He popularized, vulgarized, and musicalized the great traditions of English tragedy, and passed them along to the nineteenth century as the possession of the illegitimate drama.

At the height of Colman's career, however, the illegitimate drama found a still more powerful ally. Englishmen who in 1802 went to Paris to enjoy the peace were delighted with an entirely new kind of theatrical entertainment there, the *mélodrame*. The industrious Holcroft promptly translated its most successful representative, and "The Tale of Mystery" heralded the long ascendancy of this new species of drama in England and America. The peculiar novelties of the *mélodrame* were the supplementing of the dialogue by a large amount of dumb show and the accompaniment of both dialogue and dumb show by descriptive orchestral music; otherwise, with its songs, sensations, and mechanical devices, it resembled the preceding musical drama of Colman and others. With this new recruit, the illegitimate held

full sway. Its influence spread into all dramatic performances, and many regular plays were supplemented
by songs, music, spectacle, or machinery. From the
start, *mélodrame* allied itself to most of the paraphernalia
of medievalism and of the terrific school, but it soon
showed the capacity for absorbing varied material. Reynolds in 1812 turned Dryden's "Don Sebastian" into
a musical play in three acts written in prose; equestrian
combats, real water, cataracts, and machinery for thrilling escapes became usual adjuncts. Soon Scott's poems
and novels supplied splendid material. As each novel
appeared the theatres vied with one another in bringing
out the first melodramatization; and often several versions were acted at the same time. Macready gained
one of his first large successes with "Rob Roy" in a
version that reduced Di Vernon to a singing part (1818).
Any kind of a story, providing it offered strange scenes,
an exciting and lively action, and marked contrasts
between bad and good among the characters, lent itself
readily to a dramatization that required a minimum of
dialogue and a maximum of action, music, and machinery.
Comic scenes were, of course, *de rigueur*. "The Slave,"
by Morton, was one of the most enduring of the Colman-
esque type. The serious plot, which presents Gambia,
the slave, as the sacrificing hero, borrows from "The
Curfew" and "Oronooko," and for its great scene im-
proves upon the escape over the bridge in "Pizarro."[1]

[1] Its borrowings are noted by Genest, viii, 603. The scene is quoted
in Archer's *Life of Macready* (Eminent Actors Series), p. 40.

After Clifton and Zelinda (whom Gambia hopelessly adores) escape across the hanging bridge, Gambia climbs up the tree from which it is suspended and cuts the rope. The pursuing villains are foiled on the brink. "We are safe, my husband," cries Zelinda from the other side; but her child, safely hidden by Gambia, hears her voice, and runs from his hiding-place, — on the wrong side of the river.

Child. It was my mother's voice! Mother! mother!

Zelinda. Alas! my child!

Somerdyke. Her child! Then we triumph — seize him! (*A slave seizes the child, and, running up a point of rock, hands it to Somerdyke, who continues.*) Move one step further, and you will see him buried in the waters. Submit, or this instant is his last. (*Holding him up in the act of precipitating him.*)

Zelinda. I do submit.

Gambia. Never! (*Gambia, who has concealed himself in the branches, snatches the child up into the tree.*) Father, receive your child! (*Throws the child across the stream.*) They have him! He is safe! Ha! Ha! Ha!   (*Curtain.*)

The term "melodrama" ceased after a time to denote the peculiar species brought from France in 1802, and came to be applied to all plays depending for effect on situation, sensation, or machinery, rather than characterization. The musical accompaniment and songs became minor features; the lively action, elaborate mechanical devices, dumb show, strong contrast of virtue and evil, and the happy ending remained the essentials. There was thus created a kind of inferior tragedy aiming at no literary excellence, which has ever since continued to fill the theatres and to satisfy the larger public. This natural reaction from eighteenth century dullness and declamation to bustle, pantomime, and music did not further, as in France, any immediate development in the literary drama. There was in England no relationship between the two as between Pixérécourt and Hugo. On the contrary, melodrama in England offered nothing new, for it absorbed about all that was old. All the well-worn situations, the escapes, rivalries, sacrifices, of the English stock plays were preserved, and to these was added whatever French melodrama offered. In this way there is curiously preserved in the cheaper theatres to-day the direct results of theatrical traditions going back before Shakespeare.

The illegitimate drama also represented the prevailing tendencies of Romanticism. Its fondness for Shakespearean and Elizabethan motives, its medievalism, its terrors, its democratic and humanitarian sentiments indicate the popularization of romantic ideas. These found expression suited to immediate public approval, not in Wordsworth but Kotzebue, not in Coleridge but Colman, not in Southey but in melodrama. And as the popularization of literature has increased, this illegitimate offspring of the drama has continued to respond to changes in public sentiment and thought by a recourse to well-worn theatrical means. During the nineteenth century, melodrama has thrust tragedy from the theatres and from public favor. Crowded out by the opera and again by the novel and now by the melodrama, tragedy has tended either to assume the garb of its rivals, or to conform its appeal to a select audience.

In the period from 1800 to 1830 the novel and the

melodrama and the melodramatized novel all united to restrict the demand for pure tragedy. The breach between the theatre and literature which the eighteenth century had opened was widened. In the theatre new plays and especially new plays with tragic, romantic, or heroic plots, were adapted from Scott's novels or otherwise devised by a comparatively small group of men. These men, Reynolds, Morton, Soane, Terry, Dibdin, and others, were associated with the theatres, understood the arrangement of scenery and spectacle, were quick to foresee the taste of the audience, and pretended to little literary skill, for none was required. Their work created a new distinction in the drama, a species, melodrama, or tragedy if you please, that can be acted but cannot be read. On the other hand, the literary romanticists, while usually having no connection with the stage and despairing of its reform, by no means relinquished the field of tragedy. Wordsworth, Coleridge, Byron, Shelley, Landor, Scott, Keats, and many other lesser poets wrote tragedies, and most were not unwilling to have these acted. These plays fall into two main classes, those that were acted and carried on the tradition of tragedy in the theatres, and those that were not acted. This second class, which for the first time becomes of some importance in the history of literature, has itself several divisions. There are tragedies intended for the stage but failing to get a trial there. There are others which, while not intended for the stage, conform in the main to its requirements, and might easily be adapted for presentation. There are others, like "Cain" or Wells's "Joseph and his Brethren" or Swinburne's later plays, which violate almost all the requirements of the theatre. These form another dramatic species, the opposite of melodrama, plays that can be read but cannot be acted. Some of these various classes of closet drama influenced the acted drama, others have so little dramatic quality that they are at most "dramatic poems," but all have a connection with the tradition of tragedy. Most of the literary tragedies are indeed, despite variations in degree, alike in kind. They are all written in verse; they are all romantic rather than realistic; they mostly return to Shakespeare and the Elizabethans for models; and they nearly all disregard the stage demand. Whether they loathe the stage or ask for admittance there, they seek literary rather than theatrical excellence. At the time when the stage demanded action and was superseding dialogue and speech by music, spectacle, and dumb show, the romanticists conceived of tragedy only in terms of poetry, and wrote mainly in order to clothe their tragic themes in the beauty of verse.

The most determined attempt to reform tragedy was made by Miss Joanna Baillie, who, in the year of the "Lyrical Ballads," published the first volume of her "Plays on the Passions," containing "Basil," a tragedy, and "The Trial," a comedy, both on love, and "De Montfort," a tragedy on hatred, with a preface announcing her intention to continue the series, illustrating each of the dominant passions by a tragedy and a comedy.

Her preface, which should have found sympathetic response in the young men who at Alfoxden were polishing their own tragedies and planning a revolution in poetry, exhibits the main fallacy of the romanticists' theory of the drama. She proposed to devote a play to the illustration of a single passion, to trace this from its beginning to the final ruin, and to recognize that passion arises from within, unprovoked by any external stimulus. This absorption with a study of emotion *per se* led to a subordination of plot and all external incident, and — so she proposed — all poetic embellishment, to a searching study of isolated passion. Her first volume attracted attention, and Kemble and Mrs. Siddons played " De Montfort," but without success. She continued, however, writing and publishing, completing the series of plays on passions, and as many more "miscellaneous plays," twenty-eight in all, of which fifteen were tragedies. These present a variety of themes, one being a domestic play in prose, another dealing with witchcraft, but the favorite setting is medieval with gloomy vaults, knights, monks, singing nuns, and the moon shining through vaulted windows. Her conception of a play of passion forbids motiving of character, or integration of the development of character with action. As Hazlitt acidly observed, she manipulates her actors like a girl playing with her dolls. There are many improbabilities, and the passions are exposed mainly in soliloquies. The language avoids ornamentation to a degree that makes one wonder why it is not in prose, though there are purple patches. It rarely if ever betrays any adaptability to the individual speakers. Though the plays were designed for the stage and overflow with stage-directions and much spectacle, scenery, and excitement, the technic shows scarcely a bowing acquaintance with the theatre. A few of the plays were acted, one being melodramatized, but none proved effective. They gained, however, the admiration of Campbell, Byron, and Scott, and of a wide circle of readers. Their morality, their proximity to poetry, their definiteness of purpose won a popular appreciation for their analyses of passion, denied to more imaginative, subtle, or revolutionary poems. Her plays, if forbidden the theatres, invaded the prairies and forest primeval; and Miss Baillie was justly gratified by receiving a diploma "constituting her a member of the Michigan Historical Society."

Wordsworth and Coleridge were in 1796–97, like Miss Baillie, writing tragedies of passions[1] arising from within and ending in ruin, and, like her, they were seeking presentation in the theatres. Wordsworth's "Borderers" treats of the deep springs of villany, and was based, as he thought, on his experiences with human nature in France during the revolutionary period, but he seems rather to have made a study of Shakespeare's Iago operating in a band of Schiller's robbers, and animated by the abhorrent principles of Godwin's "Political Justice."

---

[1] *The Fall of Robespierre* (1794), by Southey and Coleridge, and Southey's *Wat Tyler* (1817), written in 1794, hardly require even mention as tragedies.

Coleridge's "Osorio," a study of remorse, also derived its inspiration from books rather than from observation. Sixteen years later, in 1813, remodeled and pruned of some of its earlier radicalism, it won as "Remorse" a fair stage success, and led a partial revival of the poetical drama in the theatres. The plot of a wicked brother who reports the death of the good brother and seeks to win his betrothed, was suggested by "The Robbers"; the inquisition, sorcery, cavern, dungeon, and other elements of the spectacle were derived from the Radcliffian school; but the main inspiration was Shakespeare. Coleridge planned a revenge play, with a characteristic modification; the avenger was to seek, instead of blood, the remorse of the villain. The elaborate plot, which might have done duty for an Elizabethan revenge play or for one of Lewis's romances, has no connection with the main theme of the play. The opening acts disclose everything, and the interest in the full awakening of remorse in the wicked brother is not contributed to by the intrigue, magic, and insurrection, nor is it made veracious in the madness to which the remorse drives. But both the beautiful descriptive poetry and the underlying searching for tragic passion inspired other poets drama-ward. "Zapolya" (1817) has little philosophical interest underlying its romantic plot, suggested by the "Winter's Tale," but it displays a conscious effort to provide the movement, variety, spectacle, and surprise needful for the stage. Coleridge gave these in an Elizabethan profusion that must have overwhelmed the managers. But even had he made the revisions that they required, he could hardly have prevented his poetry from impeding rather than adorning his melodramatic action.

Charles Lamb's single tragedy, "John Woodvil" (1802), was written and offered to Kemble in 1799. Southey's comment, "(it) will please you by the exquisite beauty of its poetry and provoke you by the exquisite silliness of its story," comes near to being the final word. The verse catches something of Shakespeare's sweetness and artlessness as well as his obsolescent words, and the few persons and the silly story catch something of Lamb's own simplicity and charity. The play is more human, though feebler, than the contemporary plays of Miss Baillie, Wordsworth, and Coleridge. Lamb imitates the Elizabethans with much more charm than they, and he utterly disdains the stage spectacle which they admit, but, like them, he seeks to explore the heart without regard to what is happening outside and discloses its secrets by means of inordinate soliloquizing. "The Wife's Trial," based on Crabbe's "Confidant," was written in 1827, and refused by Charles Kemble. This tragicomedy, as Lamb called it, in two acts, is slighter than "Woodvil" and even less adapted to the stage.

From Miss Baillie's "De Montfort" (1800) to Coleridge's "Remorse" (1813), literary tragedy made no impression on the theatre. Godwin's plays, "Antonio" (1800) and "Faulkner" (1807), failed flatly, and Tobin's "Curfew," a medley of Elizabethan motives, was the most successful acted tragedy. When Lewis tried to give his terrific vein a little dignity and blank verse, even he failed on the stage.[1]

After "Remorse" the theatre half opened its doors to literature and the poets rallied to the support of tragedy. Maturin's "Bertram" (1816) had a large success, though his other plays failed. In the next few years a half dozen wordy tragedies by Sheil were acted. Kean revived versions of the "Jew of Malta" and "The Fatal Dowry," and the most successful of Sheil's plays was "Evadne," based on Shirley's "Traitor." Milman's "Fazio," acted 1818, though not intended for the stage, came nearer perhaps than any preceding tragedy of the romanticists to meeting theatrical requirements. Fazio's wife, jealous because of his infatuation for a countess, betrays her husband, and then for the remainder of the play is wildly remorseful. In spite of the extreme improbability of both the persons and the language, the story is told with dramatic directness and affords manifest opportunities for a great actress, seized upon by Miss O'Neill and later by Miss Cushman and, in an Italian adaptation, by Madame Ristori. A still greater theatrical success was won by Kean in "Brutus" (1818), a pastiche of the plays of Lee, Cumberland, and Downman composed by the American, John Howard Payne. Sheridan Knowles's "Virginius" (1820), followed by his "Caius Gracchus" (1823), and "William Tell" (1825), gave promise of a

---

[1] In this and the two following paragraphs the bracketed dates are those of the first performances in London. Some of the plays were first acted elsewhere.

more permanent revival of the poetical drama. Knowles, an actor and a practical playwright, was also the friend and in a way the pupil of Lamb and Hazlitt, and he gained the coöperation of a great and ambitious actor, Macready. He united as no other writer of the generation had done, stage-craft and poetic ideals. "Virginius," the best of his tragedies, is still acted — excepting Bulwer-Lytton's "Richelieu," the only relic of early nineteenth century tragedy. The story, with its one great acting scene, is told after the Shakespearean model in very ornate and artificial verse. It mingles much scoffing at the rabble with romantic appeals for liberty, tricks Virginia out with a lover, and ends with the insanity of Virginius. Knowles's tragedies at the time of their presentation were only moderately successful, far less so than his absurd comedy, "The Hunchback"; and several poetic dramas by other writers fared worse. Thomas Wade's "Woman's Love," based on the Patient Griselda story, obtained a hearing in 1808, but his Marlowesque "Jew of Aragon" was hooted off the stage in 1830. But Procter's "Mirandola" was acted sixteen times in 1821, and Miss Mitford's "Rienzi" (1828) and Byron's "Werner" (1830) gained veritable triumphs.

For about a decade longer poetic tragedy continued to contend for the theatre. Its main hope lay in Macready, and its hey-day was during his two periods of management of Drury Lane, 1837-39 and 1841-42. After the success of "Werner" ("Marino Faliero" had been earlier produced in 1821), "Sardanapalus" was brought out by

Macready in 1833–34; and "The Two Foscari" later. Knowles's "Alfred the Great" and his "Bridal," an adaptation of Beaumont and Fletcher's "Maid's Tragedy," won considerable success; and "The Pledge," a version of Victor Hugo's "Hernani," in 1831 heralded new support for romantic poetry in the drama. In the years 1836–37 Macready introduced three new writers in the "Ion" of Talfourd, "Strafford" of Browning, and the "Duchess de la Vallière" of Bulwer-Lytton. Talfourd's tragedies, including two, "The Athenian Captive" and "Glencoe," later acted by Macready, are stiff and wooden, contributing little to the drama. Bulwer-Lytton's later plays, "The Lady of Lyons" (1838) and "Richelieu" (1839), were extremely successful and surpassed any preceding efforts of the romanticists to adapt poetry to the stage. "Richelieu" is by no means a great poem or free from claptrap, but it has the merit of being written to be spoken and in having its characters designed as parts of the action. The interest is not in the poetry — it reads much better with the omissions made for acting — but in the development of the character of the cardinal through the incidents. The failure of "The Blot on the 'Scutcheon" in 1843 marks the end of Macready's management and the end of romantic tragedy on the stage.

Many of these acted plays gained what suitability they had for the stage by accident rather than design. Milman's "Fazio" was published several years before it was acted, and his later tragedies were decidedly closet dramas. Miss Mitford's "Julian" made little impression on the stage, and her other tragedies, except "Rienzi," still less. Byron's tragedies, which succeeded largely no doubt because of his reputation, were acted against his wish or after his death. And the various poetic tragedies that were written at about the same time as Byron's and Shelley's were mostly composed without thought of stage presentation. The surpassing genius of the greater poets has thrown into obscurity the work of these other young men, who in the decade after Waterloo faced the world with thin volumes of verse. But there have been few times in our literary history when the Muses have been so alluring, and Melpomene had her share of devotees. In John Wilson's "City of the Plague" (1816) a young naval officer wanders about plague-stricken London, through its bacchanals and horrors, buries his mother, discovers his betrothed, the ministering angel of the afflicted, and at last finds rest with her in the terrible crowded churchyard. The poem is grandly conceived and beautifully written in verse, occasionally Wordsworthian but without affectation or over-ornament. Two other closet dramatists offer rather less sincerity and impressiveness of conception but even more of poetic beauty. "Joseph and his Brethren" (1823), by Charles Wells, for a time the friend of Keats, was published when the author was twenty-three, and fifty years later revived and rewritten because of the appreciation of Rossetti and Mr. Swinburne. Like the plays of Thomas Wade, it shows the influence of Marlowe in

verse and plan. Long drawn out and in the main undramatic, there is imagination everywhere, especially in
the remarkable scenes that depict the passion-inflamed
Phraxanor, Potiphar's wife. Of the Elizabethans, too,
was Beddoes, who studied Webster and Tourneur as well
as Shelley and Keats, and whose verse at times fairly
surpasses his masters. His "Bride's Tragedy" (1821),
written when he was nineteen, is a play only in name,
but it is a poem that joins terror and fascination as scarcely
another since Webster and Ford. Here, as in his in-
completed dramas and his "Death's Jest Book," published much later, loveliness masks with madness and
death, and mockery with passion. It seems as if he were
lavishing over strange juxtapositions of beauty and decay
all the sensuous fascination of Keats and the lingering
suggestiveness of Shelley's lyrics. One's admiration for
his genius is tempered only by the thought of the greater
things he might have done.

Earlier than these poems was Landor's "Count
Julian" (1812), which, like them, presents qualities
suited for the closet and not for the stage. As in some
of the "Imaginary Conversations," Landor takes it for
granted that his audience understands the story and the
motives of the actors as well as he himself. The reader
gradually disentangles the situations and is stirred by
the splendid poetry; but no audience could make out
what it was all about. His other poetical tragedies, written
a quarter of a century later, show no improvement of
these defects, nor do they present dramatic themes as

interesting or as powerfully conceived as those in "Count Julian."

"Otho the Great," the tragedy which Keats hoped would lift him out of the mire,[1] was devised for Kean, and apparently accepted for Drury Lane. Charles Brown furnished him "description of each scene entire, with the characters to be brought forward, the events, and everything connected with it"; and Keats merely wrote the verse up to the fifth act, when he took the entire management into his own hands. The result of this peculiar collaboration was what might have been expected. The plot and characterization follow old types; and the poetry, though not lacking in fine passages, is inferior to nearly everything else that Keats wrote in his *annus mirabilis*, 1819.

Scott's dramas are somewhat out of place when grouped with these other closet tragedies, for they are varied in character, representing a number of the proclivities that we have noticed in the romantic drama.[2] "The House of Aspen," written in prose at about the time of "Goetz," was intended for the stage and considered by Kemble for representation. Based on a German tale and showing the influence of "Goetz," it

[1] "I mean the mire of a bad reputation which is continually rising against me. My name with the literary fashionables is vulgar. I am a weaver-boy to them. A tragedy would lift me out of this mess." Letter to his sister, December, 1819.

[2] The translation of Goethe's *Goetz von Berlichingen* (1799), *The House of Aspen* (1830), *Halidon Hill* (1822), *Macduff's Cross* (1823), *The Doom of Devorgoil* (1830), *Auchindrane* (1830).

offers no important deviations from the terroristic drama. "The Doom of Devorgoil," designed for Terry at the Adelphi, is a melodrama with many songs and a mixture of mimic goblins with supernatural machinery that was found to be so objectionable as to prevent its performance. It is interesting as one of the very few cases in which a man of literary reputation undertook to meet the requirements of the illegitimate drama. None of the other plays, which are in blank verse, was intended for the stage. "Macduff's Cross" is a mere sketch in one act; "Halidon Hill" a two-act dramatization of border warfare; "Auchindrane," in three acts, is a more fully developed tragedy. "Halidon Hill" has a clearness and directness of characterization and a vigor of movement which sugggest that had the auspices been more favorable, the historical drama might have had another great exponent. "Auchindrane," though retaining a little of the Radcliffian mystery and mystification which Scott never quite outgrew, also tells its domestic story with a directness and verisimilitude not usual among the romanticists. German translation, terroristic tragedy, spectral melodrama, dramatic sketches for the closet, and domestic tragedy are all illustrated by these six plays; and their subjects and treatment also reflect the various attachments of Scott's literary career. They illustrate also the inability of literary genius to aid the theatre in this period, but they differ from most of the literary drama in their absence of subjectivity or attachment to theory.

Byron's plays, like other poetical tragedies of the time,

were written in accord with the writer's theories and counter to the prevailing theatrical practices; but Byron prided himself on departing from the methods of the Elizabethans or of his fellow romanticists, and on following the guidance of eighteenth century models. "Marino Faliero," "The Two Foscari," and "Sardanapalus," all written 1820–21, attempt regularity of plot and observance of the unities, and profess Alfieri as a model. The two Venetian plays, however, recall Otway's "Venice Preserved," and their exaggeration of strange passions is quite in accord with the general practice of the romanticists. The plots are improbable, though selected from history, and aloof from general interest, for the resentment of the old doge at the insult to his wife and the unyielding vengeance of Loredano and, indeed, all the major passions are treated with an extravagance that becomes melodramatic and renders the persons all but unintelligible. With "Sardanapalus" the case is different. The dissolute, luxurious, but nobly-aspiring hero and his better angel, Myrrha, derive from the characters of Byron and the Countess Guiccioli a truth of passion that animates the rapid and spectacular action. A tragedy of palace intrigue, after the eighteenth century type, is thus reanimated by the romantic fervor of its passion, philosophy, and poetry. Any time from "The Mourning Bride" to "Zenobia" it might have triumphed on the stage, and so it did triumph when finally acted; but it summoned only a tithe of Byron's power. Quite different from any of these three plays, his "Werner" was ob-

viously suited to its own day. Based on one of Harriet
Lee's novels, it forsakes classical structure and exhibits all the paraphernalia and emotional horrors of the
terrific drama. It was one of the greatest stage successes
of the romantic drama, but it is no more deserving,
either as a play or a poem, than a dozen of its rivals.

Byron's other dramas depart farther than any of these,
not only from fitness for the stage, but from likeness to
any definite dramatic species. Of the four, however,
all of which deal with a world of spirits, "Manfred"
and "Cain" have tragic themes and protagonists. "It
was," wrote Byron, "the Steinbach and the Jungfrau,
and something else much more than Faustus that made
me write Manfred." Nature, the ever-recurring theme
of the romantic poets, is here given something akin to
dramatic treatment. The impassioned descriptions create
a presence, not one "that disturbs him with the joy of
elevated thoughts," but "the wild comrade of Manfred's
antipathy to men." [1] The mountains become sharers
in the hero's tirades, though their nights' "dim and
solitary loveliness" is the only power that curbs his
fierce unrest. "Cain," less lyrical and far more distinct
in its presentation of dramatic conflict, may rightly be
claimed by romantic tragedy for its own. It is not merely
Byron's own personality which finds expression here,
but the revolt against convention and creed, so characteristic of the romantic movement. The demands of the
individual man against society and providence make

[1] Herford, *Age of Wordsworth*, p. 227.

up the tragic theme. The tragedy of individual passion, leaping the bounds of history, romance, or actuality, is here divorced from the theatre, divorced indeed from any semblance to the models of tragedy; but in its symbolistic and allegorical presentation of philosophical questionings still keeps close to the essentials of great dramatic art, the searching of the motives and conflicts of human passion. Cain is of the brotherhood of Marlowe's Faustus and Shakespeare's Hamlet and other tragic heroes who chafe against finite limitations, greatly seeking after knowledge and certainty, and finding the very curiosity of their discontent the weapon of their own destruction. The theme is an eternal one in tragedy, but it was left to the romanticists fully to realize its meaning, and to Byron to give it isolation and grandeur.

Shelley's "Cenci" in a different way mirrors this eternal defeat that human struggle after justice must encounter. Deeply impressed by the current tradition about Beatrice Cenci, he made this story of incest and parricide the expression of his view of life and history as a conflict between tyranny and downtrodden innocence. Nowhere else in Shelley, not even in "Prometheus Unbound," does this world drama come out of the clouds and reveal itself with such clarity and power. There is passion in the persons, climax in the situations, and directness in the language such as the romantic drama had rarely shown. The philosophical conception and the tangle of human motives do not indeed quite harmonize. Beatrice's lie and her unworthy seeking after life are bits of the story which interfere with our acceptance of Beatrice the martyr, flaws that Browning would not have admitted. On the other hand, Shelley's philosophy overrides the story, as may be seen by a comparison of the tragedy with one of the earliest to show dawning romanticism. Walpole's " Mysterious Mother," which at this time Byron was praising as "the last tragedy," treats a more horrible story of incest with the interest mainly in the plot, holding in suspense the fearful solution until the end; "The Cenci" begins with the act of incest, and then tries to carry our interest solely to the two characters, one the embodiment of all inherited evil, the other, a pure and beautiful spirit striving madly and in vain to free herself from wrong that is might. The conquest of the stage, the writing of dramatic blank verse, and the endowment of this story of crime with representational truth were tasks too large to be accomplished in a single play; but, though faulty in the details of dramatic art, "The Cenci" is, for a first tragedy, without an equal in its mastery of the great essentials of tragic poetry. The poet who shrank from comedy as from a wicked thing and who thought a story of incest possible in a London theatre, had much to learn before he could master the stage. But "The Cenci" reveals the maturing Shelley, who was opening his mind to new impressions, admiring "Cain" and "Don Juan," profiting from Æschylus and Calderon as well as Shakespeare, and who was seeing his allegories clothed in human form, and no longer only in images of mist and flame. As one

reads one wonders, — had the play not been the last as
well as his first tragedy? had it come at the beginning
instead of nearly at the close of the romantic movement?

In "Prometheus Unbound" there is even greater
achievement in the presentation of this world conflict;
and there Cain triumphs and Beatrice is purified. But
the achievement is lyrical rather than dramatic, and has
no proper place in the history of tragedy.

In all these tragedies, whether acted or not, and
whether works of genius or not, certain resemblances
have been noted. They exhibit most of the elements that
characterize the romantic movement as it stirred English
poetry from the "Lyrical Ballads" to the first publica-
tions of Tennyson and Browning. Without realism in
plot or language, and dealing always with what is unusual, improbable, and removed from the present, they
made little effort to catch the interest of the average
audience or to excite an interest common to ordinary
experience. Their reaction against the frivolity of contemporary melodrama was as decided as their reaction
against eighteenth century conventionality; but both
impulses led to poetry, passion, and Shakespeare, but
not to drama. They did not succeed in working out cause
and effect of character through incident; when they desired to gain stage effectiveness, they merely borrowed
from current melodrama or from the Elizabethans.

Elizabethan influence is usually apparent in the choice
of themes, in the devising of plot and situations, and
particularly in the figurative and ornate phrasing. The

revival of some Elizabethan plays on the stage, the vulgarization in the illegitimate drama of many of their incidents, and the general interest among readers at this time in the Elizabethan drama, all encouraged a fondness for madness, incest, battles, villany, and unrestrained passion of various kinds. In phrasing, the Elizabethan influence appears in all degrees; in the sympathetic emulation of Keats, in the amazing reproductions of Beddoes, or in the starched artificiality of the poetic embellishments of Milman, Knowles, or Procter. In general the style is redundant and florid. In such plays as were adapted for the stage, it will almost always be found that the mere curtailing of the figures, soliloquies, and episodes causes a marked improvement in the dramatic quality of the dialogue. Byron and Shelley both attempted to free their dramatic blank verse from conceits and artificialities, and to give it directness and lack of ornamentation corresponding to natural speech. In consequence, Byron's blank verse often makes a slovenly approach to prose, and Shelley's loses something of the beauty of his non-dramatic masterpieces; but on the whole, "Sardanapalus" and still more "Cain" and "The Cenci" show their greatness in this as in other respects, in the dramatic quality of their verse.

Many of the tragedies also exhibit the influence of the school of terror. The Radcliffian romances, the early German drama, and the spectral melodrama of the theatres all encouraged castles, dungeons, titans like Karl Moor, hallucinations, and ghosts. There is something of this in Beddoes's churchyards; "Bertram" is a full-fledged drama of terror by one of the masters of the school; Byron's "Werner," itself a dramatization of a tale of terror, conforms to all the stage requirements of the species. After the tales of terror had gone out of fashion, the romanticists still found it easy on the stage to revert to haunted castles, inveterate villains, and in-dungeoned heroes. But in addition to the continuing influence of "The Robbers" and the plays of "Monk" Lewis, there was arising the influence of "Faust" and of Schiller's later plays. "Faust," which furnished hints for "Manfred" and "The Deformed Transformed," seems to have been regarded as a "tale of wonder," the story of the sale of a soul to the devil being a favorite with that class of fiction; but its philosophy perhaps also had its suggestions for both Byron and Shelley. Schiller's "Wallenstein," translated by Coleridge, and "Mary Stuart" at least encouraged the prevailing fondness for historical themes and the study of passion.

Medievalism continued its sway but with some new developments. The Waverley novels, the growing cos-mopolitanism of literature, the Italian residences of Byron and Shelley, in fact innumerable causes led to an expansion of the interest in the Middle Ages into an interest in the past. Literature, whether in Scott or Keats, was carrying its search for story and ideals, for pic-turesqueness and beauty, into past ages and remote climes. The treatment of history, which had formed no part of the plans of Miss Baillie, Wordsworth, or Coleridge, now became essential to tragedy; and we find Byron keeping carefully to the historical sources of his tragedies of the doges, and Shelley adhering to a narrative of the Cenci murder, which he deemed authentic, though since proved legendary. Italian history seems to have exercised a general fascination. Miss Mitford wrote a tragedy on the Foscari independently of Byron's, as well as her " Rienzi "; and " Fazio " and " Mirandola " dealt with Italian stories. The choice, however, was mainly for grandiose historical events, as " Sardanapalus," " Virginius," " Lucius Junius Brutus," " Richelieu," and Milman's " Fall of Jerusalem." Some of these attracted by the opportunity to praise liberty, meaning Catholic emancipation and electoral reform, and the denunciation of tyranny; but they seem to have been especially welcomed because of their opportunities for rhetorical fervors.

In nearly all the plays the main interest is not in plot, as in the eighteenth century, and not primarily in story, as in the Elizabethan period, but in the delineation of individual passion. " Lear," " Othello," " Hamlet," and " Macbeth " are the models; but the passions are more distempered, more isolated, more abstracted from reason or sense than in Shakespeare. As in the Restoration and the eighteenth century, the influence of Shakespeare and the Elizabethans is most unmistakable in the prominence given to insanity and villany. But this prominence is also a natural result of the romanticists' prepossession with passion. In tragedy, they felt that

some passions must be very evil and some ruinous; hence
they devoted themselves to a study of malice and madness.
Their villains are more vigorous than those of the eighteenth century, but they, too, imitate Iago; and the mad
scenes always recall either Lear or Ophelia. The romanticists can realize passion for the moment, or display
its variable moods; but they rarely succeed in making
its extended portrayal convincing. They clung to the
idea that the only way to depict passion was to eliminate
all else. Even in the great writers passion absorbs the
interest; in the minor plays it tears itself to tatters. Tragedy after tragedy represents passions, not conflicting
but alternating, until one or the other turns to madness.
As Lewis's prologue declared, Romance "raves away
the hours." The conception of tragedy seems to be
the burning up of the soul in passion, and the poets'
main concern to describe the conflagration. The romanticists needed Lyttleton's advice, to read Shakespeare, but to study Racine.

The conception of tragedy that requires the expression
of passion working in individual men, and seeks in history or legend for examples of isolated effects of the great
emotions, clearly involves something different from a
veracious representation of life as we all see it, and something more than the confusion of passions run wild. According to contemporary philosophical criticism, as that
of Schiller and Schelling, or that of Coleridge and Shelley, tragedy should take part in the search for universal
truth; not universal in the eighteenth-century conception

of typical characters and aphoristic generalizations, but universal in the sense that, in the words of Carlyle, it seeks the "interpretation of the divine idea in the world." Tragedy should investigate, as Lamb declared, "the grounds of the passion, its correspondence to a great and heroic nature," and should also seek to find in the riots of evil or the storms of passion symptoms of the struggle of Nature to rid itself of disease and fever, the presage of a higher unity for both man and the universe. Something of this is discernible in "Remorse" or elsewhere; there is a passionate demand for ethical realities in "Cain"; but the only positive presentation of an idealistic theory of tragedy is "The Cenci."

Though tragedy thus reflects the changes working in the ideas and forms of literature, these changes are, of course, more distinctly indicated elsewhere. If we had no knowledge of other literature, and only tragedy to judge from, we could not clearly discern the far-reaching changes wrought by the romantic revival. Tragedy from 1800 to 1830 could be described as marking a return to the Elizabethans and Shakespeare, an absorption in the depiction of passion, a revival of poetic imagination in expression, an appeal to terror rather than to pity, and to the strange and mysterious rather than the reasonable; but it could not be said that the summation of these changes resulted in an extensive or enduring development.

It is not easy to find a stopping-place for a history of English tragedy. In the case of the acted drama the close of Macready's management offers a definite end, for the ensuing twenty-five years are nearly a blank as far as acted tragedy is concerned. In the case of the unacted drama, however, there is no point of marked change. The deaths of Scott and Goethe mark a stage in European literature; and the Victorian era introduces new poets and novelists, new social and political conditions, and a new foreign influence in the French romanticists. But the closet dramas after 1830 are in many ways closely related to those of the generation before. Closet tragedy in the plays of Browning, Sir Henry Taylor, Matthew Arnold, Swinburne, and others, was largely the outcome of the theatrical and literary conditions which we have been tracing. Separated from the theatre, it offers, one must fear, little that is vital in the development of the drama, however impressive it may be as poetry. The appearance of new semi-dramatic species was a natural accompaniment of the continued departure of drama from the stage. Miss Mitford and Bulwer-Lytton had written "dramatic scenes." Later Landor's genius found its truest opportunity not in poetic plays, but in prose imaginary conversations, at their best splendidly dramatic. Browning turned from the theatre to dramatic lyrics, romances, and monologues. In fact, in the work of all the romantic dramatists, including Browning and Swinburne, dramatic power reveals itself in scenes and passages rather than in whole plays. Tragedy as a literary form, it may be repeated, is dependent for its life upon the theatre. Removed from the theatre, its integrity is gone, it develops strange and varied forms. Instead of tragedy, we have "My Last Duchess," "The Ring and the Book," and the Mary Stuart trilogy.

It is this separation from the theatre that seems to have been the main cause for the failure of the romantic movement in tragedy. We may, to be sure, find other causes in plenty. The genius of its great poets was lyrical rather than dramatic. Lyrical and narrative poetry and, above all, the novel absorbed both public interest and imaginative genius. Again, there was no free play for a revolution in tragedy, because there had been no tyranny. Classicism had never dominated the drama as in other European nations. In English tragedy of the eighteenth century, blank verse, however tainted by affectation, had kept the Elizabethan fondness for figure; structure, though following after French models, had maintained the traditions of English freedom; the subjects had kept open a wide range and had not neglected the medieval field; and sentiment, if not passion, had reigned. While the German and French romanticists found in Shakespeare an incentive to something new, the English romanticists could only elevate to omnipotence one who had long been the idol of the theatres. He was for them no innovator, but rather the unrecognized tyrant who held them back from real innovation. As Beddoes recognized in theory though not in practice, "the man who is to awaken the drama must be a bold tramping fellow, — no reviver, even however good."

But if we still ask why Coleridge or Beddoes should

not have written tragedy as well as Schiller or Victor
Hugo, why the tragedy of passion, revolt, and idealism,
applied to history or legend, did not flourish in the time
of the French Revolution and Napoleon, of Kemble and
Kean, of Byron and Browning, the best answer must be
found in the fact that theatrical conditions offered no
encouragement to tragic drama, but almost forbade a
serious attempt to learn the ways of the theatre or to deal
in its debased wares.

If theatrical conditions had been favorable, if the union
of Macready and Browning could have continued, one
fancies that the romantic drama might yet have succeeded. The chronicle of English tragedy finds its climax
in the first act, with Shakespeare as its protagonist; henceforth, directed by his ghost, its action goes haltingly,
vainly awaiting another climax and another protagonist.
In Browning, it was, perhaps, nearer than ever before to
finding both. Since the Restoration, no poet had come
to the theatre so gifted with dramatic genius, no poet
so concerned with the study of the vicissitudes of human
motive, so alive to the dramatic values of crucial moments, so curious as to the meaning of passion and pain,
suffering and evil, in the drama of life. "Strafford" and
"A Blot on the 'Scutcheon" have the weaknesses of youth
and experiment, but they are the plays of a pioneer who
is not content with returning to the Elizabethans or the
Greeks, but is seeking to convey through his stories and
persons the truth that is in him. The study of Strafford
is almost the first independent and acute study of an

Englishman of history in all the historical tragedies since
"Henry V"; "A Blot on the 'Scutcheon" one of the
few plays to realize individual passions since Otway.
And the dramatic defects — the failure to meet his audience half-way, the awkwardness and garrulity of expression, the lack of repression in form, while defects that
continue in Browning's later poetry — are the very
faults for which a severe apprenticeship to the theatre
might have been the best discipline. An apprenticeship
such as Shakespeare served might have turned Browning's monologues and lyrics into dramas; but the age was
incapable of furnishing such a training, and the fiasco
with Macready was the end of the period and the defeat
of the poetical drama.

What comes after in the nineteenth century may best be
left to the future historian, who will be able to interpret
its plays in the light of a succeeding development. The
plays of Tennyson, reverting again to Shakespeare, and
the poems of Swinburne may, after all, be the forerunners
of a new revival of poetical tragedy. Or the great development in technic that has proceeded, first under the
guidance of the French dramatists, and then of Ibsen,
and the serious essays of dramatists of the passing generation may be the pioneers of a national drama of first-
rate importance in the generation to come. Certainly
Ibsen, with his revolution in both the content and the
form of the tragic drama, has been the great force in later
nineteenth century tragedy. His work as it affects England and America, however neglected, postponed, or

modified, must be the text of a succeeding chapter on English tragedy, which cannot yet be written.

NOTE ON BIBLIOGRAPHY

Genest's *Account of the English Stage* stops at 1830. A continuation of this work down to the present time is much to be desired. There is no thorough history or bibliography of the drama of this period. In addition to the histories of the theatre already mentioned, W. C. Oulton's *History of the Theatres of London*, 1795–1817, may be consulted. Memoirs of the Kembles are useful for this period, and also Macready's *Reminiscences*, ed. Sir F. Pollock (1875), Moore's *Life of Sheridan* (1825), Molloy's *Life of Edmund Kean* (1888), William Archer's admirable life of Macready (*Eminent Actors Series*), are all valuable. *Random Recollections* by Colman the younger, and memoirs of Kelly, O'Keefe, and Reynolds supply information in regard to the theatre and illegitimate drama. John Cumberland's collections, *British Theatre* (41 vols., 1829) and the *Minor Theatre* (15 vols.), are printed from acting copies, and the second comprises many illegitimate plays.

Dramatic criticism of the period includes Coleridge (see criticism of Maturin's *Bertram* in *Biographia Literaria*), Hazlitt, *A View of the English Stage* (1818); Leigh Hunt, *Critical Essays on the Performers of the London Theatres* (1807) (selections from same, ed. W. Archer and R. W. Lowe, 1894); Lamb (see *Lamb's Dramatic Essays*, ed. Brander Matthews, 1893). See, also, R. H. Horne's *New Spirit of the Age* (1844), containing criticism of Knowles, Macready, Bulwer-Lytton, and Browning.

The dramatic work of the chief poets has been studied in connection with their other poetry by many editors and critics, but rarely in its relation to the drama of the period. Professor Beers's two volumes, *English Romanticism in the Eighteenth Century* (1899), and *English Romanticism in the Nineteenth Century* (1901), deal with the German influence; C. H. Herford has an excellent though brief account of the drama of the period in his *Age of Wordsworth*; Watson Nicholson's *The Struggle for a Free Stage in London* (1906) is full and valuable. Ernest Bates's monograph on *The Cenci* (1908) discusses that tragedy and its relations to contemporary drama.

CHAPTER XI

CONCLUSION

HE questions with which the first chapter began should now have found their answers. The plays considered in our historical sketch have many common characteristics, they do separate themselves from other plays of their periods, they are connected from one period to another in a continuous development. English tragedies constitute a dramatic type, a literary form. This type has, to be sure, permitted many variations, — revenge tragedy, chronicle play, tragicomedy, domestic tragedy, sentimental tragedy, heroic play, or the closet tragedy of the romanticists — but every one of these species has had its connections with others, and in every period the tragedies of varying kinds have been related not only to one another but to those that have gone before. With changing theatrical conditions, with new literary impulses, with new views of the old traditions, with new influences from Spain or France or Germany, the type has taken new characteristics or made new alliances, but has never lost its integrity. At any time during the three centuries it would have been possible to frame a definition of tragedy that would include over nine tenths of the tragedies of the period, and the other tenth would offer only definable variations. However strong the foreign influences, tragedy has maintained the national tradition; however great the innovations, it has never broken with the past. From Marlowe to Shelley there has been an unbroken continuity in themes, stories, types of persons, nature of emotional appeal, structure, and even in the blank verse.

So marked is the integrity and continuity of the type that tragedy lends itself, better perhaps than most·other forms, to the biological analogy. The processes which we have been tracing are evolutionary. Whether we consider the main type or its varying forms, we are reminded constantly of the laws governing the origin and development of natural species. The history of the Elizabethan drama in particular affords an example of the origin, development, culmination, and degeneration of a literary species, which might be analyzed closely as Brunetière has analyzed French tragedy of the seventeenth century. Created from a cross-fertilization of Seneca on the medieval drama, it appears in dubious forms of morality and chronicle, springs into full integrity in Marlowe, reaches its culmination in Shakespeare, and degenerates under the changed environment of the social and theatrical conditions that followed the death of Elizabeth. But the analogy is not less applicable to the whole history of tragedy. The slow development of variations and new species under changing environment is found in every period, as in the formation and growth of the revenge play or in the development of the sentimental tragedy of the eighteenth century. The quick formation of species by mutation also has its parallels, as in the sudden appearance of Marlowe or of the heroic tragedy bred from the Beaumont-Fletcher play and French romance. In the persistence of the stage villain through all forms and periods, we might even discover one of Mendel's unit characters. The reversion to an earlier form appears in the return of Lee or of the Romanticists to the Elizabethans. And the tendency of individual plays to regress to the main type has been a constant and on the whole perhaps the most potent force of the development.

We may find the nature of the literary species determined by constant principles corresponding to environment and heredity in the evolution of natural species. Environment as a factor in literature has long been recognized by criticism, and has been apparent in every play that we have examined. Each period has been distinguished by theatrical, social, and literary conditions peculiar to itself and constituting the change-producing environment of the drama. Tragedy has at every stage responded to these changing conditions. And the law of heredity is also paralleled. No play has been without its inheritance. The most original, as Shakespeare's "Hamlet," Otway's "Orphan," Lillo's "Barnwell," and Shelley's "Cenci," have shown their indebtedness no less clearly, if less slavishly, than the more commonplace individuals. The classical tradition transformed the English breed as the Arabian stock has the racing-horse; the French influence changed the very anatomy of the species. Our study must surely have called attention to the extraordinary force that imitation has exercised in the creation of tragedy. It seems, indeed, the generating power. Men are forever imitating, but they cannot imitate without change. In these changes, the variations due to environment — personal, theatrical, literary, social — arise the individual peculiarities, the beginnings of new species, the element of growth. The great mass of tragedies, however, differentiate themselves only feebly or slightly from the type. They are imitations that preserve all the essential characteristics of their originals. Some ideas, some plays, some traditions, have an astonishing fecundity; other stocks, procreative for a while, soon turn barren. But, destroy the faculty of imitation, and the generation of literary forms would seem wellnigh impossible.

Thus far, perhaps, the biological analogy may be pressed, if we remember that it is only an analogy. The evolution of a wagon or a battleship might offer an equally suggestive and an equally unsafe comparison. No one should be deceived by the analogy into thinking that what we call environment and heredity in literary species correspond in fact with their namesakes in the physical world. One play does not create another. It, along with countless other things, suggests ideas and impressions which are made into a play by the author. Each tragedy is the child of a mind, whose creative processes have little real resemblance to physical generation. To call the influence of "Hamlet" heredity, and the influence of the author's newspaper reading, or of his family, or his political beliefs, environment, is merely to assign arbitrary names. Again, art, unlike nature, is careless of the type and careful of the individual. A single play may live longer and have greater generating power than a whole species. "Othello" during the eighteenth and nineteenth centuries has, perhaps, had more influence upon English tragedy than all non-Shakespearean tragedies together. Sophocles is still germinating. It is as if we now had the venerable chief of the mastodons, surviving many of the species he had originated, and still creating his offspring to confuse the evolutions of the many other species he had already aided in forming. In literature we are attempting to trace the development of species, of which individuals live forever; to discriminate the agents in a complex creative process which we do not at all understand; to call one play the child of another when it is more truly the kaleidoscopic aggregate of much reading, much observation, much experience shaken into a new form by the author's creative imagination.

Literary criticism may borrow from the natural sciences the evolutionary conception and some of its accompaniments; in particular, the demarcation of literary forms by the persistence of certain characteristics through changing conditions of nation or period, and the recognition of imitation as an important element in the creative process. It would seem, however, that further progress in the classification and explanation of literary phenomena is not to be gained by searching for additional analogies, but in the study and analysis of the phenomena them-

selves in the effort to discover the principles and laws
of the mental processes peculiar to literature.

We may put the case, then, without further reliance on
the evolution of physical species. For three hundred
years Englishmen have been writing tragedies, all much
alike, all related in origin, nature, and purpose. In our
study of their relationships, the influences governing their
creation have been grouped in two main classes: first,
that of the theatre itself, and second, that which has been
called the literary tradition. In the theatre has been included the influence of actors and audience and all per-
taining to the theatrical presentation. Changes in the
mere stage and its appurtenances have been factors
determining the very nature of tragedy. The scenery
and women actors of the Restoration compelled important
modifications in the drama; the large theatres of Kemble's
day drove tragedy from the stage and encouraged a pantomime hybrid. The influence of theatrical fashions and
traditions, always in part changing and transitory, has
been felt in every variation, advance, or retrogression of
the acted drama. Yet it is the influence of the theatre
that has maintained the integrity of form and has thus
been the main force in preserving the species. The literary
tradition, even more complex in its elements than that of
the theatre, altering and cumulative, composed of classical or French as well as English masterpieces, drawn
from the novel or other forms as well as the drama, affected by all social movements, passing through such
transformations as those of the classical and the romantic

periods, has nevertheless, on the whole, conserved the form and content of tragedy. During the periods that we have examined, blank verse, illustrious persons, the pomp of courts, the great passions of revenge, ambition, jealousy, lust, love, and hate, hideous crimes, and the conflict of potent wills have been the usual accompaniments of the actions of suffering and ruin. There has been only occasional departure from the Shakespearean conception of tragedy as representation of great personalities engaged in disastrous conflict. Shakespeare, in fact, at least since Dryden's "All for Love," has been a constant and often the dominating element in this complex and variable literary tradition. The two classes of influence, theatrical and literary, have thus proved both variable and conserving. The theatre, while crying for novelty, holds tenaciously to its traditions. Literature, while enforcing rules, precedents, prejudices, while clinging to its models and demanding imitation, yet incites to rivalry and originality, to new endeavor, variation, and excellence.

These two main classes of influence have rarely if ever run parallel. At times the theatre has attracted literature, as in the Elizabethan era, at times it has repelled literature, as in the early nineteenth century. Usually, what the stage of the day desires and what the literature of the past encourages have been quite different and often irreconcilable. In our study we have consequently had to keep in mind not only two main lines of influence, but two points of view and two standards of judgment. It is the purpose of dramatic art to bring about their reconciliation,

to harmonize the technic of the theatre, the necessities
of the drama, and the standards of literary excellence.
Our history records no attainment of such an ideal;
rather the two antinomies seem farther from final unity
in the time of Byron than in that of Shakespeare. Yet,
through the discarding of temporary fashions, the growing knowledge of structure, and the multiplication of
theatrical means, the material and experience necessary
for further progress have at least been accumulating.
Perhaps a survey of the drama of the last century on the
continent would result in a more sanguine view of the
development of the principles of dramatic art freed from
the temporalities of theatrical fashion. There is proba-
bility in Professor Brander Matthews's suggestion that in
our growing cosmopolitanism national divergencies in
content will exist with a growing agreement in form. We
may hope that this will be merely an agreement in making quick trial of new ideas, from whatever theatre derived, and that the principles of art established will not,
as so often in the past, prove pedantic and hampering.
This much seems fairly certain, — literary genius and
theatrical experience must unite in order to produce
great tragedy. From the theatre the writer must learn
dramatic art, the first rule of which is to win his audience;
from literature he must learn the elements that will give
his work lasting value. Only after an experience with
the theatre can he venture on innovations likely to be
permanent. Only if he have literary genius will he depart
in triumph from literary traditions. The double mastery

comes to one only rarely, and then only after a double service.

The relationships of tragedy, however, are not confined to the theatre or to literature. That tragedy, like other forms of literature, is an imitation of life, is a platitude whose meaning sometimes fails to impress us. But its truth has a witness in every writer of tragedy. However insignificant or thoughtless, he has been trying to put into his play something of life as he knows it, trying to find some relationships in the world of fact that will carry meaning and interest to his fellows. Whether he has been writing mainly to meet the desires of actors and audience, or has been voyaging alone toward some discovery of beauty and grandeur of human passion, whether he has been building his house of intrigue according to well-conned rules of dramatic structure, or has been copying some tangle of fact, he has been studying the ways and means of human actions. Trivially or greatly, as the case may be, he has been seeking to interpret life. Classicist, romanticist, and realist have been by different processes seeking the same end, the discovery of meaning in the facts of existence. They have all viewed the Art that they have so differently formulated, as a means of approach to Nature, the deity whom they all profess. Neither high seriousness, nor sublime theme, nor a complete philosophy is a necessary accompaniment of Matthew Arnold's definition. Whether the poet write of "the tangles of Neæra's hair" or of that disobedience that first "brought death into the world," he is attempting a criticism of life. This definition does not state the primary aim of literature, for it must first of all interest us, or its sole function, for it seeks beauty as well as truth and cannot always unite them; but it does indicate the most permanent and vitalizing element in the creation of literature, the most organic relationship that connects its many manifestations.

The greatness of tragedy depends upon its allegiance to this meaning of literature. The dramatic form gives opportunity for a close approach to the semblance of actuality. The very subjects of tragedy, suffering and disaster, discourage the seeking of mere amusement or a contentment with mere beauty of expression. They require, if not high seriousness or a teleology, at least a concern with the most interesting, inescapable, and dreadful of human facts. This baleful portion of human existence is the field of tragedy's research, where it may find grandeur and violence, malevolence and magnanimity, optimism or pessimism, harmony or anarchy, but where it can only with difficulty escape a serious attempt at the study of character and deed. No other literary form has so nobly responded to this great mission as that adopted by Sophocles, Shakespeare, Calderon, Corneille, and Ibsen. It has constrained drama and literature to their duty of research, interpretation, discovery in the almost impenetrable maze of human fact, by the very nature of its chosen field, by the preëminence of its great examples, and even by the continued endeavor of its humblest servants. As one reads through these forgotten tragedies, as when one scans closely any large field of human effort, the main impression is one of futility. Beauty is not attained, life is not revealed, everything is imitative, feeble, and absurd. Yet, even among those hundreds of eighteenth century tragedies, with their rhyming tags that neatly sum up their authors' generalizations on life, one may find reason for sympathy and interest. They record what had meaning for their day, the heroisms, sentiments, and morals that somehow stirred men's hearts and elevated their resolves. They represent some degree of temporary success in giving relations and significance to their world. The lastingly significant representation of life is found not in the many but in the few, but the mediocrities and the failures continue the effort and maintain the form that make possible the few masterpieces. The very greatest set no impassable bound, for the ever-widening expanse of tragic fact continually invites new explorers. Progress can come not by resting admiringly on the greatness of the past, but only through a free opportunity for new pioneers and discoverers. Were the achievement of English tragedy far less than it has been, the very expenditure of effort should give it some interest for study. Its history, however, includes in Shakespeare's tragedies a few of the unapproached achievements of the human mind, many other plays that for a while greatly interested and persuaded men, not a few that still have searching meaning for us, and hundreds more that have maintained an unselfish, a social, a moral inquiry into life, and that, while perishing themselves, have aided others to live. In such a history, even he who runs may read a record of human endeavor not alien to his interest.

Tragedy takes an abiding place among the great courses of continuous human activity dedicated to an inquiry into the meanings of life. Its imaginative and intellectual study of suffering and ruin must continue, however its form may alter, if the theatre is to be a social force of importance, if literature is to offer an intelligent, serious, and comprehensive view of life, if the two are to unite in something better than a trivial and selfish entertainment. Its methods may not commend themselves in an age of physical and mechanical sciences, its aim may not commend itself at a time when splendid discoveries in the physical world blur the importance of an interpretation of moral and social relations. But tragedy has survived many ages and creeds, and seems likely to survive as long as men try to understand other men, to sympathize with their troubles, and to relate these somehow to their own beliefs and ideals. In the future as in the past, when a nation or community is at a period of culminating advance, when society is most mindful of its greatness and its obligations, tragedy should find its most helpful encouragement and its greatest opportunity.

INDEX